MW01257770

"It might be a stretch to call the Earps' last escapade together in what became Sawtelle, California, a 'battle,' but their last hurrah there, and at the neighboring Old Soldiers' Home, in the early 20th century makes for a little-known but intriguing conclusion to the story of a wandering but close-knit family that revolved around patriarch Nick Earp right up until his death in 1907. Nick and son Newton were enrolled in the Soldiers' Home, and Newton's far more famous half-brothers Wyatt and Virgil showed up from time to time, but the star of the Earps "blind pig" (illicit alcohol sales) scheme at Sawtelle was none other than the often overlooked older brother James, who as 'the veteran club man of North Fourth street' was providing whiskey to thirsty veterans. The late historian and Wyatt Earp–biographer Lee A. Silva would have been proud of this successful effort by two of his old pals, Messieurs Don Chaput and David D. de Haas, to tell not only a hidden chapter in the Earp legend but also the stories of two fascinating communities—Sawtelle (which was annexed to Los Angeles in 1917) and Santa Monica—and the tale of the early temperance movement in the LA area."

—**GREGORY LALIRE**, editor of *Wild West Magazine* since 1995 and author of two historical novels, *Our Frontier Pastime, 1804–1815* (2019) and *Captured: From the Frontier Diary of Danny Duly* (2014)

"This book is delightful and most informative. The Sawtelle and Earp story is compelling, all the more because humor is constantly inserted. I laughed my head off as I read. Keeps the reader wanting to turn the page; I could just see those old veterans gravitating to the nearby blind pigs, having scorned the coffee and weak beer of the Home canteen. Of course, the Earp attempts at getting a share of all that pension money was most interesting. The photos of the Soldiers' Home are stunning—I had no idea how handsome it was. In fact, most of us don't know much about the later life of the Earps. I knew next to nothing about this Sawtelle chapter of the Earps, and it was presented in a fascinating manner. I enjoyed the Appendices—found out a lot. A great job tying up the final chapters of the

Earps. This is a needed contribution to Earpiana and to the lore of the last West; authors Chaput and de Haas have hit a home run with this book."

—**BILL O'NEAL**, State Historian of Texas, 2012–2018, and author of more than forty books

"I thoroughly enjoyed this book. When I first received this, I thought I had a general knowledge of the entire Earp saga, but trying to find a mention of Sawtelle in my Earp books proved to be fruitless! Admittedly, I have a small collection of 'Earpiana,' but I doubt if many others have any inkling of what authors Chaput and de Haas have discovered, and now to-be-preserved!

"In chapter 8, 'The Earps Cometh,' we learn more about the brothers as well as Nicholas and others. By then we are 'hooked.' I found myself having been drawn in and wanting to learn more, but a voice inside of me kept saying, 'We need a gunfight,' but that did not happen. What did happen was an explanation of how the Earps (minus Morgan) operated, trying to find that last bonanza, that last gold mine, or silver mine . . . and in doing so we get reacquainted with so many others from the Tombstone days, John Clum, Henry Clay Hooker, George Parsons, and even John Flood— all becomes mingled together into a story of attempted entrepreneurial energy which didn't pan out as intended.

"This is finally a biography of the Earps which doesn't re-hash the O.K. Corral Battle, the non-arrest of Ben Thompson, the death of Curly Bill, nor the Peoria riverboat frolics, and so many other legendary aspects of their career. It is a gathering of brand-new material, succinctly put together with enough drama to keep the reader's interest and at the same time presenting biographical information on the lesser characters to satisfy any genealogist.

"Needless to say, this is a biography of a family, a community and a period of American history to please even the most cynical reader. It is a 'must have' for anyone who appreciates good writing and fascinating history."

—**CHUCK PARSONS**, independent historian and author of seventeen books

"David de Haas and Don Chaput have made a significant contribution with this exposition of a previously unexplored chapter of the Earp story. Most people know about the Earps because of their shootout with the Clantons and McLaurys in Tombstone, Arizona; and most never get past the stories surrounding that event. Over the past twenty-five years knowledge about the Earps has not only produced previously unknown information but also has changed the shape, form, and meaning of the Earp story.

"De Haas and Chaput have added a new chapter to the Earp story. In the process, they have also shed light on the dynamic of the Earp family. The brothers Earp—including half-brother Newton—remained close and were as a group remarkably strong-willed, as was their father, Nicholas. The Sawtelle conflict also reveals the restless quest for success that seemed to consume them all and confirms the trouble they had walking the line between law, order, and respectability on the one hand, and the vices on the other.

"This new book also reveals that Newton was Nicholas's son by more than blood. One important contribution here is the insight provided into the life of the most mysterious Earp brother—James. He has been treated as an invalid saloonkeeper, with a minimal part in the Earp story. But this book contributes to my suspicion that he always played a larger role, even at Tombstone, than he is generally credited with having. Another contribution lies in the book's revelations about the ongoing connections between the Earps and their former associates and friends from Tombstone.

"Truly understanding any historical subject requires context. What de Haas and Chaput do is to give readers insights into the lives and character of the Earp brothers, but beyond that, they offer a case study of the moral debate that raged at the turn of the twentieth century over gambling and liquor—a time when men like the Earps were asked to choose between the codes they had lived by and organized demands for social reform. Sawtelle was not the only place struggling with vice at the time, but its experience helps us to understand the process while expanding our knowledge of the Earps."

—**GARY L. ROBERTS**, Emeritus Professor of History, Abraham Baldwin College, and the author of *Doc Holliday: The Life and Legend* and co-editor of *A Wyatt Earp Anthology: Long May His Story Be Told*

"This is an interesting account of the final attempt of the Earp family to obtain their bonanza for the future, a story that hasn't been told before. I'm sure it will be of interest to Earp fans and those interested in the development of Southern California and the West."

—THOMAS SITTON, former head, History Division, Natural History Museum, Los Angeles, and author of many books and articles

"There is some good research here! Contains several events in the Earp lives of which I was unaware, and I appreciate this very much. The fascinating story of the Earp family continues to grow with on-going research into not only the famous or infamous brothers, Wyatt, Virgil, and Morgan, but also the parents of the boys, their siblings and other close connections. In this book authors David D. de Haas and Donald Chaput present an almost totally new story of the Earps lives in California in the areas of Los Angeles, Sawtelle, Santa Monica and other locales. The interesting accounts of Nicholas Porter Earp and eldest son Newton Earp in the Old Soldiers' Home have rarely been told, and certainly not to this depth. When you add in brothers James and Warren Earp, you have an Earp family history of the late 1800s into the new century of the 1900s. This book will appeal to not only the fans of the Earp brothers but also to those who are interested in the history of southern California as well as the lives of Civil War, Indian Wars, and Spanish-American War veterans."

—ROY B. YOUNG, Vice-President and Journal Editor, Wild West History Association, author of numerous books and co-editor of *A Wyatt Earp Anthology: Long May His Story Be Told*

The Earps Invade Southern California

The Earps Invade
Southern California

❖━◈━◇━━◈◇━

*Bootlegging Los Angeles, Santa Monica,
and the Old Soldiers' Home*

DON CHAPUT *and* **DAVID D. DE HAAS**

UNIVERSITY OF NORTH TEXAS PRESS
DENTON, TEXAS

10 9 8 7 6 5 4 3 2 1

Permissions:
University of North Texas Press
1155 Union Circle #311336
Denton, TX 76203-5017

The paper used in this book meets the minimum requirements of the
American National Standard for Permanence of Paper for Printed Library
Materials, z39.48.1984. Binding materials have been chosen for durability.

LIBRARY OF CONGRESS CATALOGING-IN-PUBLICATION DATA

Names: Chaput, Donald, author. | De Haas, David D., 1956– author.
Title: The Earps invade Southern California : bootlegging Los Angeles,
    Santa Monica, and the Old Soldiers' Home / Don Chaput and David D. de Haas.
Description: Denton, TX : University of North Texas Press, [2020] |
    Includes bibliographical references and index.
Identifiers: LCCN 2020010289 | ISBN 9781574418095 (cloth) |
    ISBN 9781574418187 (ebook)
Subjects: LCSH: Earp, Wyatt, 1848–1929—Family. | Criminals—California,
    Southern—Biography. | Alcohol trafficking—California,
    Southern—History—20th century. | Prohibition—California,
    Southern—History—20th century. | Soldiers' homes—California—Los
    Angeles—History. | Sawtelle (Los Angeles, Calif.)—History. | Santa
    Monica (Calif.)—History. | LCGFT: Biographies.
Classification: LCC F860 .C45 2020 | DDC 978/.02092—dc23
LC record available at https://lccn.loc.gov/2020010289

The electronic edition of this book was made possible by
the support of the Vick Family Foundation.

DEDICATION

The authors would like to dedicate this book to the following individuals:

Our mutual best friend Lee A. Silva, discussed further throughout this text and references, who introduced us to one another, provided inspiration, and without whom this book obviously never could have been written.

Don would like to also dedicate the book to his family, his friends, and his many colleagues who over the years have encouraged his interests in the American frontier. The discussions, the arguments, and the laughs have made this most enjoyable.

David would also like to dedicate this book to (in addition to all those mentioned in the acknowledgement section) his wonderful wife Mary who has been his "proofreader" for so many years (nearly 40) through multiple medical journal and western article publications. She has also weathered his Wild West fascinations and endured annual summer vacation "historic" road trips throughout the country in search of Wyatt, Doc, Billy, Pat, Kit, Davy, Wild Bill, Geronimo ..., as have his children Lindsay, Heather, and Lance. Of course, to them, the summer "historic" educational road trips were actually referred to as "torture trips," but still they all withstood. Sadly, for them, Wyatt and Doc never made it to Hawaii, London, or Amsterdam .... And now, his three (and another on the way) grandchildren Ethan, Jacob, and Asher; all of whom have had to put up with his Old West obsession through their fledgling years, and time away from "grandpa," in the writing of this book.

The Angel of History:[1]

"His face turned towards the past. Where we perceive a chain of events, he sees one single catastrophe which keeps piling wreckage and hurls it in front of his feet. The angel would like to stay, awaken the dead, and make whole what has been smashed. But a storm is blowing in from Paradise; it has caught in his wings with such a violence that the angel can no longer close them. The storm irresistibility propels him into the future to which his back is turned, while the pile of debris before him grows skyward. This storm is what we call progress."

"... Every image of the past that is not recognized by the present as one of its own concerns threatens to disappear irretrievably."[2]

WALTER BENJAMIN,
German philosopher

We need to "weigh the costs of these disappearances and identify what paths we might take to ensure that their histories better become our concerns moving forward. Failure to do so risks a future of repeated rediscovery of past harms ..."[3]

JEREMY A. GREENE, MD, PhD,
Johns Hopkins University School of Medicine,
Baltimore, Maryland

CONTENTS

ILLUSTRATIONS

PREFACE

by David D. de Haas

Donald Chaput and I have been good friends for many years after having been first introduced to one another by our mutual best friend and Old West author/historian Lee A. Silva, who passed away in August of 2014. Since that time, we have collaborated on several small projects and are currently working on a few more. In 2015 Don "officially retired" from writing after having published more than a dozen books (his last being *Empire of Sand* in 2015) and many more magazine/journal articles. Communications between the authors have continued through in person visits, email, and phone calls. Although now retired (he gave his entire research collection to me and author/historian Garner Palenske a few years back), Don continues to imagine more and more ideas for potential future projects.

A twenty-five-year-old fan letter/query to Don, and a Virgil Earp token, led the authors through an Internet search, a Wild West discussion board entry from a year earlier, and ultimately the rediscovery of the sparsely known/published fact that Virgil Earp had actually teamed with his surviving brothers one last time in Sawtelle, California, for a brief period before his death in Goldfield, Nevada, in 1905. Further research led to the accumulation of enough provocative and previously unpublished new material to write about this last Earp family escapade, and eventually this book; please see chapter 9 "Enter V.W. Earp; Virgil Joins the Revelry" for more detail on its origins.

As scholars of the Old West know, Virgil was one of the legendary Earp brothers involved in what historians designate as the most famous gun battle in Wild West history,[1] the so-called "Gunfight at the OK Corral," on October 26, 1881, in Tombstone, Arizona. He, along with his brothers Wyatt and Morgan, and renowned gunslinger Doc Holliday, faced down six

Cowboys including Ike and Billy Clanton and the two McLaury brothers, Frank and Tom. Also, on the scene and affiliated with the Cowboys, were William Claiborne and Wes Fuller, who retreated as the fight commenced. Both Don and I have written about this famous shootout in the past.

This book is not just another story about Wyatt and the Earp family. It is also the story of Sawtelle, California, and its Old Soldiers' Home, early Santa Monica, Los Angeles, prohibition,[2] and the Earp family's (seldom publicized) ties to them all. The Earps fought the battles of the Wild West in its legendary boomtowns— Dodge City, Tombstone, Wichita, Fort Laramie, Tucson, Deadwood, Cheyenne, Prescott, El Paso, Fort Worth, and Yuma to name just a few—for over fifty years, with mediocre success. In the early 1900s they had one last chance together as a family, in the Los Angeles/Santa Monica/Sawtelle areas, at their anticipated big bonanza: "The Battle of Sawtelle." The brothers all appear to have been scheming together one last time, one concluding episode in the Earp legend, and one last hurrah for the Earp family.

In this same time period, Earp family patriarch Nicholas Porter Earp was an influential resident of the Old Soldiers' Home, which was adjacent to where the new townsite of Sawtelle, known as "Soldiers' City," was being developed, just west of Los Angeles and east of the beautiful and upcoming new seaside resort city of Santa Monica. Nick, the tough old trailblazer of this renowned family, died in the home, after living there for about six years, in 1907, and is buried in the affiliated adjacent Los Angeles National Cemetery. The Earp boys' half-brother Newton spent seven years in the home too, and brother James lived in adjoining Sawtelle. Their presence there was strong in the early 1900s.

The authors have never intended this to exclusively be a story of the Earps, and hope instead those reading it are interested in learning a new account of Sawtelle and the Old Soldiers' Home (which eventually morphed into the modern day West Los Angeles V.A. Medical Center complex/ campus) and its 1800s military (Mexican-American War, Indian Wars, Civil War, Spanish-American War, ...) veterans, as well as the history and developmental years of early Santa Monica, Los Angeles, and their neighboring cities, including Hollywood, Malibu, and Beverly Hills. Also, a prominent theme throughout this book is the drive towards prohibition, which led to illicit alcohol sales ("bootlegging") and hidden backroom underground bars known as "blind pigs" or "speakeasies." Los Angeles County and Sawtelle, to their detriment, and that of its neighboring cities, were drowning in such institutions in the early 1900s, as unscrupulous scavengers, most often military veterans themselves, preyed upon the Home's elderly soldiers and their pension incomes. This murky episode in American history significantly influenced and swayed the early evolution of these prominent Southern California cities.

When I was a freshman math/biochemistry major at UCLA in the mid-1970s, I was relegated to the infamous (even comedian Bob Hope joked about it in one of his nationally televised primetime monologues in 1975) distant off-campus "lot 32" parking lot, as were most other newcomers to the university. This forsaken lot, about one mile southwest of campus and from which students are bussed to the main campus, overlooks the Los Angeles National Cemetery, which is adjacent to the Old Soldiers' Home (currently the Veterans Administration's West Los Angeles Campus), from its southeastern border. This was a view I visualized daily as I arrived for and departed from school, but did not at the time fully appreciate its historical significance. It did intrigue me and made an everlasting impression during my formative years as a young premedical student. Little did I know at the time that mythical Wild West frontier marshals Wyatt and Virgil Earp, and their brothers and father, whom I had regularly watched throughout my childhood portrayed in the movies and on television, had frequented that very ground in the early 1900s, right next to my college campus! The area is currently surrounded by the ultra-luxurious urban sprawl of Bel Air, Westwood, Brentwood, Century City, Malibu, and Beverly Hills, some of the wealthiest and most desirable real estate on the planet, and, in stark contrast to the dusty dubious frontier towns I had always envisioned them inhabiting. The opportunity, first proposed by coauthor Don Chaput to research this historical landmark and actual Wild West history in my hometown, the cultured Los Angeles area, and learn more, over forty years later, was most definitely an enticing prospect.

One thing led to another, and here is the "another": the book (a sort of "Guys and Dolls"[3] west coast style)[4] which eventually came of this joint research and discussions between Don and me, two close friends from differing generations with similar historical fascinations, but somewhat divergent interpretations and approaches.

PROLOGUE

What was a bonanza? In the nineteenth-century American West, the Spanish word was usually associated with mining. Good times were either here or would be soon. The mine (gold or silver) was about to produce the good stuff. A mine or town "in bonanza" was a throbbing place, with so much profit on hand that even marginal people or low-lifes could expect a piece of the action. Into the twentieth century, the word bonanza broadened, coming to mean the approaching of good times; things are "looking up."

It's good to be around during a bonanza. The Spanish word *borrasca* is the opposite, good times are in the past; the mines are not producing enough. This is when the investors, the faro dealers, the merchants, the prostitutes, ... are looking elsewhere.[1]

ACKNOWLEDGMENTS

The authors would like to acknowledge and thank the following individuals without whose input and assistance this book would not have been possible – Bill and Karon (RIP) O'Neal (retired two-term Official Texas State Historian), Chuck and Pat Parsons, Charlotte and Roy B. Young, Dr. Gary L. Roberts, Kenneth (K.t.K.) Vail (Morgan and James Earp authority/researcher/biographer), Greg Lalire (Editor *Wild West Magazine*), Sara Crown (Archivist of the Santa Monica History Museum/Research Library), Nicholas Cataldo, Ian Rosen (Librarian, Santa Monica Regional Library), Rosemarie Knopka (Librarian Archivist, Digitalization and Special Collections Department, Los Angeles Public Library), Julie Huffman (Los Angeles Central Library; History and Genealogy Department, Genealogy Librarian), Ronald Chrisman (Director; University of North Texas Press), Garner Palenske, Kate Fitzpatrick (Archivist & Librarian; Arizona Historical Society, Tucson), Susan (RIP) and Lee A. Silva (RIP), "Texas by God and the Twin Territories" internet discussion board and its participants, Mary de Haas (editing/proofreading), Pete Martinez ("Lead" – New Directions for Veterans; V.A. West Los Angeles Campus), Ed Chaput (technical support), John Boessenecker (manuscript critique), Tom Sitton, Antoinette Chaput (proofreading/editing), Lance de Haas (technical support — i.e. assisting Dad with the formatting and pagination), Michael Esquerra, Lindsay Esquerra, dust jacket artist Gary Zaboly, and editor Karen DeVinney (University of North Texas Press).

In addition to those above, David would like to also acknowledge some of the amazing Wild West historians he has met/befriended on this nearly 30-year Old West historical journey. Each of whom have shared a bit of their vast knowledge, and making him a better and more informed historian/researcher/author in the process, and thereby contributing to this book. Most importantly, they are great friends all; i.e., his group of "fellow sophisticates": Peter Sherayko (actor/author/collector/firearms authority; Caravan West Productions; *Tombstone* movies' "Texas Jack"), William and Paula Jean Hunley (The Bird Cage Theatre, Tombstone, Arizona), Michael Hickey (Talei Publishers; RIP), Rose (Talei Publishers; RIP), Paul (RIP) and Karen Cool, Mark (RIP) and Harriet Dworkin, J.P. (grandson of legendary Wild West Sheriff Pat Garrett; RIP) and Star Garrett, Anne Collier, Tom Gaumer, Garth Gould, Tom Moy, Troy Kelley (with whom I made my first trip to the Old Soldiers' Home/Cemetery), Randy Lish, Kevin and Bev Mulkins, Arthur Goldberg (RIP), Rose and Robert DeArment, Suzanne and Michael Wallis, Lee Simmons (RIP), Paul Marquez, Gordon Anderson (Tombstone Larian Motel), Robert Palmquist, Ron Fischer (RIP), Glenn (RIP) and Jane Boyer, Miguel Corona and Jody Davis, Naomi and Marlin Wertman, Billy Clanton Naylor, Jan Devereaux and Bob Alexander, Elaine Patterson Bennett, Rita and Daniel (RIP) Patterson, Mary and (McLaury biographer) Paul Johnson, Ron Woggon, Alan Blanchette, Donna Dycus, Ron Lawson, Don Taylor (Tombstone Town Historian), Karen Holliday and John Tanner (RIP), Jeff Millet (Graphic Publishers), Jeff Wheat, Linda Wommack, Robert ("Bobby") McDearmon, Larry and Ruth Ball, James and Margaret Bailey, Robert Devere (whose amazing Tombstone family ties date back to the 1880 Earp days there), Thom Ross, Jane Eppinga, Joe Cesario, Ben Harleman, Bob and Joy (RIP) Paul (gg Grandson of legendary Arizona Sheriff Bob Paul), Brian Ostberg, Carmen Brody, Christine Rhodes (Retired Cochise County Recorder) , Jeffrey (with whom the De Haas family made their first trip to Tombstone) and Cindy Roth, Dakota and Sunny Livesay, Stuart Rosebrook (Editor *True West Magazine*), Marshall (official Arizona State historian) and Vanessa Trimble, Dale Hector, Scott and Christina Seaman, Marshall and Louis Libert, Dennis and Mary Lee McCown, Dick (Richard) Derham, Harry ("Mick") and Ingrid McNeer, Rick (RIP) and Shelby Mosolf, Jerry and Ann Fields, Jim and Jodi MacGregor, John Don Church, Julie Ann and Bob Ream, Leah Alden Jaswal, Lisa Lach Chiles, Joe Gallagher, Walt and Vickie Ross, Richard and Ellyn ("Dolly") Ignarski, Richard Weddle, Rick Mielke, Jim Schiffer, Scott Nelson, Sharon Cunningham, Steve Gatto, Bob Pugh, Butch Badon, Clair Cavoto Homan (Albert Fountain gggranddaughter), Corey Recko; Donna, Madison, and Louis Harrell;

Carroll and Jane Moore, Larry Knuth, Long Branch Beltrao, Michael Bell, Mike Mihaljevich, Nicholas Narog, Michael Lanning, Eli Lizzie, Norman Wayne Brown, Paul Andrew Hutton, Terry Ike Clanton, William Nicholas, Bill Koch, John Rose, Wyatt (Wyatt's gg grandnephew) and Terry (RIP) Earp, Phyllis Eccleston, Leon Metz, Tim Fattig, Drew Gomber, Joe and Sue Harvey, Allen Hatley (RIP), M.D. "Doc" Ingalls (RIP), Gary McLelland, Irisse and Richard Lapidus, Peter Brand, Wayne Sanderson, the Wild West Collectors Facebook page and all its members and active participants, Jim (also with me on my first visit to the Soldiers' Home in the early 2000s) and Lynda Groom, Mark (*True West Magazine*; Editor *Tombstone Epitaph* newspaper) and Patty Boardman, Doug and (Ike Clanton biographer) Rita Ackerman, Ben (prolific author and retired Tombstone Town Historian) and Mary Traywick, "Texas Jack" James and Carrla (RIP) Wright, Ida Saunders (RIP), David and Joanie Bruce (and Rocky), June Robertson, Roger Myers, Bob Cash, Ol' Minor Larry Arrendale (RIP), Clell and Arlene Furnell, David Rodgers, Peter Vourakis, Gary and Rachel Ledoux, Scott and Alice Dyke, Jerry Lobdill, Michael Pitel, David Lauterborn (Managing Editor *Wild West Magazine*), John (J.R.) Sanders, David Wright, Barb Chiero, Chris Swinney (Tombstone movie stunt coordinator), Julia Bricklin, Scott Malin, Robert Keith (actor, event promoter), Kurt House, and on the fiddle Rex Rideout (*Cowboys and Aliens*).

CHAPTER 1

The Wandering Earp
Band of Brothers

The Earps, in many ways a typical Western family, naturally preferred bonanza over borrasca. It was all a matter of timing. Sometimes the Earp timing was perfection, at other times a bit off the mark.

Nick Earp, father of the Earp brothers and head of the clan for half a century, did his best to aim for the high points and avoid the low periods of Western prosperity. He joined an Illinois military outfit during the Mexican War and spent some grueling months south of the border. He returned to Monmouth, Illinois, served as a constable, and later farmed in Iowa and served as town marshal of Pella for a few years. During the Civil War, while sons Newton, James, and Virgil were in uniform, Nick was helping out on the home front, recruiting and training local troops and serving as a local deputy provost marshal. He diddled around in Illinois and Iowa, working himself into positions of trust, responsibility (and income) for decades, even making a trip to California with his family to get in on the good times. He floated back to the Midwest, tried Missouri for a few years, then bolted back to California, trying to ensure that he and his boys would get a piece of the action. One can look deep in Western historical sources to find a family that more than once "moved West," but Nicholas Earp was one of those Western wanderers in search of the true bonanza. He believed that west of the Mississippi, he and his family would find success.[1]

Certainly, Nicholas Earp at first believed the Midwest would be where the Earps could make a mark. He tried to do so, carrying his sons, cousins, and a passel of Earp relatives along the way. They spent some years in Illinois, Iowa, even Missouri, later Kansas, trying to create successful lives in farming and law and order that could fit in with Earp goals. It almost meshed, but not quite. In the Midwest, Nick, Virgil, Wyatt, James, even Morgan obtained positions of military, law enforcement, or other slots that could have led to advancements. But for Nick, and the rest of the Earps, these positions were either not high enough, or not interesting enough.

In May 1864, Nick took his first California venture, heading a convoy of wagons which reached there in December. Apparently, the Golden State was not very golden at this point in time for the Earps, as in 1867 they returned to the Midwest. The new locale would be around Lamar in western Missouri, where they farmed, Nick was a justice of the peace, and young Wyatt put in his first "official" stint as a lawman in November 1869.[2] Most of the late 1860s and the 1870s saw various members of the Earp family shift from Missouri to Illinois, Texas, and Kansas, where Earp time was spent on farms, in saloons, and wearing badges.[3]

By the late 1870s, the Midwest had lost its allure for the Earps. Morgan would explore the Dakota goldfields, then find a lawman position in Butte, Montana. Virgil was establishing himself as a stage driver, miner, and constable in Prescott. In 1877, Nick had again moved with the remnants of his family to California. By time of the 1880 census, the Nick Earp family was running a small farm near Temescal, which was then in San Bernardino County.[4]

The other Earps, though, would never give up their California connections. Virgil and Wyatt had a look at the Cripple Creek, Colorado, excitement, but were not impressed. Wyatt, James, and Warren spent some time in the Idaho goldfields, but all soon headed south again. Virgil's remaining time was mostly in Colton, until his death in Nevada. Wyatt's career paths were many, but all of them meant returning to California. He would deal in cards, real estate, and horses in San Diego, do much of the same in San Francisco, where he also refereed an infamous prizefight, take time out to do well in the Nome Gold Rush, then tried a brief turn at saloon operations in the Nevada mining town of Tonopah. Yet, roughly from 1902 until his death in 1929, Wyatt's life mostly revolved around summer months in Los Angeles, and during the winter, operating his small gold and copper claims in the Whipple Mountains of San Bernardino County.[5]

Earp information is pretty easy to find, as interest in the Tombstone and Dodge City eras, or a few of the sporting world events (boxing, gambling, horse racing, etc.) Wyatt was involved in, get many Internet hits, as well as books and articles.[6] Yet, the Earp wanderings in the West are more interesting when we consider how and when they achieved, came close, or missed out on the bonanza timing.

The Earp brothers touched all grades of the bonanza-borrasca situations. Even old dad, Nicholas, found his niche, if not bonanza, in Colton, California, drawing his veterans pension for the Mexican War, enjoying decent status for his law enforcement roles in Illinois, Iowa, and Missouri, and some income for his judicial services in San Bernardino County.

Wyatt had an "unfortunate period" in 1871 when he was arrested for cattle theft in the Indian Territory.[7] In 1871-72 the boys were in Peoria, where Virgil tended bar, and Wyatt and Morgan did some card playing as well as a bit of pimping.[8] From then on, though, eyes looked Westward. James had already spent an "exciting" period in Montana (bar tending, larceny, and jail break).[9]

What James did in Montana gives some insight into the James described by friends and family who knew him well. The severely wounded Civil War veteran was not about to go back to Iowa whining. He headed to Deer Lodge, Montana, where in the census of 1870 he was identified as a waiter.[10] This was probably the beginning of his long "service" career in the restaurant and saloon business. But James was busy, with many interests. He was arrested for larceny early in 1871, escaped jail (along with a horse thief or two), and was later caught fifty miles from Deer Lodge.

Cause of this ruckus is unknown, but it had no impact on his local reputation. A long memoir by another pioneer in 1873 says of James, well known around Deer Lodge, "Ah! poor 'Crummie,' I knew him well." This raconteur, using the James nickname, also used these words: "With a roll of greenbacks in his pocket, or minus even a nickel, he was ever the same—light-hearted, rollicking, and generous to a fault." This particular account was focused on a bad experience in a faro game, which caused James to head out to Utah for a time.

James would be back a few times to Montana, never shying from the crowd, usually involved in saloon life, but also plugged in to what mattered locally. In 1894, when folks around Butte were split in two factions, one included James C. Earp, a speculator in Butte for years. As late as 1902, the *Butte Miner* mentioned that those with area mining interests included James Earp, formerly of Deer Lodge.[11]

The James Earp of Montana was the James of Fort Worth, Wichita, Dodge City, Tombstone, San Bernardino, Nome, and greater Los Angeles. He was a well-known, well liked sporting man, frequently mixed up in those events and activities that interested men of that world.[12]

In Wichita and Dodge City, Wyatt, James, Morgan, and Virgil spent time, their income related to their talents; they were hustlers, bar tenders, gamblers, and officers of the law. The Wichita "Earp party" included the boys as well as a few wives and other women (prostitutes) named Earp who helped provide some income. Parts of 1877-78 were spent in Fort Worth, where James and Wyatt were particularly active in the world of saloons, both as customers and employees.[13]

The next major stop for the Earp boys was at Tombstone in 1879-82, where Virgil, Wyatt, and Morgan were peace officers. The Earps and their friend Doc Holliday were involved in the famous shootout near the OK Corral, which was followed by the ambushes of Morgan and Virgil by the notorious Arizona/New Mexico "Cowboy gang," and then Wyatt's retaliatory vendetta ride. After some "events" in New Mexico and Colorado, Wyatt, James, and Warren headed for the goldfields of Idaho in 1884, and Virgil and James hit the faro tables of Calico, California, in 1885. Virgil and Nicholas settled in Colton for a few years, where they handled "justice," Nicholas becoming justice of the peace in 1884, and son Virgil town marshal and running a detective agency for most of the late 1880s. By 1887 Wyatt was in San Diego, where for a few years he was a sporting man as well as dealing in real estate. He shifted to San Francisco in 1891, where he would remain for a few years.[14]

James and wife Bessie lived in San Bernardino in 1886-87, while he was in business with the Earp & Anderson Saloon. Bessie, whom he had married in Illinois in 1873, died in San Bernardino in January of 1887. James spent a few years salooning in Montana and then joined Wyatt in San Francisco in 1896.[15]

Wyatt and Virgil spent a few weeks in Cripple Creek, Colorado, in 1895 before realizing that the excitement there had already passed. The next meaningful, profitable venture for Wyatt, James, their wives, and a few other relatives was the era of 1900-1901, when the profits of the Nome goldfields helped enliven the Dexter Saloon, in which Wyatt and James had a major interest.[16]

Some of the above locations, such as Tombstone, Idaho, and Nome, were in the bonanza category; others, like San Diego and San Francisco, were "holding actions," while they really missed their timing in Calico and Cripple Creek.

One aspect of the Earp family that should be emphasized is the "California syndrome." The fact that a famous shootout concerning the Earps took place in Arizona, or that Wyatt Earp got rich from a saloon in Alaska, or that Virgil Earp died while serving as a deputy sheriff in Nevada, ignores a major point: for the Earps, California was to be (they hoped) the Promised Land. Other places in the West would interest the Earps temporarily (Kansas, Nevada, Montana, Alaska, Idaho, even Baja California), but California remained the base. For the Earps, the months in Arizona, Nevada, Idaho, or Alaska, pale when compared to the decades in San Bernardino County, San Francisco, San Diego, Sawtelle, and Los Angeles. The year 1880 is a good year to highlight the California-centrism to the Earp family. Nick Earp would move the family to Colton, which would be an Earp focus for two decades, as Nick operated a saloon there and also worked helping to keep the peace and as a recorder. The Earp sons Wyatt, Virgil, and James would only be in Tombstone a few years, and even in that time were in frequent contact with the family in Colton. As the Earps traipsed about through the late 1800s and early 1900s, there are occasional mentions of them elsewhere. Wyatt may have had a faro bank in Baja California, Virgil gave Prescott a second try, and Wyatt, Virgil, and James were all intrigued with the mining towns of Goldfield and Tonopah, Nevada. California, though, was the touchstone. Only Morgan and Warren[17] would have limited California time, both getting killed in Arizona saloon shootings, Morgan in an 1882 ambush in Tombstone, Warren in a saloon brawl in Willcox, Arizona, in July 1900. For the Earp family, where options existed, California was the end of the line.

And how is this related to Santa Monica and Sawtelle? The Earp family had roamed the Wild West for four decades, and at the turn of the century, in the early 1900s, the newly emerging Santa Monica–Sawtelle areas were to be their final shot at a major bonanza; it would involve all the surviving members of the Earp family, including Dad.

CHAPTER 2

⬧━◉━◦━━━◦━◉━⬧

The Birth of Santa Monica
and the Old Soldiers' Home

Southern California in the 1880s experienced what was probably the largest land boom of the nation during the century. The Transcontinental Railroad was completed in the 1860s, but the rail connection between San Francisco and Los Angeles in 1876, followed by the San Bernardino rail line in 1883, permitted a fantastic publicity push for Southern California. Huge amounts of available land for building as well as for citrus, and other fruits and grains, led to hundreds of thousands of new arrivals, who took advantage of the new transportation, irrigation, and the erection (much of it on paper) of dozens of new communities. The boom would collapse in the late 1880s, caused by national financial as well as local situations. However, Santa Monica was less impacted than other local communities. Her birth preceded the Boom by a few years, and the Pacific Ocean was an ingredient that was not shared by the locations farther inland.

The beautiful beaches of Santa Monica and the investment smarts of Senator John P. Jones, Colonel Robert S. Baker, and others led to the development of this major Western community. The building boom, improved transportation connections with Los Angeles, and the moderate increase of population pointed to a heady future for Santa Monica. A major problem for the city fathers, though, was booze. They felt there was too much of it, most of it involving the veterans from the Soldiers' Home, just a few miles away. The great Santa Monica dislike of booze appealed to the Earp family, and they saw it as a way to create family riches.

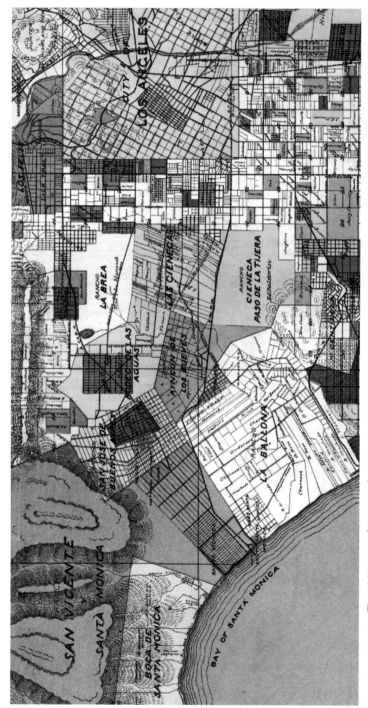

The 1888 map of Los Angeles County contains one of the earliest noting the National Military Home, which is in the Rancho San Jose de Buenos Ayres. *Library of Congress.*

Senator John Percival Jones of Nevada, a Santa Monica founder, the man behind the locating of the Soldiers' Home. *Press Reference*, 1915.

Robert S. Baker, a Santa Monica mogul and a leader in the founding of the Soldiers' Home. *Wikipedia Commons.*

The Santa Monica evolution was not rapid, the plat being recorded in 1875, and incorporation following eleven years later. Santa Monica Precinct and later Santa Monica Township were sliced off from northern La Ballona Township. In this early period, then, the nearest neighbor of Santa Monica Township to the east was Los Angeles Township.[1]

An interesting sidelight of the celebration in July 1875, when Santa Monica was launched, was that the main guest of the day was renowned orator and politician Tom Fitch.[2] A few years later, Fitch would be in Tombstone, the lead defense attorney for the Earp faction following the O.K. Corral shootout of October 1881.[3] Fitch was known as "The Silver-Tongued Orator of the Pacific" for his inspiring speeches and debates. He had been a colleague and friend of author Mark Twain, in the mid 1860's in Virginia City, Nevada, when they both wrote for local newspapers.

Tom Fitch, well-known Western orator, speaker at Santa Monica's founding, and Earp attorney at the Tombstone shootout hearings. *History of Arizona,* 1884.

He represented and defended Mormon religious leader Brigham Young, known as the "American/Mormon Moses," and who was the second president of the Church of Jesus Christ of Latter Day Saints, founder of Salt Lake City, Utah, and first governor of Utah, in Salt Lake City, Utah, in the early 1870s, in his polygamy-related lawsuits.

Fitch had also been a friend of "The Big Four" railroad tycoons, Leland Stanford, Charles Crocker, Collis Huntington, and Mark Hopkins, who built the Central Pacific Railroad. He was there at Promontory Point, Utah, on May 10, 1869, for Leland Stanford's hammering of the "golden (last) spike." He would in later years accompany Stanford on his second U.S. Senatorial election campaign trail and speak throughout the tour on his behalf. Ironically, forthcoming Tombstone, Arizona O.K. Corral gunfight justice of the peace to be, who would also be involved in litigation regarding the Mormon Church in the 1870s, Wells W. Spicer, was also in attendance for the golden spike ceremony that May day.[4] This ceremony celebrated the merging of the Central Pacific Railroad, built from the west coast heading east, and Union Pacific Railroad, built from the east traveling west, "officially" creating our nation's first transcontinental railroad. Later that day, Fitch would accompany Stanford and several other prominent dignitaries, on "the first through train" heading west from Chicago, and arriving in Reno, Nevada, in "26 hours and 30 minutes"; "considerable enthusiasm took place."[5]

In the late 1870s Fitch served as an advisor to the territorial governor of Arizona and former (the newly formed Republican Party's very first) presidential candidate John C. Fremont, known as "The Pathfinder" for the expeditions he led into the American Western wilderness in the 1840s.[6]

Fitch worked for years on newspapers in San Francisco as well as at the *Los Angeles Times*. The citizens of four Western states and territories elected him to their legislatures.[7] In the early 1890s, he defended Ed Tewksbury in his murder trial after he shot and killed Thomas Graham in ambush en route to the Hayden flour mill/home, Tempe's first buildings, in Tempe, Arizona, near present-day Arizona State University, to conclude the infamous "Pleasant Valley War (Graham/Tewksbury Feud)" and become famed western novelist Zane Grey's *"Last Man"* standing after that bloody, long-standing conflict.[8] In 1901, he earned a significant paycheck representing the Queen Liliuokalani of Hawaii (in her "sea and beach sand case").[9] Quite a Wild West resume![10]

The lead mogul in the Santa Monica land doings was Colonel Robert S. Baker, who gobbled up much of the four local ranchos,[11] including three which would in part become the Old Soldiers' Home (Rancho San Jose de Buenos Ayres - main, Rancho San Vicente y Santa Monica, and Rancho La Ballona).[12] He was soon joined by John P. Jones, a Nevada senator with huge success in Nevada mining and a keen interest in railroads. The Baker and Jones interests would control local events into the 1890s.[13] Baker's wife was Arcadia Bandini de Baker, a Californio[14] and heir of the Bandini family, one of the most prominent ("favored") rancho families in the state. She was also the widow of Abel Stearns, the largest landowner in Southern California. This gave Baker additional local status and clout.[15]

Arcadia Bandini de Baker, of a prominent Californio family, lent high status to local doings. *Overland Monthly*, July, 1895.

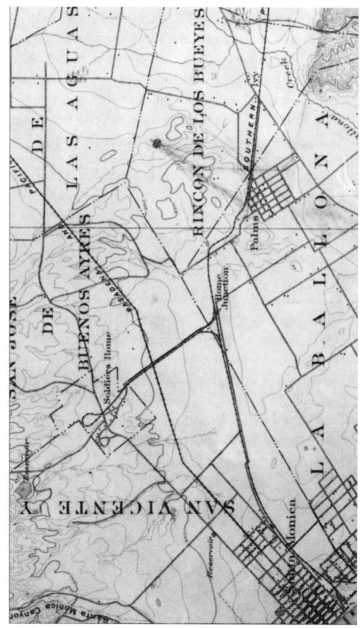

Santa Monica and the Soldiers' Home in relation to the historical ranchos.
United States Geological Survey, 1902.

In the next few decades, matters changed rapidly in Santa Monica. Although rail service to Los Angeles began in 1875, there were dozens of squabbles among competing railroad companies, as well as plans for piers and wharves. Things perked up for Santa Monica during the California land boom around 1888, but it at least didn't subsequently collapse again, as in so many other California locations.

An interesting aspect of the Santa Monica past is one seldom discussed. Although known as a major tourist destination on the Pacific Coast, that was not the intention of its founders. Colonel Baker and Senator Jones aimed to make Santa Monica the industrial center of Southern California, maybe even replacing Los Angeles. If this were not possible, maybe Santa Monica could at least be the major port for Los Angeles. Despite what Santa Monica did to disparage and mock the San Pedro area, that location remained the choice of Los Angeles for all major port developments. Even with such an ally as Collis P. Huntington and his Southern Pacific Railroad, Santa Monica was not up to the San Pedro challenge. In other words, the beautiful beaches and fancy shoreline of Santa Monica are only there today because she failed to attain her industrial hopes.[16]

Just as one Earp contact—Tom Fitch—had been associated with the birth of Santa Monica, another Earp contact—George W. Parsons—was most responsible for Santa Monica losing the port competition to San Pedro. Parsons, the Earp supporter and diarist of Tombstone doings, had moved to Los Angeles and became prominent in mining circles. He was a founder of the Chamber of Commerce, its secretary, and head of several mining organizations. Through speeches, writings, committee work, and an appointment by the governor, Parsons managed to get most people convinced that the future of transportation for Los Angeles led through San Pedro, rather than Santa Monica.[17] Baker and Jones, therefore, lost out in their efforts to create an industrial empire at Santa Monica, and mostly what they had to show for their efforts was a huge amount of rancho acres.

This was when the role of Senator Jones came into play. Following the Civil War, a series of homes for veterans had been established, mostly in the East and Midwest. The first was opened in Maine in 1867, and a few were opened in the following decades. These veterans' homes provided food, shelter, clothing, and medical care, mostly for men incapacitated in

This huge dining hall was just one of dozens of structures on the grounds of the Soldiers' Home. *Overland Monthly*, September 1888.

Dining area in the late 1890s. H. F. Rile photo, Santa Monica Public Library.

some way because of the Civil War or Indian War-era service. Authorities in Washington, D. C., decided to expand on the Pacific Coast, where many veterans had settled. In 1887 the Board of the National Soldiers' Homes of the United States visited California, as they were considering a Pacific Branch. The locations considered included San Bernardino, Santa Monica, Salt Lake City, San Diego, even Catalina Island. In the Los Angeles area alone, there were a dozen or so locations vying for the right of a Soldiers' Home.[18]

The outcome was as easy to predict as a hare outrunning a turtle. Here was Senator Jones, a Pacific Coast power, one of the wealthiest men in America, with several decades of Washington experience, who just happened to be part owner of thousands of acres of vacant land near Los

"The Balloon Route." This is the cover of *Newman's Directory of Los Angeles*, 1903.

Angeles and the Pacific Ocean. It would be exceedingly difficult today to ascertain all the favors that most certainly were called in, what congressional committees were put under pressure, whose arms were twisted. However, Jones's cash up-front was part of the arrangement, and his party doubled the amount desired. The result was that almost 700 acres of the old San Vicente Grant, owned by Baker and Jones, would be purchased for a soldiers' home, official name to be the "National Home for Disabled Volunteer Soldiers." The area was about four miles east of Santa Monica and twelve miles west of Los Angeles. If one was ever to have uncertainty regarding the significance of Senator Jones to the process, the architectural files of the Home in the Library of Congress could be consulted; there it is clearly stated that "Jones assisted in drafting legislation which established the institution."[19]

The property deed for the new institution was recorded in 1888, and it was clear from the wording that although Baker was a big man in town, the huge acreage in his care was through his wife. The seal of the deed is by the name of Arcadia B. de Baker, "by her attorney in fact, Robert S. Baker."[20]

There is an Earp connection with this founding of Santa Monica worth some words. Senator Jones (along with Robert S. Baker and wife Arcadia Bandini) were the key players. At this time Jones, a multi-millionaire based on mining fortunes in Nevada, was a power in the United States Senate. Yet, a few years earlier in the early 1880s, Senator Jones had been linked with Wyatt, Virgil, and James Earp as co-owners of property adjacent to downtown Tombstone. S. B. Comstock, a major speculator and owner of the Grand Hotel in Tombstone, seems to have brought Senator Jones into the investments. These claims were in and around Treasure Hill and included the Comstock, the Mountain Maid, the Daisy, the Grasshopper, and one claim named the Senator Jones.[21]

In 1880-81, Wyatt Earp twice would act as guide and bodyguard for Senator George Hearst as he was considering mining property in Pima and Cochise counties. Hearst, like Jones, was enormously wealthy, based on mining, and an influential United States Senator. In the 1880s Wyatt Earp had business, personal, and legal connections with Senator Hearst, Senator Jones, and Thomas Fitch, three significant nineteenth-century contributors to Western history.[22]

CHAPTER 3

The Birth of Soldiers' City

By December of 1888, the Old Soldiers' Home's first barracks had been erected, and in the following few years other barracks, chapel, library, hospital (ca. 1889), dining hall, and other facilities followed, as well as the development of huge garden areas and livestock grounds. Not only did Baker and Jones profit from the sale of some rancho land, but the city of Santa Monica became the leading beneficiary of the financial windfall. There would be thousands of veterans at the Soldiers' Home getting monthly pensions. Also, hundreds of employees would be receiving pay checks which would find their way to Santa Monica merchants.[1]

In a major publication of 1894, *Tourist's Guide-Book to South California*, George Wharton James mentioned the Soldiers' Home, "where upwards of 1,500 soldiers of the late war are whiling away their old age amidst three hundred acres of flowers, lawns and orchards." The "whiling away" aspect of Soldiers' Home life was not to be for many of the veterans.

By the mid-1890s, then, Santa Monica was moderately increasing in size, and the new Soldiers' Home had been mostly constructed and housed a thousand veterans. There were practically no buildings between the Soldiers' Home and Santa Monica. Surely some use could be found for these vacant rancho acres.

Knowing a good thing, Roy Jones, son of Senator Jones, and Robert F. Jones, the Senator's nephew, became interested in the land adjacent to the Soldiers' Home. The Jones family, along with William T. Gillis and R. C. Gillis of Santa Monica, incorporated the Pacific Land Company in September of 1896. The Gillis brothers were involved with several other

Southern California land developments, including the Santa Monica Bank and the Santa Monica Land & Water Company.[2] The new firm decided that a community next to the Home could be a profitable venture. They organized such a community, and trying to curry favor, suggested it be named Barrett, after the manager of the Home, General Andrew W. Barrett. The new community was called Barrett Villa. Lot sales for Barrett Villa were announced in the *Santa Monica Outlook* of March 31, 1898: average acre costs were $150 to $200, and lots were $50 to $100.[3]

The post office authorities vetoed the name choice, stating it could get confused with another California place-name, Bassett, a township near San Gabriel. In a compromise they decided to name the planned town Sawtelle, after William E. Sawtelle, an officer and part owner of the Pacific Land Company. Mr. Sawtelle lived in the new community and also headed the Sawtelle Water Company. He was also a founder and long-term vice-president of the Citizens State Bank of Sawtelle. Yet, although Mr. Sawtelle would remain "plugged-in" to the new community bearing his name, he moved into Los Angeles in 1905.[4]

One of the confusing oddities of the community names was that Barrett was not the "head" of the Soldiers' Home. The person in charge there was Col. J. G. Rowland, and his official title was Governor. Barrett, the state adjutant-general, was the local manager, the fellow appointed by the Board of Managers in Washington to keep an eye on things.

The Pacific Land Company decided they needed an experienced hand for the new community and turned to Stephen H. Taft to be the

Sawtelle's first home/building; erected in 1897.

Stephen H. Taft, a Midwest clergyman, was recruited west to become "administrative head/town agent" of the new community of Sawtelle. *Los Angeles Herald*, August 6, 1899.

administrative head of what would develop in Sawtelle. Taft was an elderly Midwestern clergyman, whose only experience had been as head of a small college in Iowa. It boggles the mind to consider that this zealous prohibition advocate would father what would end up becoming, as we will learn, such a center of illicit alcohol sales activity (usually referred to as bootlegging, a blind pig, blind tiger, and later a speakeasy).[5]

The town's population was easy to compute—the place had no residents, and much of the land was devoted to a barley crop. The first house was erected in 1897, and by 1902 the population of Sawtelle was around 500. State law and policies of the Home dictated that no alcohol could be sold within one and a half miles of the Home. This meant, then, that the new community of Sawtelle was a prohibition town.

Another factor was at play in the evolution of the Soldiers' Home as well as the growth of the new town of Sawtelle. There was another veterans' home in California, at Yountville in Napa County. However, the Napa Home had a combination of private, state, and federal funding, and in 1897, when the feds bowed out of it, this became the Veterans Home of California. The *San Francisco Call* newspaper pointed out that any veteran was eligible for the Soldiers' Home near Sawtelle, but there was

Assemblyman Robert Bulla of Los
Angeles sponsored legislation to
prohibit alcohol sales near the Soldiers'
Home; it had the opposite effect. *Men of
Achievement*, 1904.

little space left and the waiting list was long;[6] some veterans opted for the
lesser-equipped facility near Napa.

It was in 1895 that Assemblyman Robert Bulla of Los Angeles introduced the legislation, which was approved, that would have a serious
impact on saloon life, crime, and entertainment in greater Los Angeles.
The new state law would prohibit the sale of any alcohol within one and
one-half miles of lands "occupied by any home, retreat, or asylum for
disabled volunteer soldiers, or soldiers and sailors" in the state of California. Specific fines and jail time were authorized for those convicted.
Why Bulla was so concerned is not known. It was certainly not because of
vice dens in Sawtelle; the first residence in the new community was not
erected until 1897. This first residence was the home and office of the Rev.
Stephen H. Taft, the new community's agent, and a pioneer in the anti-saloon movement. He was obviously not the threat that Assemblyman Bulla
had in mind.[7]

Although much was made of this law over the years, it should be
realized that not all things in life were related to the Soldiers' Home. The
same year the legislation was passed (1895), laws regarding liquor sales
and distance from state prisons and the state university were also passed.

Many of the veterans moved from the Soldiers' Home to nearby Sawtelle.
West Coast Magazine, February, 1912.

The state law regarding sales of liquor and distance from the Home seem to have been topics of conversation and planning in the vicinity. Even in March 1898, in the first notice of lots for sale in Barrett Villa, this sentence appeared: "Being near the Soldiers' Home, it is by United States authority, forever protected from the moral and social curse of the saloon."[8]

The living situation in the Soldiers' Home was seldom clearly explained in the local newspapers. Thousands of veterans would live at the Home, but the new community of Sawtelle soon saw relatives of the veterans move in, and many of the veterans themselves bought property in Sawtelle. Many of them had "sleep out" arrangements, taking some or all of their meals in town, yet turning to the Home for some meals and almost always for medical care. Veterans who left the grounds of the Home needed a pass, but this was easily arranged.[9]

A typical example would be W.W. Bunce, a Civil War veteran from Iowa who had worked as a carpenter in Arizona for years. He entered the Soldiers' Home in 1902 and arranged for his wife to live in a cottage in Sawtelle. Then, for a few years, Bunce operated a small store on North Fourth Street, selling fruit and vegetables. When Bunce died in December 1904, he was buried in the Home cemetery, and his wife continued to live in Sawtelle.[10]

Entries in the Sawtelle city directory over the years show how this community differed from others in the country. The compilation for

1906, for example, listed the occupations of residents as Real Estate, Attorney, Grocer, Farmer, and so forth, but interspersed were the notations of "Veteran" or "Old Soldier." This is not the type of information that would have been included in directories of North Dakota, South Carolina, or Massachusetts. Along these same lines, in 1907, on Oregon Avenue in Sawtelle, there were two pension attorneys, who were obviously kept busy with veteran requests.[11]

The Soldiers' Home population had a steady growth, and by time of the Inspector General's report of 1902, there were almost 2,000 veterans registered. Added to this was a substantial number of civilian employees. For the hospital buildings alone, there were ninety-six employees. So, the veterans' pensions and the employee wages meant a lot of money in circulation in and around the new community of Sawtelle. Another interesting gauge of population growth was published in June 1909. There were 2,350 veterans "sleeping in the ground," 2,216 members in the Home, and 1,372 veterans away on furlough.[12]

One of the aspects of having an institution of thousands of elderly people is that deaths were common. The *Evening Express* stated that around 300 old soldiers died in the Home every year, "average nearly one a day." It seems that almost daily the many local newspapers carried obituaries, dateline "Sawtelle."[13]

The Pacific Land Company arranged the sale of inexpensive small lots in town, where some veterans and veteran families built modest homes or cottages. Some of the many employees at the Home also chose to live in Sawtelle, and some of the business places were owned and operated by Home residents. Another unusual aspect for veterans living at the Home was the opportunity for side jobs in the gardens, on the farm, or in the hospital. The money was little enough, but it gave a boost to their pensions, and probably made their days less boring.

AN "OUTRAGE" AT THE SOLDIERS' HOME.

INEBRIATED VET (just up from Santa Monica): "I say, Guv(hic)nor, I'l
never offer yer (hic) 'nuther drink—never! Any man that would pour out good
(hic) whisky like that ain't fit (hic) to command a Soldiers' (hic) Home!"

From earliest days, some Santa Monica folks resented the veterans coming to town to carouse. *Los Angeles Times*, September 22, 1889.

CHAPTER 4

Malibu Attacks!

By 1900 Santa Monica was experiencing reasonable growth and was becoming known as a tourist destination. The city, though, believed its growth and reputation were thwarted because of the presence of saloons; there was a vigorous local movement to ban them. This may appear contradictory for a community trying to enhance its status as a tourist destination, but it was entirely in keeping with a major national thrust towards prohibition. For example, Pasadena in that era was a major world tourist destination with its fine climate, orange groves, mountain railway, and fancy hotels. Yet, Pasadena, too, was a strict anti-alcohol community.

In Santa Monica, saloons and the old veterans were an unwelcome combination practically from the opening of the Soldiers' Home. As early as August 7, 1889, the *Times* reported that the veterans had just received some pension money and a few were in Santa Monica "in a little toot." Also, Santa Monica did not lack appropriate places; by the late 1890s, there were more than a dozen saloons in town.

The major figure in Santa Monica's anti-saloon movement was Frederick Rindge, a leading businessman and owner of the finest ranch lands in Malibu. When some merchants, officials, and residents of Santa Monica took the position that income from liquor licenses was essential to the city, Rindge countered. Rindge asked how much money the liquor licenses brought in; when told it was $2,500, he immediately wrote the city a check for that amount. He promised to continue to bankroll the local prohibition cause.[1]

The *Times* gave a lot of space to Rindge, quoting him on religion, Santa Monica politics, even the sections of the Bible dealing with

MILLIONAIRE PHILANTHROPIST
EXPIRES SUDDENLY IN NORTH

Frederick Rindge, a major financial figure in greater Los Angeles, a vigorous opponent of alcohol, and a leader in Santa Monica's anti-saloon work. *Los Angeles Herald*, August 30, 1905.

wine. The column was headed, "Rindge's Anti-Saloon Views." He also expressed his own perplexity when he described his travels in Germany where he saw "a great many good clean virtuous people drinking their beer without thought of wrongdoing, but, for all that, the beer habit is the curse of Germany." This way of life, obviously, was just fine with Germans.[2]

In an election in April 1900, residents of Santa Monica voted on the saloon issue. The opponents of booze won because: "The no-saloon workers, with Frederick H. Rindge in the lead, displayed great energy and kept a lot of carriages running."[3] Santa Monica did not prohibit the sale of alcohol, but limited the hours of service, and stipulated that alcohol could only be served with meals. This was obviously patterned after ordinances and policies of Pasadena, where the Carlton Hotel was for years the only place where alcoholic beverages could be served, provided they were part of a meal.

Santa Monica would continue to ponder the saloon question, but after 1900 the legal questions of alcohol, saloons, and the old soldiers would more and more be problems of the community of Sawtelle and the County of Los Angeles. It is true that many of the arrested veterans or the blind pig (illicit alcohol) operators of Sawtelle were sent to justice court in Santa Monica. However, in prior years it was often for violations or troublemaking in Santa Monica; this gradually shifted, as dozens of these justice court cases were handled in Los Angeles, Long Beach, and other Los Angeles County communities.

The situation in 1900, then, was that Santa Monica had a limit on the number of saloons, and state law prohibited the sale of alcohol near the Soldiers' Home, meaning, of course, that booze of any kind could not be sold in Sawtelle, which was adjacent to the Soldiers' Home. This meant, then, that the thousand-plus veterans in the Home, as well as their guests, couldn't even buy a bottle of beer. This was a situation ready-made for moonshiners, unlicensed merchants, and criminals. The Los Angeles area had a surplus of these types, and the Earp family would be part of the crowd willing to provide liquid refreshment and entertainment for the veterans.

The War Department had its Inspector General look over the Pacific Branch in 1902, and the report is not only good history, but indicates the local potential for skullduggery. After praising the buildings, overall facilities, and discipline, he wrote that the number of drunks was insignificant, there were few trials, few sentences, few fines. He did point out, though, that "in regard to amusements, it has not fared well, as it has practically no facilities for the amusement of the men. . .no room for billiards or pool, no rooms for cards, chess, checkers, dominos, or other similar games, nor is there any bowling alley." Well, he was right, but almost at that very moment things were about to change, and thanks to the developments in the new community of Sawtelle, the old veterans would finally have many choices to brush off the boredom.[4]

The comments in the annual reports for the Pacific Branch are indeed revealing. In 1893, before there was a community of Sawtelle, the Soldiers' Home handled forty-six cases of "drunk and disorderly." In 1907 there were 171 trials for drunkenness, and the arrests for drunkenness and absence without leave were 517. We must remember that these were internal matters of the Soldiers' Home, and had nothing to do with drinking, arrests, or confinement by township or county officers, or arrests for drunkenness in the cities of Santa Monica, Los Angeles, or Long Beach.

Not an easy job; Home Governor
Andrew Smith was shot by a
disgruntled veteran. *Los Angeles Herald*,
September 29, 1898.

The entire concepts of discipline, attitude, and arrests were not merely philosophical concerns. They involved the lowly as well as the fellows on top. General Andrew J. Smith was the governor of the Soldiers' Home at Santa Monica (Los Angeles/Sawtelle) in 1898, when a disgruntled veteran blasted away at him, hitting him with five bullets in September 1898. Smith lived, but the attempted assassin, Albert Bradley, was "dishonorably discharged." This may have been Smith's fault. Years earlier, when he had headed the Soldiers' Home in Leavenworth, a veteran resident had attempted to blow up his home.[5]

In May 1901, Southern California received an ego boost when President McKinley visited such local sites as the tin production near Temescal, as well as some of the tourist locations at Pasadena. High on the list was the Soldiers' Home at Sawtelle; McKinley was no doubt their

A huge crowd gathered at the Home for President McKinley's visit in May 1901.
Postcard view.

most important visitor ever. As would be expected, the newspapers gave tremendous coverage to such a presidential tour, and fortunately there was no notice of any blind pig goings-on in or around Sawtelle.[6] On the other hand, there were "pickpockets at work." Two members of the presidential party, Secretary Wilson and Colonel Charles A. Moore, were relieved of their pocketbooks. The good news was that the pickpocket was apprehended, and he was not a resident of the Soldiers' Home.[7]

The period 1900-1902 was when the Earps looked at Sawtelle and saw attractive prospects. We must consider the players at that time. Father Nicholas Earp took a back seat to no one. He was a Mexican War veteran, and wherever he lived in the next half century, he was "known." In Illinois, Iowa, and Missouri he had been a constable and a justice of the peace. He went to California twice, both times as leader of a caravan. When he settled in Colton, San Bernardino County, he served for years once again as a justice of the peace and was also president of the Pioneers Society. Folks didn't "cotton to" Nicholas Earp, as he was forceful and always elbowed his way to the front. He fathered a collection of sons who also were not wallflowers.[8]

Virginia and Nicholas P. Earp of San Bernardino County.
Lee A. Silva Collection.

Nicholas lost his wife of many years, Virginia Cooksey, in 1893, and shortly thereafter remarried. By mid-1900, though, Nick was feeling his years. Youngest son Warren had just been killed, and Nick was thinking that maybe his final years would be spent in the care of the government, at the Soldiers' Home in Sawtelle; he had been on the pension rolls since 1894. Some of his friends were there, and the recent Spanish-American War meant that another crop of veterans was in the making. By this time, it was well known that Santa Monica had killed the booze racket, and that the new town of Sawtelle was coming to the fore, as a place to cater to the drinking and gambling whims of the residents of the Soldiers' Home.[9]

There is no record of a meeting where the entire Earp clan got together and decided that Sawtelle was the family's last good chance at a bonanza. But the Earps, no matter how scattered geographically, remained in touch, and San Bernardino County, where Nicholas still watched over things, was the family pivot. Nicholas decided to enter the Soldiers' Home, and all four of his remaining sons would have a role in the Sawtelle shenanigans.[10]

The Earps could certainly feel some attachment to the Soldiers' Home. Nicholas was a Mexican War veteran, and of the boys, only Wyatt lacked military service. The eldest son, Newton, served four years in the Civil War, rising to sergeant in the 4th Iowa Cavalry, and was wounded in action. James and Virgil had each served several years at the front in the Civil War in Illinois regiments. James, one of the first Illinois soldiers to get wounded in action, would be an invalid for half a century because of his wrecked shoulder.

Newton had farmed for years in Garden City, Kansas, where he also became their first chief of police. He spent some time in the Soldiers' Home in Fort Dodge, then in the 1890s moved to California, later to Nevada. His wife died near Winnemucca in 1898. Newton then moved to San Francisco where he did carpenter work near the city. By this time Newton was in his sixties and was still in frequent contact with his father and brothers. It appeared to be a reasonable decision in the Earp family that Newton would join his father Nicholas as a new resident at the Soldiers' Home.

The question was, then, who would run the show in nearby Sawtelle? Wyatt, Virgil, and James knew all aspects of saloon life. They had each owned and worked in saloons from Illinois to Texas to Arizona, California, Idaho, and Alaska. Wyatt, though, believed he had spotted a livelier place than Sawtelle. With his major winnings from the Dexter Saloon in Nome, Wyatt decided to head for a richer bonanza, the new gold-mining community of Tonopah, Nevada. Virgil, in 1900 a candidate for sheriff in Yavapai County, Arizona, had just proved up on his land claim in the Kirkland Valley, and was thinking of projects nearby or possibly in Nevada.

James became the man. In late 1901 or early 1902 he was living in Sawtelle and drawing his pension check there. Within a few months both

James Earp was a Civil War pensioner for years. The dates 1901 and 1902 indicate his move from San Francisco to Sawtelle. *National Archives.*

Nicholas and Newton were adjusting to life in the Soldiers' Home, only yards away from Fourth Street, Sawtelle, where James was planning his booze and poker moves. Wyatt and Virgil would visit Sawtelle from time to time to enlarge the Earp presence.[11]

By 1900 James was by far the most experienced of the Earps in saloon operations. He was the most extroverted of the family, was a live wire, had an unusual sense of humor, and had been involved in saloons, whore house operations, and gambling set ups from Texas to Montana to Alaska. In late 1896 in San Francisco, James and Wyatt were at the racetrack where James, drunk and angry, was forcing a fight with Riley Grannan, one of the nation's most notorious gambling "plungers." Grannan had been a leading loud-mouth, and anti-Wyatt, regarding the Sharkey-Fitzsimmons fight. This San Francisco fight of December 2, 1896, one of the most famous boxing matches in American history, saw Wyatt Earp the referee giving the nod to Tom Sharkey on a blow beneath the belt, a controversial decision that was discussed for years. Just prior to the bout, Wyatt was nearly arrested for carrying a concealed firearm into the ring. One news account stated that James Earp was "a wild Arizona dead shot," and he drew his gun at Grannan. Wyatt managed to stop the challenge and apologized to Grannan for his explosive brother. In other words, James Earp was not just a man pouring drinks; he was a lively participant in saloon and other sporting affairs.[12]

The Earps were ready to launch their Sawtelle operations. The following seems to have been the chronology. Wyatt sold his portion of the Dexter Saloon in Nome to Charlie Hoxie, and apparently made a hefty bundle in the transaction. In mid-November 1901, Wyatt and Josie were in San Francisco, where Wyatt attended a boxing match. In mid-December they were at the Hollenbeck Hotel in Los Angeles. Wyatt was always the front man, so we can assume James followed Wyatt from Nome to San Francisco. Sometime in 1901, James shifted his pension address from San Francisco to Sawtelle. This was for $17, and obviously James intended to add to that amount. [13]

Father Nicholas in San Bernardino County does not seem to have spent much time with his new wife, as by 1900, Nick was living near Redlands with the family of daughter Adelia. He had recently had his pension boosted to $12.[14] In June 1902, Nicholas was admitted to the Soldiers' Home, and Newton's admission followed in October.[15]

One of the unknowns of James's life in this era is female companionship. His wife Bessie had died in San Bernardino in 1887. Yet, sailing to, and returning from Nome in 1900-1901, he was accompanied by "Mrs. J. C. Earp." At Sawtelle, and later in San Bernardino County, there is no further mention of this Mrs. Earp, so we remain in ignorance.[16]

The first decade of the twentieth century in greater Sawtelle is what concerns us, not the operation of the Soldiers' Home, nor the goings-on in the schools and churches. We are looking at folks on both sides of the law who were aware of the steady flow of pension money that the old veterans would receive. By 1900 over a thousand veterans called the Home their home, and within a few years this would increase by several thousand.

Although many parts of Sawtelle would be involved in this money grab, the main activities took place in, on, and around Fourth Street, the closest point of entry for the Soldiers' Home veterans, from the Home, into town. This was also where James Earp set up shop. In September 1898, when the new community was just being formed, Fourth Street was the first roadway to be created to the Soldiers' Home.

Fourth Street, early 1900s, Sawtelle's action place, where James Earp, P. J. Flynn, and others operated blind pigs. *Postcard view.*

When Wilshire Boulevard was completed in 1906, it sliced through the grounds of the Soldiers' Home and west to Santa Monica (assimilating the former Nevada Avenue) and the Pacific Ocean.

Los Angeles Herald, April 14, 1906.

The most important roadway in the area was developed in 1906, when Wilshire Boulevard, from downtown Los Angeles, was made to slash through Soldiers' Home property, connect with Nevada Avenue, and go on to Santa Monica and ultimately the Pacific Ocean. Nevada Avenue's career ended.[17] Although this became the "big road," during the era 1900-1910, nothing surpassed North Fourth Street (modern day Sawtelle Boulevard) in Sawtelle for activity (liquor, prostitution, card rooms).

CHAPTER 5

Almost Paradise

The Soldiers' Home with its hundreds of acres and dozens of major buildings abutted the new community of Sawtelle. People who considered themselves in-the-know about Los Angeles usually considered the two entities interchangeably. They were only inches apart but were light years away in style, law, and the routine of life.

Susie Miller, who took control of *The Veteran-Enterprise* in 1904, tried to pretend that the Home and Sawtelle were one and the same.[1] The newspaper was partially successful in this smokescreen, as there was a vigorous interchange between the two entities. The thousands of veterans shopped, walked, even lived in Sawtelle, and there were dozens of organizations and societies which met regularly in both locations. They were bound together socially and culturally but were often undone by legal considerations. The one place was a federal bastion, the other, a county-township-municipal conglomeration.

Of the thousands of veterans in the Home, hundreds had been natives of such distant places as Georgia, Oregon, Alabama, Idaho, Texas, New Hampshire, and so forth. The word spread across the land via correspondence and articles in newspapers, books, and magazines. The Soldiers' Home near the Pacific Coast was a beacon, praised from coast to coast for a dozen different reasons.

An article in Maine about Southern California claimed: "When all has been said the fact remains that Santa Monica is the favorite and popular all-the-year-round resort of the State." To make certain that more than beaches were intended, the following was included:

This postcard view of the Soldiers' Home in the early 1900s has the Santa Monica Mountains as the background; the Pacific Ocean is to the left. In the foreground to the left is the Chapel which, although in great disrepair, is one of the few buildings that was there at the time of the Earp family, and still remains to this day. Compare to isolated chapel photo page 154, modern chapel page 157, and dust jacket. *David D. de Haas, MD, Collection.*

Barracks Buildings and Park, Soldiers' Home, Cal.

Old Soldiers' Home Barracks; early 1900s. *Postcard view. David D. de Haas, MD, collection.*

What will be in time one of the finest public parks in America is the National Soldiers Home, at Sawtelle, about three miles from Santa Monica. The Home has quarters for nearly 3,000 soldiers, of which number about 2,800 are on the roll. There is always great activity among the older soldiers to get transferred to this Home, on account of the beauty of location and mildness of climate.

Such endorsements nationwide for Santa Monica as well as the Soldiers' Home were not to be found for the nation's other homes for veterans.[2]

The booze question was ever-present. The *Veteran-Enterprise*, the "voice" of the veterans, in each issue carried advertisements from the leading Southern California booze dealers. A typical issue in 1904 had a pictorial ad of the Maier & Zobelein Brewery, a wine and liquor ad from A. Gunn of Los Angeles, C. F. A. Last of Los Angeles boasted of his wine and spirits, and H. C. Akin of Santa Monica reminded folks that he was a wholesale liquor dealer.

If the above does not seem too contradictory, consider further that the "town agent" of Sawtelle, the Rev. Stephen H. Taft, and his wife Etta, were state leaders in the prohibition movement. In the decade of 1900-1910 there must have been a hundred lectures, meetings, parades, and similar gatherings, both in Sawtelle and at the Soldiers' Home, pushing the prohibition movement and passing around anti-saloon petitions. Add to this mix of contradictions that Sawtelle had more arrests for illegal liquor sales than any other part of Los Angeles County. In the *West Coast Magazine* of February 1909, an article was entitled, "Sawtelle-The Home Mecca." Newspapers, magazines, and many public officials were complicit in downplaying the local booze situation.

The temperance and booze drinking at and around the Soldiers' Home came together in an incident in November 1905 when, at the Soldiers' Home, Mrs. Marion Boyd was giving a temperance speech. In the audience, there was a difference of opinion between Major Horace Russell and Gustave Krusen, so shortly after the speech, Major Russell pulled out his pocketknife and stabbed Krusen. Krusen survived; Russell was arrested, and eventually appeared before the superior court in Los Angeles where he was given a year's probation. The affair was interesting enough to be reported to veterans in Kansas.[3]

In that same November, the Women's Christian Temperance Union (W. C. T. U.) held a meeting at the Soldiers' Home and fifty veterans took the pledge; they even formed an auxiliary unit to be active at the Home. The fifty fellows may have been sincere, but they didn't seem to represent the general attitude of the 2,000+ veterans at the Home.

In this same era, when incorporation of Sawtelle was being considered, it was pointed out that "the everlasting liquor question is understood as having been the paramount issue in the election."[4]

How many times James Earp was caught up in the controversies, sweeps, and arrests is hard to say. As early as 1903 he had been referred to in the press as "the well known club man of North Fourth Street."[5] Some accounts of the raids and crackdowns refer to as many as a dozen or so operators sent to justice and police courts in Santa Monica or Los Angeles. However, usually only a few people were identified in the newspapers, and few justice court records have survived. From what we do know, we can surmise that James was either arrested, warned, or cautioned at least a half-dozen times.

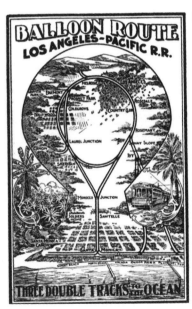

LOS ANGELES–PACIFIC RAILROAD

BALLOON ROUTE

The Greatest Trip for the Money in California.

Leaving Los Angeles over Sunset Boulevard

Passing through Colegrove and Hollywood, the newest and finest Town in Southern California. Sherman, Sawtelle, Soldiers' Home, Santa Monica, Ocean Park, Palms, Playa Del Rey, North Manhattan, Manhattan and Hermosa Beaches and Redondo, returning via the shortest route from the ocean, through the southwestern residence section of the city, making a ride of over 65 miles of foothills and valleys, orange groves and roses; ocean bluffs and beaches with a surf line —twelve miles—more attractive than on ANY SHORE.

OFFICES

LOS ANGELES PACIFIC Bldg.
316 WEST FOURTH ST.

Stops at the Soldiers' Home and Sawtelle are shown on this Balloon Route map of the early 1900s. At the bottom of the illustration can be seen the Pacific Ocean, Santa Monica and its pier, and the Arcadia Hotel. North of the Soldiers' Home and Sawtelle can be seen Morocco Junction (modern day Beverly Hills), Hollywood, and Griffith Park.

General LaGrange headed the Soldiers'
Home in the early 1900s. *New York
Tribune*, April 3, 1894.

Between 1902 and 1906, when Nicholas and Newton were in the
Home and James was living and operating in nearby Sawtelle, the paper
trail indicates that in some ways they resembled their fellow citizens.
They were registered voters of Los Angeles County, as were many other
"denizens" of Sawtelle, seeing no great contradiction in peddling illegal
booze, maybe even on the same day as casting a vote.

The Voter Registrations for the 4th Supervisorial District included
both the Soldiers' Home and the community of Sawtelle. These few pages
over the years provide a quick glimpse of the high and the low, the politician and administrator, as well as the crook and con man, along with
the hundreds of veterans who cared to vote. Nicholas Earp was admitted
to the Home in August 1902, and at once he entered into local politics
as well as registering to vote. Over the years James, a Sawtelle resident,
registered, as did Newton, a Home resident.[6]

The Precinct No. 1 page of registered voters for 1906, shows, in close
proximity, James Earp, Horatio Bolster, and John Dupree, three of the
leading illegal booze sellers in town. A few spaces distant on the same
page are James Keener, marshal of the new town, plus Frank C. Langdon,
head of the Board of Trustees of Sawtelle, and James J. Nellis, a leading

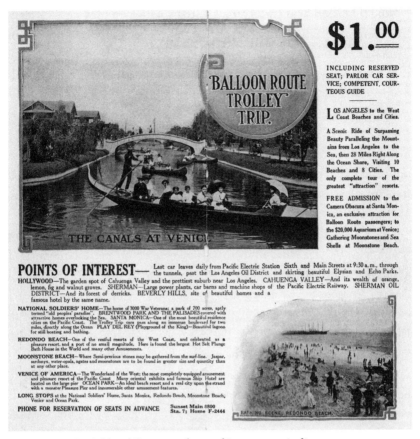

The Soldiers' Home was featured in most tourist literature.

merchant whose son would soon become a Los Angeles County supervisor. The new community certainly had a wide mix of occupational types.[7]

There were dozens of federal and state Soldiers' Homes in the nation, and in one way the one near Sawtelle was not unique. The big and the small, the rural and the urban, it mattered not; alcohol was the leading problem. For example, three of the larger ones, Togus, Maine, with 2,626 members; Dayton, Ohio, with 5,500 members; and Sawtelle, with 3,200 members in 1905, all listed "drunkenness and disorderly conduct" as the leading problems. However, the Sawtelle situation was different because of the state law. The Sawtelle environment meant that criminal action often accompanied a binge, whereas in the other Soldiers' Homes internal discipline or perhaps discharge were the only consequences.

The composition of the veterans in the Soldiers' Homes varied widely. In general, if a fellow had had some military service, was disabled (or later, just in need), he could apply to any of the many homes throughout the country. The Pacific Branch at Sawtelle had veterans by the hundreds from Florida, Michigan, Idaho, Arizona, Maine, Texas; you name the place. This is not something you would find in the Soldiers' Homes of Fort Dodge, Kansas, Milford, Nebraska, or Marshalltown, Iowa. Often the promise of better climate was a factor, but a number of accounts point out veterans making choices related to scenery, nearness to a metropolitan area (Los Angeles), or being able to hear the surf and visit the Santa Monica beaches.

As an example of this situation, in early March 1905, Governor LaGrange of the Pacific Branch was instructed to permit no further admissions until told otherwise. [8] This was not the case in Maine, South Dakota, Wisconsin, or Kansas. An even more telling instance was the case of William T. Wells, who had artillery and cavalry service in the Civil War. He later had a long career with the railroads in Utah and retired to San Francisco. In November 1911, he was visiting in Ogden, fell ill, and was taken to the Soldiers' Home at Sawtelle: "It was Mr. Wells' great desire to be laid to rest in sunny California, and circumstances seemed to favor his wish and bring peace to his last moments." He died days after his arrival.[9]

Santa Monica's relationship with the Soldiers' Home did not end just because the new community of Sawtelle emerged. Santa Monica's merchant and legal apparatus was closely linked with the Home, and the "Balloon Route" (the Los Angeles Pacific Railroad "Trolley" which began service in 1901) included Hollywood, Beverly Hills, Soldiers' Home, Sawtelle, and Santa Monica. Furthermore, the beaches, shops, and saloons of Santa Monica were much closer than any Los Angeles attractions. Alcohol and gambling existed in Santa Monica, but saloon licenses were carefully monitored, and officers of the law enforced things. In April 1904, for example, gambling machines were banished from saloons and stores. The *Times* suggested the money grabbing devices were patronized by "men who could ill afford the drains which the machines made on their pocketbooks." Veterans from the Home would have been in that category.[10]

The nearness to the town meant that veterans would be in Santa Monica daily. In August 1904 children playing by a haystack in the polo grounds found the body of Thomas Sexton. Beside the body were an empty wine bottle, a box of strychnine pills, and some pension papers detailing his Civil War service with a Pennsylvania regiment.[11] In 1905 there was much coverage of Walter Vandercook, a Spanish-American War veteran in the Home, who became acquainted with Ruth Hilliard, the beautiful young daughter of a fellow veteran there. He moved into Santa Monica to be near her and became a local photographer. He may or may not have been a victim of alleged multiple midnight assaults by enemies/secret admirers of the young lady, who were giving her "unwelcome attentions." Ms. Hilliard had enlisted him to protect her, after she had received several undesirable "annoying" anonymous letters, which contained "improper proposals." Vandercook was probably mentally disturbed. Pages of press coverage and hours of police time were wasted on a non-event. This was just another of the hundreds of connections that Santa Monica had with the Home.[12]

Some events are more than curious. In Justice Summerfield's court in October 1909, "Howell G. Trogden, a member of the Soldiers' Home, and wearing medals given him by congress for valor, attacked Joseph F. Gough, a Santa Monica policeman." Gough had to go to a hospital for his scalp wounds, and Trogden was taken to the county jail. His reasoning was that he had been mistreated by Gough and other Santa Monica policemen.[13]

Trogden was an administrator's nightmare. He was an authentic hero, receiving the Medal of Honor for deeds in the Siege of Vicksburg in 1863. By the turn of the century, though, Trogden was off the rails. He was in many a fracas in Santa Monica and Los Angeles, and once, in San Francisco, he whipped out a pistol and broke up a meeting of anarchists. He frequently, in public, criticized the Soldiers' Home, especially the administrators. He was discharged from the Home and died in Los Angeles on December 2, 1910.[14]

The Santa Monica relationship with the Soldiers' Home was very positive, yet at the same time dismal. For many people in California, and the West, the Soldiers' Home meant fantastic climate, architectural splendors, attractive gardens and grounds, sunny beaches, and the major resort city of Santa Monica. For the city of Santa Monica, it also meant clogged justice courts and too many tipsy veterans.

In June 1901, for example, in the Santa Monica court of Recorder Wells, eight cases of drunkenness were handled, and Justice Guidinger dealt with five cases of disturbing the peace. Justice A. L. Jenness was also busy, the *Herald* reported that "many old soldiers, almost too intoxicated for locomotion, were, however, not arrested, but instead put aboard the electric cars for the home."[15] The *Times* reported a case handled by Justice Jenness. A Santa Monica housewife complained that elderly veteran Henry Fraser had crawled under her house, "ostensibly to see and hear whatever might be of interest as it percolated through a crack in the floor."[16]

Drunkenness, humor, and confusion were part of an incident in Santa Monica in October 1904 when Justice Jenness dealt with the case of Thomas Folk and Martin Freeman. These veterans wandered into Santa Monica, loaded up on liquor, borrowed money from each other, but forgot who borrowed what, and sued each other. One veteran was deaf, and his "attorney" was a pre-war barrister "who is now a member of the home, where he waits on the table." Nothing came of the case, other than more bad publicity for the Home and for Santa Monica.[17]

An event in June 1905 pretty much summarizes the way Justice Jenness considered and decided on questions regarding Sawtelle. He was dealing with Mrs. Mattie Mitchell, arrested on the alleged robbing of veteran William Folk. He felt the evidence was too thin, so he released her. "The merits of the blind pig allegation were not gone into." Jenness, and other local court officials, needed a big bundle of evidence even to attempt to rule on Sawtelle and blind pig concerns.[18]

Alexander Milne, a Soldiers' Home member, was in a Santa Monica lodging house in January 1902, had been drinking heavily, and asked to have Henry Akin visit him. Akin did so, but shortly thereafter a physician was called, and Milne died. In his pockets were twenty cents and two morphine phials. Of more than passing interest here is that Henry Akin was probably the leading saloon and wholesale liquor dealer in Santa Monica. These, and dozens of other incidents, indicate what a mixed blessing for Santa Monica was the Soldiers' Home.[19]

There were tons of incidents and circumstances of the Soldiers' Home and Sawtelle that involved wives, women, or marriages, but they were a bit outside the realm of criminal activity or booze use. Yet, these incidents do indicate that the local Soldiers' Home was different from the other homes in the country. Sawtelle was created precisely because there was vacant land next to the Soldiers' Home. Therefore, it became possible to erect hundreds of small, inexpensive cottages where wives, or sometimes entire families, could live next to the Home.[20] These veterans were old, and the number of deaths large; therefore, widows were large in numbers. Many cases of "true love" developed, as widows and available veterans tried to make something of their remaining years. One report of 1906 suggested that there were hundreds of veteran families living in Sawtelle, some of them "new" families. Much was made of certain incidents like the wedding in 1904 of Major Hiram Rogers and Mary Jane Thompson, a recent widow. He was a Mexican War veteran and they would be the "oldest bride and groom in history of county." [21]

Another unusual "made in Sawtelle" marriage was in 1909 when Varnum Westcott, eighty-one, who served in the California Cavalry during the Civil War, married a twenty-one-year-old widow, Electa Bessie Hawkins. Her father, C. E. Chase, was also a resident of the Home, and this cinched their relationship. Although all these folks had interesting pasts (her husband was hanged for murder in Arizona), the marriage is mentioned here as an example of the role Sawtelle could play in match-making. Westcott bought a home in Sawtelle where the couple lived after the wedding.[22]

One couple re-married at Sawtelle. Mrs. Giles Burgess claimed her frontier soldier-husband deserted her, so she divorced him and returned to New York. In 1909 she read an account of controversies at the Soldiers' Home at Sawtelle and "rushed across the continent" to be with him again, after twenty-five years. They were remarried. [23] Most typical of the marriages of veterans, though, was that two elderly folks decided they wanted company. The *Los Angeles Herald* publicized with a photo, Mr. and Mrs. Lewis Cass Bell: "Begin Life Again, Though Gray and Wrinkled With Age."[24]

A similar story of "renewal" occurred in March 1906. Captain Enos Bailey, the undertaker at the Soldiers' Home, requested leave to go to

Tourists visit Soldiers' Home Library October 1910. Many groups and organizations considered a visit to the Soldiers' Home a must. Courtesy of the California History Room, California State Library, Sacramento, California.

Michigan. Mary Billings was a widow, and they had known each other as children. So, "Civil War Veteran to Marry Former Playmate."[25]

One of the frequent occurrences of the Home which involved alcohol was suicide. There are a variety of reasons for taking one's life, and an aged veteran, often disabled, can easily supply some of these reasons. In the existence of the Home, the numbers of suicides must have been very high. One example which combines a few of the factors was that of John Beyer in late June 1904. Beyer, an Ohio Civil War veteran, had been admitted to the Home in 1894 and was one of the best employees of the dining hall. He started drinking, "could not seem to let go," ran out of funds, and was found drunk and dead in a ditch at Morocco Junction (Beverly Hills).[26]

The situation of Lutellus Doolittle highlights why Sawtelle and Santa Monica had so many lawyers, not just dealing with criminal affairs, but with the hundreds of cases where elderly veterans were really helpless. Doolittle had served in an Illinois infantry regiment, later lived in San Diego, was admitted to the Home in 1904, and died there in February 1905.

In a complicated case which reached the California Supreme Court, the question was if Doolittle was "himself" when he signed his will in the Home Hospital. Was he lying in bed, sitting up, sort of reclining; did he make his mark properly; did he see the paper when he marked or signed? Was he drowsy? Was he aroused to sign the will? At this time there were several thousand elderly veterans, many of them in poor health, in greater Sawtelle and in the Home, so we can imagine the high number and variety of issues that would arise when they reached the end of the trail. [27]

The "dens of Sawtelle" and phrases like "drunken veterans" were not the only words and subjects about the Soldiers' Home. This huge complex of buildings with several thousand residents was not only well known, but it became a major tourist attraction as well. Sandwiched between Los Angeles and Santa Monica, pierced by Wilshire Boulevard, and having a rail station on the famous Balloon Route (so named as the route on a map took on the shape of a hot air balloon) assured that the Soldiers' Home would be one of the most visible places in Southern California.

Nicholas Earp's letters from the Home would be read to members of the San Bernardino Historical Society, and folks from there and Colton would visit him at Sawtelle. Historian Fred Holladay wrote about Judge John T. Knox of San Bernardino, who went into the Soldiers' Home around the same time as Nicholas, and how they enjoyed talking over old times as they were confined to the Home hospital at the same time.

This is the type of information that flowed throughout most communities in Southern California. From the late 1890s on, excursions were made from San Bernardino, San Diego, Van Nuys, Pasadena, Riverside, and dozens of other communities. Veterans organizations, historical societies, and fraternal organizations would make annual trips by rail, bus, touring car, and private auto. These groups would do this as a major outing, or more often as part of a holiday or military commemoration. A typical outing occurred in April 1904 when a group from San Bernardino went to the Soldiers' Home via the Los Angeles Pacific Railway to help celebrate Appomattox Day with the veterans.[28]

In November 1910, Inspector-General and Chief Surgeon, Col. W. E. Elwell, from the Washington headquarters, inspected the entire Pacific Branch facility, which included more than a thousand veterans in their

This view of Sawtelle blind pig thugs and scavengers was part of the useless newspaper campaign to stamp out Sawtelle vice. *Los Angeles Times*, March 15, 1904.

uniforms, all the horses, farm wagons, ambulances, and anything else that could move. The presentation was such a major event that special grandstands were erected to accommodate the many visitors.

Such was the unusual double-pronged reputation of the Soldiers' Home and Sawtelle. An enormous contingent of elderly veterans were housed in a massive, well-maintained, attractive arrangement of buildings; nearby, debauchery, card playing, illicit alcohol sales/drunkenness, and other shenanigans took place.

On the other hand, service in the nation's wars, and adjusting to life decades later may sound like considerations for the prophets, but life was going on. The nitty-gritty of daily life was noted by Oregon's *Daily Capital Journal*. The meals at the Soldiers' Home in Sawtelle were said to contain a heavy daily dose of oleomargarine. "Attention has been called to the fact that congress has placed its ban on oleomargarine in foodstuffs but considers it good enough for the veterans."[29]

CHAPTER 6

The Den of Evil

The numbers of arrests, encounters, and searches by officers of the law were staggering. Many accounts would state that at any time there were more than a dozen blind pigs in operation. A search in justice court records, jail placements, and newspaper accounts would show more than a thousand such cases during 1900-1910. This does not mean that Sawtelle was a vile place, a den of evil. It only indicates that Sawtelle was adjacent to an institution housing a sizable group of elderly men with time on their hands, and a little pension money to relieve their boredom.

The activities of the veterans and their "providers" were many. Sometimes officials tried to prevent "gambling of all kinds, from poker to dice games for cigars." Joseph Schultz, owner of five acres and a "good grocery store, by no means a poor man," was arrested for selling whiskey. In one haul by constables in 1906, in addition to many blind pig arrests, four soiled doves were arrested and fined $20 each. Sometimes the booze was too much for the old boys. In June 1905, one veteran visited the home of Mattie Mitchell, "a Negress," where he died of a heart attack. She was arrested, not for the death, but because she was seen stealing from another veteran "while he slumbered on her bed."[1]

The drive for money led to creativity. Dave Smith was arrested because a search of his wagon revealed not only fruit and soda water, but liquor and beer. Another young fellow was referred to as a "walking blind pig," as he had several bottles that he would offer to veterans he would meet on the street. On one occasion in 1903, Constable Lederer arrested three men operating a blind pig in the alley between Third and Fourth Streets.[2]

Fifth Street, early 1900s, also a place of some illegal booze action. *Postcard view.*

That drinking and trouble often went together was demonstrated in Santa Monica in June 1906. James Sullivan, a Soldiers' Home resident, got boozed up and went to Santa Monica's Linda Vista Park, where Constable F. M Culp arrested him for being drunk and disorderly. The "inebriate veteran" was thrown into a patrol wagon, taken to city hall where he resisted, and was handcuffed. This was too much for Constable Culp, who "DROPS DEAD AFTER MAKING AN ARREST" (*Herald* headline).[3] The *Outlook* praised the work of the deceased constable, and of Sullivan reported that "the human derelict was loaded into a wagon and hauled to the city jail."[4]

James Boyle, a resident of the Soldiers' Home, turned himself in to authorities in Santa Monica stating that he "beat-up" John Manning, a fellow veteran at the Home. Manning, who started the fight, had been "in his cups." Unstated, even unasked, was where Manning could have obtained the booze that led to his condition. The answer was too obvious—only yards away from the Home grounds, at the beginning of Fourth Street.[5]

Alcohol and prostitution were leading sources of revenue for the boys, but gambling was not far behind. In March 1904, a raid found three gambling halls, a "house of prostitution," four poker tables, and booze everywhere. One group of ladies were provided by "an old soldier with one eye." Storefront names seldom revealed all interior activities. A drugstore clerk was arrested for selling whiskey, and Horatio Bolster, local barber, was frequently arrested for the same offense. One cobbler usually had his coffee pot loaded with whiskey, for veterans who often needed "shoe repairs."[6]

Most of the publicity and mystique about "wild life in Sawtelle" deals with alcohol and gambling, as though those were the only activities of interest to the veterans. Yet, there were dozens of women engaged in prostitution; some would say hundreds. In one raid early in 1906, for example, constables arrested Mrs. Gibbons on Ohio Street, where she had a merchant house advertised as "Plain Sewing." Two other nearby disorderly houses were raided at the same time. And this was on Ohio Street, nowhere near as lively as the doings on Fourth and Fifth Streets.

The merchants, especially those on Fourth Street, had dozens of tricks in order to disguise their activities. Barbers, grocers, cobblers,

Veterans playing checkers at Soldiers' Home. This was the preferred image
advocated by Home authorities. *Postcard view.*

druggists—many of them had their favorite gimmicks. Jean Gustave
supposedly ran a cigar stand. Yet, on his property could be found bottles
and cans of liquid, as well as cards and other gambling devices. He was
highly mobile and could quickly shift locations.[7]

Amid all this boozing and arrests, there existed in Sawtelle as well
as in most parts of Los Angeles County, a thriving organizational thrust
for those interested in prohibition. This major national movement had
some of its better successes in Southern California, but Sawtelle was not
one of them. In one paragraph in 1905, the *Los Angeles Herald* mentioned
that a lecture would take place at the Soldiers' Home that evening by a
speaker from the Women's Christian Temperance Union. Sentences later,
in a seemingly unrelated statement, it reported on three arrests for illegal
whiskey selling and that there were about two dozen blind pigs operating
in Sawtelle. We could say that the Home and nearby community of Sawtelle were living proof of the need for a prohibition movement.[8]

Along these same lines, in October 1904, when the Prohibitionist
Dr. E. S. Chapman gave a temperance lecture at the Baptist Chapel in
Sawtelle, he ran free busses from the Soldiers' Home to the chapel. Many
veterans took advantage of the free ride, but the newspaper suggestion

was that they could also have stopped off instead at one of Fourth Street's places of entertainment.[9]

Although there was considerable coverage of the blind pig problem in the local press, some of the writing was casual, often pointing out that the old boys were just having fun. Yet, in addition to large amounts of money being siphoned from the veterans, drinking indeed did have its dark side. In May 1906 two veterans died of the stuff. James Williamson, "a discharged member of the Home," was on his deathbed from time in a blind pig, and Franklin VanDake, a veteran, was "stricken in Sawtelle" and taken to the Home hospital, where he expired. The *Times* article reporting these incidents was headed "HELL'S POISON IN BLIND PIGS."[10]

The Soldiers' Home management knew they had a problem, with a few thousand veterans in residence, and where the greatest excitement may have been a game of checkers. For a time, there was a canteen, and a mild form of beer was available. In late 1905, Governor LaGrange promised "soft beer," with less than 3 percent of alcohol for the canteen. However, none of these efforts could match the fact that a few yards away, where Fourth Street began, there were people in Sawtelle offering good beer, whiskey, a deck of cards, and usually a place to gather.

Although our account deals mostly with booze, cards, and related activity, this only accounts for a part of the deeds that involved the Soldiers' Home residents. Some could be considered comical, such as George Kellogg, discharged from the Home and sent to the Asylum in Patton (nearly eighty miles away) in 1906. He didn't like it there, stole a bicycle, took it to Colton, then tried to head back to Sawtelle. They found him (but not the bicycle), didn't let him back in the Home, and he died in Los Angeles the following year. [11] In December 1907, John Krip of the Home wrote several articles describing the President of the United States and administrators of the Home as "a lot of decayed politicians." He was kicked out of Sawtelle.[12]

Visits to town and elsewhere, as well as furloughs, meant that Home administrators were constantly faced with tales of bad news from nearby. In October 1905, Herman Walker, eighty-seven, a veteran visiting Long Beach, was despondent over his memory loss and threw himself in front of an electric car. James Smith, an elderly Wisconsin veteran, decided to take in the sights in Los Angeles in June 1905 and was hit on the head with a cleaver in a Los Angeles saloon. William Moore and William McAtammey visited Los Angeles in September 1906, got drunk, were robbed of hundreds of dollars, went to court, but were drunk again the next day. In February 1909 Joseph Gilbert, inebriated, was creating a scene on Oregon Avenue in Sawtelle when a policeman tried to take him to jail. Gilbert resisted, threw the policeman to the sidewalk, and was only handled when another policeman arrived. These incidents were not highlights, not sagas, but merely a few of the many dozens of cases where elderly veterans, out on their own, got into trouble.[13]

Unfortunately for the Home, serious, vicious encounters even occurred on the grounds and in the buildings. A noteworthy attack occurred in August 1902 when Fred Gerant, probably mentally disturbed, obtained some liquor, grabbed a revolver, went into the steward's room where Captain H. D. Lasher was at his desk, and pumped three bullets into him. Lasher survived; Gerant was ruled as insane and discharged the next year. [14]

Charles Albee had a more unfortunate end. Albee, who had served in a California Regiment in the Civil War, didn't get on with John Condon, a veteran from New York. Albee complained of Condon's behavior, and once clubbed him on the head with his cane. Condon, prone to drink, in late June 1905, just before dinner, walked up to Albee, placed a revolver to his chest, and fired. Albee died the next day. Condon was tried in Superior Court in Los Angeles and was convicted of murder in September; he was soon sent off to San Quentin. [15]

Another violent booze event happened in October 1907, as Richard Murphy and Lewis Crane argued over who was the braver. Crane attacked Murphy with a knife, and Murphy shot Crane. Both survived. Murphy was taken to court in Los Angeles and allowed to plead guilty. The *Los Angeles Herald* had this telling comment: "From the testimony it appears that liquor flows quite freely among the old soldiers at the home in Sawtelle."[16]

Yet, despite alcohol's causing so many disputes and a number of fatalities, the high number of men in the Home assured that violence could be caused by a number of factors. In July 1914, Charles Lakel, age seventy-two, and Mortimer Broderick, fifty-eight, were in the Home, arguing over home rule in Ireland. They clinched, and Lakel fell thirty feet from the balcony and broke his neck in the fatal plunge. [17]

In this era of illegal booze, veteran dissipation, and similar goings-on, it was unusual to find a public voice that seemed to understand the situation. That voice was General George B. Loud, prominent New York figure in veterans' affairs and a trustee of the New York operation. He gave a speech in Sawtelle criticizing the prohibition movement that closed the canteens of the Soldiers' Homes in the country. He proclaimed he would like to banish liquor from the universe, but that can't be done just now. Yet, "canteen abolition at the soldiers' homes has led the inmates to seek liquor elsewhere and almost invariably when filled with the worst poison imaginable, they are subject to robbery and assault."[18]

Contrast that realistic language with the Sawtelle W.C.T.U. push in 1907 to keep the canteens closed, as it was planned to have "reading and game rooms where coffee would be served to take the place of the canteens." Needless to say, this Boy Scout approach was of little interest to the veterans.[19] The period from 1900 until World War I saw the canteen issue ever present across the nation, wherever there was a Soldiers' Home. From Sawtelle through Leavenworth to Togus, Maine, arguments

The six old soldiers now in the County Jail for skylarking at Sawtelle.

Some of the bad guys, old soldiers in County Jail.
Los Angeles Times, December 30, 1907.

and proposed legislation about prohibition, canteens, soft beer, real beer, rationed beer were constant. The *Los Angeles Herald* published an article datelined Washington, regarding proposed legislation, headed, "OLD SOLDIERS MUST GO DRY." This didn't happen.[20]

To have or not to have a canteen was a quagmire for the veterans as well as for the Home administrators. One could argue, as many did, that if the men had a canteen at the Home, even if it only served "near-beer," life would be smoother (and quieter) for all. It is easy to conclude that the blind pig operators in Sawtelle would be opposed to a canteen at the Home. Yet, there were other angles to consider. If the veterans were sipping near-beer at the home, they wouldn't be in Sawtelle playing cards or using the pool rooms, therefore angering local merchants. The *Los Angeles Evening Express* asserted an even more potent anti-canteen argument of some veterans: "The governor of the soldiers' home wants every one of the 2,000 men down there to spend his money at the canteen."[21]

CHAPTER 7

◆━◆━◇━◆━◇━◆

Sawtelle: A New City

Law and order existed, but they did not prevail. Sawtelle, with its first house erected in 1897, had no legal existence. If the manager of the Soldiers' Home needed an officer of law, he had to look afar. There is no clear way to summarize (or understand) who ran the law-and-order show in greater Sawtelle. Various justices of the peace from Los Angeles, Santa Monica, even Long Beach, were involved, which is why constables from these jurisdictions made most of the arrests. Yet, the many publicized goings-on in Sawtelle often became so embarrassing that county officers felt they had to act. For example, in October 1905 a deputy district attorney and a slew of constables from Los Angeles made a Sawtelle raid and confiscated barrels of beer and some whiskey; they made some street arrests, including a few fellows from Mallory's pool room. This time the prisoners were taken to jail in Long Beach. The raid was triggered by a complaint from the manager of the Soldiers' Home.

The law and order brigade of greater Sawtelle, such as it was, evolved as a series of layers. From the beginning, in the Soldiers' Home itself, there were individuals invested with police powers. In 1889, for example, there were a police sergeant, three guards, four watchmen, and a dining room sergeant. These, then, were federal officers, but had no jurisdiction beyond the Home grounds. By the early 1900s there were several dozen law officer types for Home property, as the veteran population had expanded significantly. The governor of the Home would hold court each morning to consider disciplinary or related cases.[1]

The *Times* covered "The Governor in his Court," a pension-day affair, held in the guard house. The heads of the units in the barracks would

60

J. V. Brighton, Arizona lawman who killed Ike Clanton, was subsequently a Soldiers' Home inmate and a police officer in Sawtelle. *San Francisco Examiner*, February 25, 1894.

bring in a half-dozen or so miscreants, who explained to Governor LaGrange how they had gone wrong. Drinking alcohol, either in the Home or in nearby Sawtelle, was the usual tale, although debts and loans also were frequent causes of friction among the veterans. LaGrange oversaw discipline, and "no pass" or "no furlough" were common punishments. The few more extreme cases led to expulsion from the Home.[2]

The title of the head of the Soldiers' Home is hard to pin down. Most were referred to as governor, yet many times their military rank, of general or colonel, was used. Sometimes they were referred to as "manager," yet that was the local title of a member of the Board of Managers. Usually, the word "governor" was used for the big guy at the Soldiers' Home.

Outside the Home property, the legal authority at first was held by the several justices of the peace in the townships of Santa Monica and Los Angeles, with an occasional call for help from as far away as Long Beach or Pasadena. These justices of the peace had as officers of the law a constable, and the justices and/or the constable could hire deputy constables if the need arose. As the population of Sawtelle grew, both Santa Monica and the Los Angeles justices of the peace put more deputy constables on the payroll. After all, at times quite a bit was going on in Sawtelle.[3]

Aside from these law-and-order types, the County of Los Angeles would get involved with their police officers. With cityhood in 1906, Sawtelle had its own police force, which tried to work closely with Los Angeles County personnel. We can see, then, that the men with the badges could be federal (Home personnel), township (constables), county (sheriff deputies), or city (Sawtelle town marshal).

Becoming a new city, but having an inadequate jail, led to a series of problems for Sawtelle. In one expose in December 1907 it was revealed that the constable was arresting veterans right and left, on minor charges, then taking them to the Los Angeles County Jail, which had the needed capacity. The constable's eager action was related to the fact that he was paid a fee for each arrest, and also received mileage for the trip to the county jail.

The inability of the city to handle the booze situation shows up in the role of Civil War veteran Milton Miely, a bicycle bootlegger. Miely would ride around the Home, then the streets of Sawtelle, receive orders (and cash), then ride into Santa Monica and make some purchases. He would return to Sawtelle and drop the bottles "at designated places where they were awaited with delightful anticipation." The *Los Angeles Herald* announced that Miely would be spending a few days in the county jail, but this was a minor interruption to a bicycle bootlegging system that he had been operating for some years and which more than likely was quite profitable.[4]

Several names appear frequently in the arrest, trial, and fines events. Justice Albert Jenness of Santa Monica had to send many a constable to Sawtelle before his death in 1907. By that time he was serving as a Santa Monica Police Judge. Jacques De La Monte was a deputy constable, then constable, for Los Angeles Township for a decade and often planned and assisted in Sawtelle raids. Jonas (J.V.; "Rawhide Jake") Brighton, well known frontier detective and deputy sheriff, who in 1887 had tracked down and killed the Earps' Tombstone nemesis Ike Clanton,[5] was an officer in the Home, and later a policeman in Sawtelle. Henry Laird was a civilian employee at the Home, but later served as a deputy constable for Santa Monica Township. Charles Lederer, a recent Spanish-American War veteran, lived at the Home off and on but also worked as a township

constable. James Keener, a Sawtelle grocer, became a constable, then for
the new city of Sawtelle in 1906 became their first city marshal.[6]

There existed an absurd, confusing nature of the local legal jurisdiction as demonstrated when John Dupree was arrested on Fourth
Street, Sawtelle, on a gambling charge by a Long Beach policeman. The
information of the gambling violation came from Santa Monica, during
the investigation of the robbing of a veteran. John Dupree was carted off
to the county jail in Los Angeles. That's a lot of geography in those two
sentences.[7]

The law and its enforcement were not so clear-cut because there was
no official Sawtelle until the incorporation vote in 1906. Until then, the
Soldiers' Home property and all the land west to Santa Monica was part
of Santa Monica Township. This explains why many of the blind pig and
other criminal violations were handled by the justice of the peace or police
judge in Santa Monica. After Sawtelle became a city in 1906, the next
major change came in December 1909, when the Township of Malibu was
created, which included all the land north of the City of Santa Monica.
According to the *Times* "it will not be necessary to take civil and criminal
cases from Sawtelle and the Soldiers' Home to Santa Monica for trial."
In other words, a case of blind pig operation, or illegal gambling devices,
could be sent to the City of Sawtelle or to the Township of Malibu.[8]

Unanswered by such specific legal and geographical statements is why
so many of the alcohol and gambling violations between 1900 and 1906
were handled by justice courts in Los Angeles, Long Beach, or other venues. We do know that the officials of the Soldiers' Home were frequently
frustrated by the drinking and gambling goings-on and leaned on any of
the nearby township or county officials to lend a hand.[9]

Even geography and distance were brought into play to clamp down
on the blind pigs. At one point in late 1907, even after Sawtelle cityhood,
Deputy Marshal A. F. Young suggested that those violators in the future
might be sent to a justice court in Pasadena for hearings and trial. This
could prove a major factor. Pasadena, some twenty miles away, would be a
costly and time-consuming combination on top of any fines or jail time.[10]

Did the arrests and fines help to defang the perpetrators? Apparently
not. Some fellows, such as John Dupree, were arrested and fined at least

ten times. With so much money in circulation, modest fines didn't slow the action. Another example is Horatio Bolster, who in one brief period in 1906 was arrested four times. "Baby," as he was called, was old, and "a regular cell has been reserved for him in the county bastille."[11]

Could cityhood put a damper on Sawtelle dirty doings? Some people believed so, and there was a strong push towards that end in 1905-06. In an election held in November 1906, voters decided to incorporate as a city. They now had officials and began planning their own jail. Surely most problems were behind them? Not at all. Practically from the beginning there were moves for "disincorporation." Many (probably most) citizens of Sawtelle were unhappy with city status. There were new regulations (no cows in the streets, for example), taxes seemed too steep, there were questions of whether veterans at the Soldiers' Home could/should vote, and so forth. The dissatisfaction with cityhood would remain with Sawtelle until some political turmoil beginning in 1918; Sawtelle was incorporated into the city of Los Angeles in 1922.

Meanwhile, though, what did city status mean to blind pigs, illegal gambling games, and prostitution? Not much. True, Sawtelle would now have its own constables, its own jail. However, Sawtelle still had, adjacent to it, an abundance of lonely, bored, elderly veterans. Also, who lived in the town of Sawtelle? Many of the residents were veterans, and many were employees of the Soldiers' Home.

The weird jurisdiction system for Sawtelle was evident in February 1907, shortly after the new cityhood. A "joint jail" in Sawtelle was assured, as Los Angeles County agreed to put in a few thousand dollars for a concrete jail, which Sawtelle would keep in repair and use "as a city prison." Food would come from the city of Sawtelle, but blankets from the County of Los Angeles. This would be just one of many situations that led to controversies among Sawtelle, the City of Los Angeles, and the County of Los Angeles.[12]

Another thing that happened with cityhood is that the new officers for a time believed they had power. They passed an ordinance that meant a "dry town," and suggested this "will mean absolute dryness." The state law already prohibited the sale of all types of alcohol; the new ordinance prohibited "the mere possession of over one pint of whiskey or other

Oregon Boulevard, probably 1905, the main drag, would become Santa Monica Boulevard in modern times. *Postcard view.*

intoxicating liquor." This ordinance was quickly quashed by the local courts, and the Sawtelle veterans no doubt had many a laugh at the overreach of the amateur politicians.[13]

Although there were a variety of political jurisdictions, there were reasonable instances when officers from several jurisdictions could have been involved. In September 1902 "robbers" stole some tools from the local railroad company, forced open the Sawtelle post office door, and made off with $34 worth of stamps and pennies. To solve the case, two secret service men, a police detective, and a deputy sheriff were given the case, in other words, federal and county officials.[14]

Cityhood brought other surprises to city officials. In May 1907 the city recorder had to deal with seven blind pig cases, the result of a major raid. Involved in the raid was a woman detective, Rosalind Caswell. Her husband Earl was also working undercover. Rosalind would move around the Sawtelle streets, flirt with the fellows, and apparently was so good at the game that one old boy thought the court summons was a marriage license. The shock for city officials, though, came when the Caswell bill was presented in June for $623.65. This included money for meals, $141 "for automobile hire," funds for "whiskey at May's" and "drink at Flynn's," as well as $2 for "backing F. Ransom at poker game." Running a city could get expensive.[15]

In those brief periods when the city of Sawtelle promised to get tough on blind pigs, there was still no shortage of booze in the area. In a period of drought, several of the veterans would get together, pool their funds, then "send one of their number to Santa Monica. There the wholesale house keeps constantly on hand the popular brands. This method of irrigation is practiced to such an extent that one veteran is kept almost continuously on the go between Sawtelle and the beach."[16]

There is abundant evidence that the new city of Sawtelle was only lukewarm about clamping down on drinking, gambling, and prostitution. In mid-April 1909 city trustees admitted that appropriations for City Marshal Millard Young were so inadequate that he had to work several shifts a day, as "there has been no money to pay extra men." Yet, Young was then named deputy constable for Sawtelle and of Santa Monica Township. That was the solution: more badges, a hint of glory, no money.[17]

CHAPTER 8

❖═◈═◇═◆═❖

The Earps Cometh

The local newspapers frequently stated that evil men were standing at the gates of the Soldiers' Home, taking advantage of these veterans, grabbing their pension money. The reality was that the veterans enjoyed going into Sawtelle and having a good time. Furthermore, many of the "villains" castigated by the press were veterans. Some of the leading "entertainment providers" in Sawtelle were James Earp, John Dupree, and P. J. Flynn. All three were Civil War veterans, residents of Sawtelle, and in good standing with their Soldiers' Home buddies. Some, like James Earp, even had relatives living in the Home.

It might be reasonable at this point to ask how the Pacific Branch compared to the other Soldiers' Homes in the nation at the turn of the century and into the first decade of the 1900s, at least so far as law and order, blind pigs, and other similar activities. In general, crooks, shady types, or adventurers were interested in getting a share of the pension money. For example, the *Leavenworth Times* reported that pickpockets and other crooks were arriving, as it was pension time at the Soldiers' Home. "The police are giving all suspicious characters short notice to leave town."[1]

However, most of the Soldiers' Homes were in out-of-the-way locations, such as Johnson City, Tennessee; Grant County, Indiana; Togus, Maine; Montgomery County, Ohio. A major exception to this was the Home in Milwaukee, Wisconsin. One estimate for 1894 was that within one mile of the Milwaukee Soldiers' Home there were fifty-two places of business peddling booze. There was obviously a lot going on there, legally and otherwise.[2]

At this time, the only known (recognized by Earp authorities) view of James Earp. *Lee Silva Collection.*

The Sawtelle area Soldiers' Home differed in many ways from other institutions for veterans. The population was huge, it was of recent origin, and the adjacent community only came into existence because of the Home. And, in an unusual development, those individuals most involved in organizing the card rooms, blind pigs, and whore houses were themselves veterans, residents either of the Home or of nearby Sawtelle.

The Soldiers' Home, Pacific Branch, actually became a tourist site, well positioned on the famous Balloon Route, the interurban which took passengers from Los Angeles locations to Santa Monica, with a stop along the way to pose with military-clothed veterans at various Home buildings.

In this era, the Soldiers' Home was well-known nationally, praised for its fine buildings, extensive grounds, gardens, and farm, and for its efficient hospital and other facilities. A typical instance of the far-and-wide impact of the Home occurred in 1913, when the *Arizona Republican* reported that Civil War veteran Elias N. Pegg just left for the Home in Sawtelle for an eye operation.[3]

The Home was frequently featured in photographs carried in the local press as well as in regional and national magazines. This important

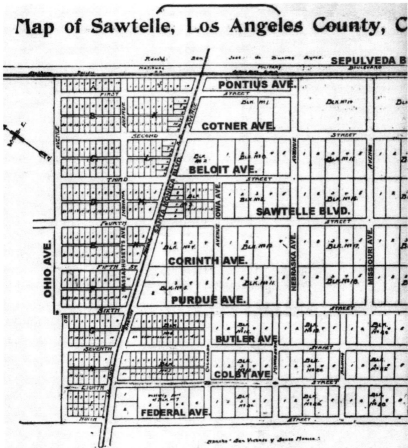

This 1901 map has modern street names superimposed. Sawtelle Boulevard
was actually Fourth Street, and Santa Monica Boulevard was Oregon Avenue
in our story/time period. Wilshire Boulevard is just to the left (west) of our
map (Ohio Avenue) and was completed in 1906 when it merged with Nevada
Avenue and finalized its new twentieth century path from downtown
Los Angeles to the Pacific Ocean.

institution, though, was adjacent to Sawtelle, which led to the following assertion:

> The most pitiful sight in all the southland today is not the soldiers' home, a splendid series of fine mansions surrounded by a magnificent park and beautiful gardens, but the town of Sawtelle beside it, where many of the wives and daughters of the old, well-cared for veterans eke out a miserable existence in old shacks and tumble-down structures, taking in washing for a living, or running blind pigs and otherwise ministering to the animal desires of some of the male pigs, some of these same old favored wards of the nation.[4]

Seemingly, James Earp adjusted fairly well to his new life in Sawtelle. After returning from Nome with Wyatt, he headed to San Francisco, while Wyatt opted to open a saloon in Tonopah, Nevada. In 1901, though, James shifted his pension payments to Sawtelle, as he had decided to throw in his lot with that community, knowing his father Nicholas and brother Newton intended to move to the Soldiers' Home.

Although his specific location is not known when Wyatt visited him, in 1903, James was declared "the veteran club man of North Fourth street."[5] As maps of Sawtelle indicate, this was the "gaming" part of town.[6] For those of us familiar with father Nicholas's personality,[7] we don't need documentation to accept that Nick would encourage his fellow veterans to "stop in and say hello to Jimmie" on the way into town.

Nick and his boys were tight as glue, and the first few years he was in the Soldiers' Home, Nick was in his usual self-assertive role; he needed to be noticed. As soon as he was enrolled in the Home, he was appointed a delegate to the Los Angeles County Democratic Convention. His letters to the Pioneer Society were usually reprinted in the *San Bernardino Sun;* he was former president of the group. This is the kind of fellow on the Home "inside" that we can conclude was pushing Jim Earp's whiskey and card activities in Sawtelle.

Wyatt and Virgil visited Los Angeles several times during this era, with their wives. Sometimes they were hosted by brother James, and a few newspaper notices indicated that they also went to the Hollenbeck

Hollenbeck Hotel, Los Angeles, Cal.

The Hollenbeck Hotel in downtown Los Angeles, owned by the Bilicke
family, the usual choice for the Earps and visiting Arizonans.
David D. de Haas, MD, Collection.

(LOS ANGELES COUNTY)
Sawtelle News Notes

SAWTELLE, April 5.—W. W. Bunce will shortly depart for San Francisco on a visit to his 15-year-old son Frank, who recently enlisted in the navy and is at the training school on Goat Island.

J. B. Taylor, a veteran of the Home, has purchased the 'bus line plying between that place and Sawtelle.

B. F. Garrison has left on furlough and will pass the time in San Francisco.

M. Drullard has sold his residence and two lots on Eighth street and Ohio avenue to Mr. Alger, lately from Nebraska.

The five-acre tract on Second street and Virginia avenue has been sold by Mr. Bobst to William Holly of Santa Ana.

Henceforth the barber shops of Sawtelle will be closed Sundays.

Wyatt Earp of Tonopah, Nev., is here on a visit to his brother, the veteran club man of North Fourth street.

Wyatt and brother James apparently were whipping up some booze business in Sawtelle. *Los Angeles Herald*, April 6, 1903.

Hotel, owned and operated by their former Tombstone acquaintance and staunch ally, Albert Clay (A.C.; "Chris") Bilicke, who had owned Tombstone's Cosmopolitan Hotel (along with his father Carl Gustave "Gus" Bilicke) and backed the Earp brothers after their legendary O.K. Corral gunfight, testifying at the Spicer hearings that Tom McLaury appeared to have a gun visible in his pants pocket just prior to the altercation. The Earp brothers and their wives, along with Doc Holliday, moved into the Cosmopolitan for their security immediately after the street fight, and the wounded Virgil testified during the Spicer hearings from his sick bed there. Gunfighter "Buckskin Frank" Leslie, a bit over a year prior to that, on June 22, 1880, had been involved in one his many infamous gunplays (with Mike Kileen) in this same hotel. Virgil Earp would be shot in ambush

A. C. Bilicke, Tombstone; was
a downtown Los Angeles hotel
operator. *Lee Silva Collection.*

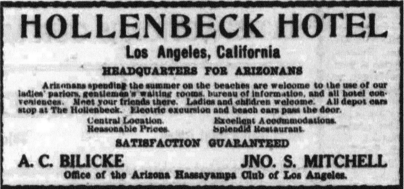

The Los Angeles Hollenbeck Hotel, "Headquarters for Arizonans," was run
by Earp Tombstone confidant A.C. Bilicke. *Daily Arizona Silver Belt* (Globe),
ads running throughout 1907.

on December 28, 1881, while making his way back to the Cosmopolitan,
and Morgan Earp's funeral was also held in (and cortege commenced from)
this hotel on March 19, 1882.[8] After Wyatt's subsequent revenge "vendetta ride," he and his posse would return to Tombstone to close out their
affairs, and would be in the Cosmopolitan Hotel when notified by Bilicke

Adelia Earp (Edwards), sister of the Earp brothers, so helpful to James in his later
years. "Rarely (never before) seen" photo. Purported to have been taken in 1877
(age ca. 15); prior to her April 12, 1877, wedding in Sterling, originally named
"Peace," Kansas. This during an Earp family (all save for Wyatt and Morgan who
remained in Dodge having left Wichita) excursion through Kansas on their way back
out to California. Leaving from Dodge City in Fall 1876 to Peace (Sterling), Kansas,
and departing there, after Adelia's wedding, May 8, 1877, reaching Prescott, Arizona
in early July 1877, where Virgil and Allie left the wagon train before Nicholas and
family proceeded onward to San Bernardino and Riverside, California. Provenance is
exceptionally strong; from the Parke/Seltzer/Don "John" Church collection. Please
see Lee A. Silva, *Wyatt Earp: A Biography of the Legend, Volume II*, Part 1 for extensive
details, and two huge notebooks full of documentary evidence in the collection of
David D. de Haas, MD. See also Wild West Collectors Facebook page December 18,
2018, and especially January 1, 2019, for much more background information
(provenance) regarding this collection, which has provided other recognized photos
of the Earps. *David D. de Haas, MD, Collection.*[10]

that Sheriff John Behan and his deputy Dave Neagle were in the lobby, along with other armed deputies, and with a warrant for their arrest. Wyatt and his posse would brush by Behan and his officers and depart town, for the final time, uncontested. These were among the reasons why Bilicke's Hollenbeck was the well-known downtown L.A. "watering hole" for former Tombstone residents in the early 1900s.[9]

The Earps had an especially fine reunion in Los Angeles in 1903, where Bilicke entertained many of the family. He even made a special effort to go and collect Nicholas from the Home, so he could join Wyatt, James, Virgil, and their wives, as well as sister Adelia and her husband. It is also most likely that Newton was part of the get-together. Adelia praised the doings of Bilicke, who had set aside "a comfortable green room" for the occasion. The tenor of the meeting can be gathered from Adelia's report of Virgil's booming voice, "Deelie pour some coffee now, and put some of that there whiskey in."[11]

On September 6, 1903, the *Herald* published a letter critical of the Earps, in particular of Wyatt Earp. The phrase "Bad Man of Other Days" was part of the heading, and the article included absurd Earp doings in Dawson and other Klondike places that no Earp had ever known. In response, in the *Herald* issue of September 9, George W. Parsons vigorously

Moving from Tombstone to Los Angeles,
Earp confidant George W. Parsons
became a leading figure in the Chamber
of Commerce and with the Mining
Exchange. *Sunset Club*, 1916.

Wyatt's Northern Saloon, a short-lived Tonopah operation. *Lee Silva Collection.*

defended the Earps, ridiculing the "bad men" usage, and pointing out that the Earps had been peace officers "defending and enforcing the law in the face of death." Parsons had known the Earps in Tombstone, had ridden in posses with them, and was still in contact with the family.

This incident was clarified in the Parsons diary entry of September 19, when he wrote that he had a "good swim at Santa Monica." He also met with Wyatt Earp, who "thanked me for my defense of him. He has killed a few but they ought to have been killed & he did a good job." This information from Parsons suggests that Wyatt Earp was in the environs of Santa Monica and Sawtelle on a visit to Dad and brothers James, Virgil, and Newton.[12]

There was never any indication that Wyatt was interested in having any role in the Sawtelle operations. He and other investors had opened a Nevada saloon, the Northern, on February 8, 1902. He seemingly did everything right, brought in new bar equipment, and advertised in the appropriately named newspaper (*Tonopah Bonanza*). The Northern was two buildings away from the Miners Exchange Hall. Wyatt's hopes had been so high that he had even planned a stage line between Tonopah and

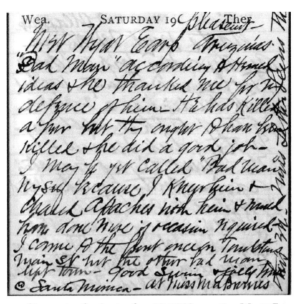

George Parsons diary entry for September 19, 1903; meeting Wyatt Earp near Santa Monica and the Soldiers' Home. *Arizona Historical Society.*

Ray. Few things, though, worked out well for Wyatt and Josie in Tonopah. In fact, Josie spent most of her "Nevada time" visiting with her relatives in Oakland and San Francisco.[13]

Wyatt not only failed in Tonopah, he quit Nevada and shifted to Arizona Territory. He opted for the near-desert, and he was soon in Cibola in Yuma County, running a small ranch. This was some miles southwest of Quartzsite, and in November 1904 Wyatt was elected the local constable (less than a dozen votes were cast). Ranching was boring, and by mid-1905 Wyatt was in the Whipple Mountains working a copper claim in the fall, winter, and spring months, living in various locations about Los Angeles in the summer. Mining would occupy most of his time until his death in 1929.[14]

It was in 1906, while living at the Hampden Arms Hotel in Los Angeles, that Wyatt would meet a young John H. Flood who would become a loyal friend and have a huge influence throughout rest of his life (and thereafter), and his wife Josie's, until her death in 1944. It would be Flood who would attempt to write Wyatt's biography for publication. The attempt failed, but did eventually lead to Stuart Lake's seminal 1931 book *Wyatt*

Hampden Arms Hotel, Los Angeles, where in 1906 Wyatt Earp first met John Flood, his friendly but incompetent biographer. *David D. de Haas, MD, Collection.*

Sawtelle Old Soldiers' Home (Pacific Branch National Home for Disabled Volunteer Soldiers; Los Angeles County, California) 1907 brochure featuring the park-like grounds and one of the barracks buildings in the background. Earp confidant John H. Flood's personal copy (likely given to him by Wyatt and Josephine Earp); given by him to historian John Gilchriese. Currently in the *David D. de Haas, MD, Collection*.

Earp Frontier Marshal, published shortly after Wyatt's death, and upon which, along with Walter Noble Burns's 1927 classic *Tombstone: An Iliad of the Southwest*, many a subsequent Hollywood Earp movie was based; including 1993's influential *Tombstone* starring Kurt Russell as Wyatt Earp and Val Kilmer as Doc Holliday. It would also be John Flood (who died in 1958) who would, in the 1950s, be tracked down by historian/collector John Gilchriese, and subsequently pass on down to him many first-hand stories of Wyatt and the Earps, and many of Wyatt and Josie's personal possessions and letters. Many of these are now in the collection of second author de Haas, and some are featured as illustrations in this book.[15]

CHAPTER 9

Enter V. W. Earp:
Virgil Joins the Revelry

Virgil and Allie seemed to have given considerable thought to the promise of Sawtelle, and apparently lived there part of 1902 and 1903. Virgil, candidate for sheriff of Yavapai County in 1900, withdrew his name. He had moved into Prescott from his ranch in the Kirkland Valley. His left arm was practically useless from the assassination attempt in Tombstone in December 1881, and in 1896 he had suffered a dislocated hip and other injuries while working the Grizzly Mine outside of Prescott.[1]

Several press accounts mention lengthy visits of Virgil and Allie to Sawtelle during the coming years. The *Los Angeles Herald* on April 23,

Virgil Earp, who supported brother
James in the Sawtelle blind pig operation.
Lee Silva Collection.

This token fascinated the authors, which began their collaborative research which culminated in this book. *Hal Dunn Collection.*

1903, reported that Wyatt and Virgil were visiting friends and haunts in downtown Los Angeles. Nothing like this could happen, of course, without their spending time with James, Nicholas, and Newton in the Sawtelle environs.

During the last few decades, new information has surfaced to indicate that not only was Virgil Earp interested in the potential "Sawtelle bonanza," but he acted on his beliefs. Shortly after 1994, when Chaput published his *Virgil Earp: Western Peace Officer*, data surfaced about Virgil's Sawtelle interests, and in 2018, when de Haas joined the search, additional information was uncovered to suggest that Virgil, too, had seriously joined James, Nicholas, and Newton in the effort to obtain some of the Soldiers' Home pension payments. It is time to examine those more recent research efforts.

Hal Dunn wrote to Chaput, commenting on the Virgil biography, and asking if there was any information in the files about Virgil's life in Sawtelle. He also supplied photos of a token, which on the obverse showed "V. W. Earp, Sawtelle," and on the reverse, "good for five cents." This was all news to Chaput, who was familiar with the Earp family's connection with the Soldiers' Home, but was unaware that Virgil had any role in this. The token was aluminum, in fairly decent condition, and had a diameter of 22 mm. Dunn theorized that it had been manufactured in Los Angeles around 1902 by the Los Angeles Rubber Stamp Co. They exchanged further correspondence, and Chaput provided Dunn with additional

Sawtelle information, including data on James and Nicholas being registered voters there.

When de Haas concentrated further on the token background, he obtained more from collector contacts, the literature, and from internet sites that examine many aspects of Western history. The Earp material, the amount and diversity of token production, started to provide the kind of insight we needed.

The token's "history" fit in perfectly with the known Earp family treks/doings/timelines. Dunn was a prominent Nevada personality and collector, had served for years as sheriff of Carson City, and had also been a member of the Nevada Gaming Control Board. The token had been found in a Goldfield dumpsite via metal detector by Lee Howard, who was for years a serious collector of Nevada mining artifacts. Howard sold the token to a local antique dealer, from whom Dunn had purchased it in 1974. Dunn died in 2006; over the years he had expressed the thought that this had to be one of the rarest and most valuable of Western tokens. Very few had been made, and it is obvious that the token was taken from Sawtelle to Goldfield when Virgil moved there in 1904. To this day, only five or six of these tokens have surfaced.[2]

A few years after the token made its appearance, another token, of a related nature, came to light. This was another "V. W. Earp, Sawtelle" obverse notation, and on the reverse, "good for one ride." This, an eight-sided brass token, was intended for a horse-car ride. Hildreth Halliwell,

A second Virgil Earp token was subsequently uncovered; Virgil's "free ride" token of 1903-04. *HolabirdAmericana. Coin World, 2012.*

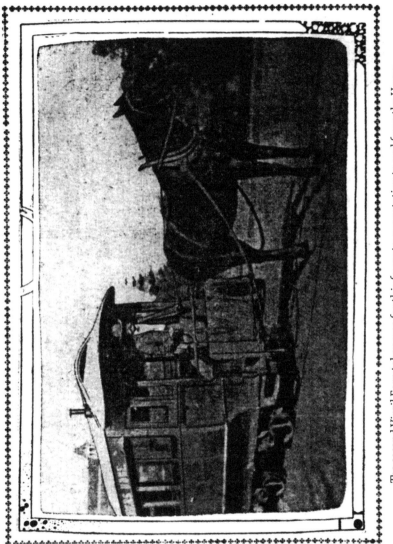

The second Virgil Earp token was for this fancy transportation to and from the Home. *Los Angeles Herald*, June 26, 1904.

in an interview in 1971, claimed that Virgil had made money at one time working as a "bus driver," but was no more specific than that.[3]

Quite possibly, Virgil's Sawtelle activity ("bus driving") involved the horse-car line between Santa Monica and the Soldiers' Home. The horse-car line, the Santa Monica and Soldiers' Home Railroad, a project of the Vawter family, opened in the 1880s, and was an important link between those locations. There were many changes in name and equipment over the years as it shifted to steam, then to an electric system. It became part of the Pasadena to the Pacific line, and then was engulfed into the Los Angeles, Pacific Electric Railway Company. By the time the Earp brothers were pushing their "ride" tokens, the horse-car portion was a mere novelty, a relic of interest mostly to tourists and veterans. For years the lone employee was George W. Seaver, and his heavy obligation was to make at least one round trip a day, pulled by the company's lone horse, Bonnie (sometimes referred to as Barney). The route, more than four miles, took less than an hour. Seaver, or the veterans, would periodically feed the horse doughnuts, apples, pears, even watermelons.

Seaver was another of "our boys," a Civil War veteran who had served in a Massachusetts artillery unit and lived in the Soldiers' Home most of the time. His role in life would fit with those who suggested a "blind pig" conspiracy in greater Sawtelle. Old Nicholas Earp, the "inside man," James Earp, one of many who had a card game going and some refreshments at hand at his Fourth Street gaming venue, and horse-car driver Seaver, expediting or arranging stops by venues operated by fellow veterans. This may not have been a conspiracy, but maybe cabal would be a better term. Everyone in the Soldiers' Home, in Sawtelle, and in Santa Monica, knew what was going on, but putting a damper on the blind pig activity was too great a challenge.[4]

The mumbling about conspiracy was not idle talk, and merchants, horse-car drivers, veterans out for a stroll, even casual residents—all were involved. The phrase "blind pig trust" was even used. This was a union, or understanding, and a "system of signals was in vogue, by which information was passed from one to the other when attempts were to be made to raid places under suspicion."[5]

In his article Dunn adds that his further investigations led to knowledge of a least six of these Virgil tokens. He also comments on this lack of certainty:

> It is not unusual to be unable to find business directory listings, newspaper advertisements, or mention in local histories for many token issuing merchants. These are the realities of research. Businesses opened and closed between directories and business names changed, sometimes almost overnight. Partnerships were formed and dissolved, often producing new names or combination of names on tokens. In the history of the West, merchants and sometimes towns, if some of those places could be called "towns," are gone without a trace. Other merchants left behind little to be remembered by— sometimes only a token or two dug from some long-forgotten dump.[6]

The business of Virgil Earp being involved in the Sawtelle events rests on some pretty solid information that ties in with what we know about the tokens. Mrs. Virgil Earp was in California in June 1902 visiting relatives;[7] she may have visited folks in San Bernardino, Los Angeles, or Sawtelle. In August Virgil was in from his Kirkland Valley ranch, visiting Prescott for the first time in two years.[8] There was apparently a destination in mind. The *Weekly Journal-Miner* reported in October, that Virgil "left today for Sawtelle, California, where he expects to remain for three months."[9] This fits in perfectly with the *Los Angeles Herald* statement quoted earlier of April 23, 1903, that Wyatt and Virgil were seen visiting in downtown Los Angeles with former Arizona acquaintances.[10] Such a trip to Los Angeles, of course, meant that Wyatt and Virgil would go to Sawtelle to see James, Newton, and Nicholas and encourage some card room and similar activity. The count here is five Earps.

These sources suggest that at best, Virgil envisioned a "quick assault" on Sawtelle, helping brother James. Part of that plan included the V. W. Earp tokens, as well as some sort of public relations jobs for Virgil, such as strutting along Fourth Street, or wandering into the Soldiers' Home and visiting with Dad, Newton, and other veterans. The evidence is strong that Virgil spent some months of 1903 helping brother James bring in some of that pension money.

One absurd but understandable thing about these tokens is that they are often identified as "saloon tokens." Such tokens were very common in the United States, more so in Western communities. However, to be a "saloon token," one must have a saloon. Because of the exclusion zone, there were no saloons in Sawtelle, and no matter how arrogant or cocky the entrepreneur, none issued a "blind pig token." What Virgil (through James) was pushing with these tokens was that the Earps were ready to serve their patrons at their Fourth Street venue, products unidentified.[11]

◇–◇— —◇–◇

CHAPTER 10

The City of Angels

Radical temperance leader Carrie Nation's nation was getting up a head of steam in the early 1900s, as the prohibition movement throughout the country was widely known, recruiting many members in various anti-saloon movements, and in general becoming a major political and social force. In Southern California, too, there were pockets of vigorous anti-saloon agitation. Communities like Pasadena, Redlands, Riverside, and Alhambra were leaders in the fight against alcohol, and other places such as Santa Monica were not far behind trying to stamp out devil rum. Los Angeles, though, was not one of these temperance strongholds.

By this time Los Angeles was a city of several hundred thousand, and the policies that evolved there towards alcohol differed widely from surrounding communities and have much to do with the situation regarding drinking, gambling, and other vices that tended to prevail near the Soldiers' Home, especially in Sawtelle. City and county officials were fully aware of the many ways that alcohol could impact a community. A drunk was a drunk, and it was agreed that use of alcohol was often accompanied by gambling and prostitution. It was also known that in specific instances, alcohol was associated with violence, burglaries, rape, and murder.

The Police Department report for 1905 listed 5,519 arrests for "drunk," 109 for gambling, 547 for disturbing the peace, 313 for battery, and so forth. Practically all of these arrests were alcohol related, and these were just the arrests. There were obviously hundreds of other cases of "near-arrest" or warnings given to patrons of various establishments.[1]

With this kind of awareness of the impact of alcohol, how did the Los Angeles city fathers consider and tackle the issue? The first thing they

acknowledged was that taxes and licensing regarding alcohol and establishments brought in sizeable amounts of money—so much so that they
decided to keep the money coming in, but put in place a series of laws and
policies that would control or minimize the damage.

In 1899 the city council passed an ordinance limiting the number of
saloons to 200, and saloons were prohibited from operating in residential
districts. The license fee was originally placed at $75 a month, and this
was aside from tax revenue for property, for alcohol, and so forth. Soon
other measures were passed which prohibited placement of tables and
chairs in front of the building, women and minors in the building, and

The city of Los Angeles continued to ignore the anti-saloon lobby.
Los Angeles Times, February 18, 1906.

INTERIOR VIEW OF A PEACE OFFICER'S SALOON.

Constable George Brown was one of the few lawmen who was also
in the booze business. *Los Angeles Herald,* March 24, 1901.

doorways and windows which permitted viewing into the structure from
the outside.

That Los Angeles was not your normal city was obvious early in 1901
when Constable George Brown was given a saloon license for a "notorious
dive" on Court Street. Humorously referred to as a "mixologist-consta-
ble-bartender-saloonist," George had expert help in his brother Edward,
a plumber. Their well-publicized opening took place in March, with some
well-wishers wondering if Constable Brown would arrest Bartender
Brown if violations occurred. Constable Brown was a busy man, as he
also operated a collection agency, dealing mostly with saloons and whore
houses. There may have been some problems with these unusual arrangements, but it shows the way in which the Los Angeles Police Commission
felt they could control such activities.[2]

It was generally agreed that Los Angeles had a decent grip on its saloon culture, that there were a minimum of violations, that residential areas were free of saloon life, and that the city profited financially from the setup.[3] It was even grudgingly admitted by the leading medical journal of the region that "the city of Los Angeles is wedded to high license," and not much could be done about it.[4]

In order to oblige this fairly positive reputation, Los Angeles officials had to clamp down on the illegal activity. Blind pigs were bad— bad for the reputation, bad for the city budget. For example, in June 1901 the Police Commissioners ordered the closing of most "social clubs." These clubs, supposedly for members only, actually allowed anyone to enter, but no liquor license was needed. This was particularly aimed at P. J. Flynn and his Army and Navy Club. Flynn closed shop, and within a year was the leading blind pig operator in Sawtelle.

In May 1905 Police Chief Auble vowed to close all blind pigs in the city, and he started at once by arresting men in three pharmacies. [5] In October 1906 the police commissioners acted at once when a delegation of residents from West Washington Street complained of a blind pig in their area. In November 1906 John Vusich, "King of the Slavs," was shot by a policeman in a fracas at the Austrian Hotel on San Fernando Street; Vusich had been running a "secret bar" there.[6]

These examples indicate that Los Angeles was sincere in its efforts to control the sale of alcohol, because that was the promise to those in residential areas, and because it helped the city budget. The *Los Angeles Times*, the *Los Angeles Herald,* and the *Los Angeles Evening Express* published hundreds of articles in this decade on blind pigs and similar operations, but the majority of these offenses were outside the city limits— the Sawtelle area was the greatest contributor to these booze-related columns.

Southern California was in many ways in the forefront of the prohibition movement. Many of its cities had chosen prohibition, and statistics indicate that Los Angeles, with more than 1,000 members, was the country's largest group of the Woman's Christian Temperance Union. Eagerly awaited, then, was the visit of Carrie Nation, who arrived in Los Angeles in February 1903, then moved on to a tour in San Francisco. Her visit was well publicized, but not overall very successful. She didn't do any "hatchet-wielding" in saloons, couldn't get cooperation from various churches,

Carrie's Los Angeles visit did not live up to the vigorous images.
San Francisco Call, March 1, 1903.

didn't have a fairground to use, and had to lease a building and charge admission. One unusual thing she did was visit a "cribtown" and asked the police chief to close the cribs. He couldn't do that, he replied, because the girls would merely go to another part of town and upset folks there. In all, Carrie Nation didn't blaze any new trails in Los Angeles.[7]

One unusual effort in the city was the organization of the Los Angeles Coffee Club Association. Several locations began operating in 1904. They had a reading room, games of chess, dominoes, and checkers, toilets and washrooms, and even free telephone use. Hundreds of thousands of meals were served at nominal charge. The report of the City Auditor praised the group, and it was pointed out by the superintendent, O. D Conrey, that "the clubs are to counteract the influences of the saloons as far as possible." Within a short time, there was little to be heard of the Coffee Club, suggesting that replacing of the saloon would not be an easy task.[8]

This period of Los Angeles saloon life can clearly be seen in events of 1905 and 1911. In an important election in 1905 a prohibition ordinance was defeated by a vote of two to one.[9] It was a crushing blow to anti-saloon people, as "Los Angeles in Favor of High License." In 1911 there was another vigorous campaign by the prohibitionists in Los Angeles and efforts to carry the anti-saloon measure to the voters were praised. "There was time to reach the voters. We believe they were reached: but they were not persuaded. Quite a majority of the voters in Los Angeles do not want prohibition."[10]

Los Angeles authorities did not seem to consider Chinatown when they either legislated or from time to time "cracked down" on illegal gambling or drinking. There were occasional "raids," but it was usually a case of let things ride, so long as they didn't get out of hand. Sometimes the illegal places were closed, yet nearby were fan-tan clubs as well as lottery operations. "Chinatown is honey-combed with gambling houses," there was a big syndicate involved, and so forth. This hands-off attitude of the Los Angeles Police Department was another way of keeping control, just as they rigidly controlled the saloon licenses in city residential areas.[11]

The city of Los Angeles had devised and carried out saloon laws and policies that were approved by the citizens as well as the officials. This circumstance did not apply to Los Angeles County; and it certainly didn't apply to Sawtelle, either when it was under the jurisdiction of Santa Monica Township (County), or of the new City of Sawtelle starting in 1906. Sawtelle was cursed, or blessed, by the laws and policies that prohibited sale of alcohol in the vicinity of the Pacific Branch of the Soldiers' Home.

One of the strangest and most confusing statements appears in John Main's *The Booze Route*, in which he praises cities like Long Beach, Whittier, Pasadena, and Sawtelle because they had no saloons. To have Sawtelle listed as a no-saloon city was quite absurd. Because of state law, Sawtelle had no choice in the matter.[12]

"Gun Man" Appears for the Defense.

Wyatt Earp "Gun Man" testifies in Corwell murder trial Los Angeles in 1908. This illustration gives us an idea of what Wyatt looked (and dressed) like during our time period. *Los Angeles Times*, January 23, 1908.

Although Wyatt, James, and Virgil were well familiar with Los Angeles, it was Wyatt who was most closely connected with that scene. And, he was a well-known figure. In 1907-08 there was a spicy murder trial in which Estelle Corwell was accused of murdering George Bennett, someone she lived with, but who "was not her husband." The trial lasted more than six weeks, and she was found not guilty because "Bennett was shot while endeavoring to prevent Mrs. Corwell from committing suicide." Wyatt Earp was a bit player— his only testimony being that, yes, indeed, he had known her, in Arizona. Not only was Wyatt given more news space than he deserved, but his visage was splashed across the pages of the *Los Angeles Times* on January 23, 1908.

Wyatt's major Los Angeles event was the bunco charge of 1911. Wyatt, Harry Dean, and Walter Scott ("Death Valley Scotty") convinced J. Y. Peterson, a local real estate dealer, that they had a sure thing in a faro game at the Alexandria Hotel. By use of a faro box, and marked cards, they could all make a fortune. The play was to have Peterson, by using marked cards, cheat several players of $2,500, which he would later share with Earp, Dean, and Scott. Peterson pretended to go along with the scheme, but secretly went to the police. On the appointed date, in the hotel room, Wyatt opened the door and the policemen walked in, arrested them, and took them to the police station. Anyone interested in following the details of this complicated convoluted scheme may read about it in newspapers of the time from New York City to Albuquerque to San Francisco.[13]

Nothing much came of this, but it was a legal quagmire. Charges and considerations included such things as conspiracy, vagrancy, swindle, fake faro outfit, and gambling. There was some jail time, bail, charges reduced to vagrancy; then in September the trio appeared before a police judge. By this time there was no question of guilt. Dean pled guilty and was released with a suspended sentence, so long as he promised to leave town. Death Valley Scotty, pled guilty, changed his mind and asked for a jury trial. Police Judge Henry Rose (soon to be mayor of Los Angeles) dismissed the charge against Wyatt. According to the *Los Angeles Times*, Wyatt was in the room when the police entered, but claimed he was not connected with the game, and "had simply dropped in by accident. No evidence against him was secured."[14]

Some of the newspapers that covered this bunco event were the *New York Times*, the *Evening Star* of Washington, D. C., and the *Topeka State Journal*. Even the Swedish language newspaper *Vestkusten* of San Francisco informed its readers of these goings-on in Los Angeles referring to Wyatt Earp as "revolverman."[15] One of the puzzling newspaper articles appeared in the *Tonopah Daily Bonanza*. Wyatt was mentioned as a "shotgun messenger, Arizona marshal and gunfighter of early days," without a hint that a few years earlier Wyatt had operated a saloon in Tonopah. Wyatt's remaining years in Southern California would lack this kind of excitement.[16]

CHAPTER 11

Exit Virgil Earp; Goldfield Beckons

Whatever high hopes Virgil had for Sawtelle, they evaporated in late 1903 or early 1904. By then he was looking elsewhere for excitement. Within a few months, Virgil gave up on the Sawtelle opportunity. The *San Bernardino Sun* reported that Virgil "was about the Court House yesterday." Virgil was obviously not pushing drinks or dealing poker in Sawtelle anymore.[1]

In June 1904 the "Colton Saloon War" erupted, a ridiculous phrase about a town with only a few poorly attended drinking holes. The city fathers entertained applications from four individuals for an additional saloon license. One of these applying was Virgil Earp, but he didn't get the nod; John Teuschman did. Justice of the Peace Nicholas Earp was no longer in town, which considerably diminished the Earp influence. The *Los Angeles Times* reported that there were "herds" of blind pigs in Colton,[2] but was not certain if the word "few" or "many" was appropriate.[3]

By this time, Virgil had moved on from the Los Angeles area, and in early September was once again visiting relatives in San Bernardino. Virgil Earp outfitted himself with fine prospecting gear and was heading for gold and copper claims east of Needles.[4]

Nevada interfered. Gold had been discovered at what became Goldfield in 1902, and the next year a mining district was organized. By late 1904, Virgil and Allie were in Goldfield. Already the place was booming, but Virgil's poor physical condition meant no mining activity, and his finances did not permit opening a saloon or any kind of business.[5]

However, they needed an income. Because of his reputation and friendly personality, Virgil was named a deputy sheriff of Esmeralda

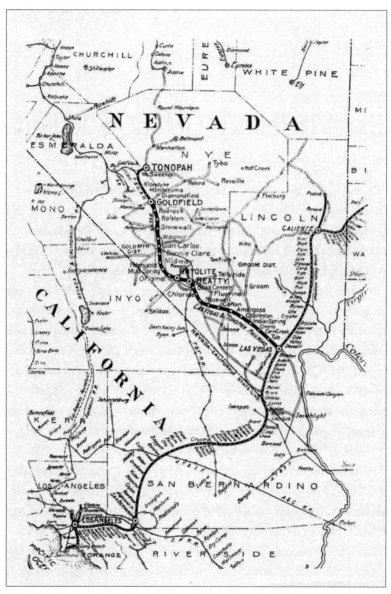

Los Angeles was the supply point for the Nevada mines in bonanza; including
Goldfield and Tonopah, where Wyatt and Virgil Earp would spend some time in the
first decade of the twentieth century. *From Don Chaput, Virgil Earp, 1996.*

Goldfield, Nevada was in bonanza in 1905, but it did Virgil little good, as he died of pneumonia later in the year. *Putnam's Magazine*, March 1907.

County in January 1905. He was also designated a special officer for the National Saloon. The former town marshal of Tombstone, leader in the West's most famous shootout, was now relegated to a saloon bouncer.

Virgil didn't figure in any of Goldfield's many exciting events, although he occasionally tried. In March 1905 an important fight was being promoted for two Nevada boxers. Virgil did the planning, and Wyatt, who was visiting, was touted as referee. Virgil rented a big tent for the affair, but the fight plan was soon scrapped.[6]

Within months, Virgil's battered body began failing him, and he physically deteriorated. By October he was in the Miners' Union Hospital, where he died of pneumonia on October 19. There were dozens of Virgil obituaries in the Western press, reporting the obvious things about Tombstone and Colton, as well as about Nicholas and the Earp Boys. In all of this praise and summarizing of Virgil's life, the only comments about Sawtelle were that father Nicholas was in the Soldiers' Home there and brother James lived nearby. Virgil's efforts with his Sawtelle tokens had left nary a trace.

Virgil's obituaries are indeed mixed. The Bisbee column describes Virgil as an evil, disgusting "bad man," who finally got what he deserved. The Prescott newspaper devoted several columns to his life, pointing out what an outstanding lawman he was, a helpful citizen, and so forth. The *Los Angeles Herald*, using a Sawtelle dateline, was pretty straight forward, and mentioned that his father was in the local Soldiers' Home. Not a hint that Virgil had joined with brother James, splashed tokens around Sawtelle, and drummed up some booze and poker business.[7]

CHAPTER 12

Fellow Sophisticates from the Wild West

James may have had better spies, or folks on the lookout for him, because while several of his Sawtelle blind pig associates had had multiple arrests, neither James nor Virgil were regular fodder for the newspapers of Santa Monica and Los Angeles.

However, it is possible that brother Virgil's death in October 1905 caused James to lose focus. A southern California newspaper article headlined "JIM EARP, GUN FIGHTER, JAILED." James, not "packing a gun" at the time, was arrested by Los Angeles police, and charged with being drunk and disorderly. Because he obviously posed a threat to no

"Gun fighter" James Earp, drunk he was.
Bakersfield Morning Echo, December 5, 1905.

one, he was kept only overnight and discharged in the morning for "some turkey and other Thanksgiving cheer." Naturally there followed some comments on the Earp boys, their role as gunfighters, and their Arizona reputation.[1]

One of the fascinating unknowns of this era is whether any relationship existed in greater Sawtelle between the Earps and Jonas V. ("J.V.") Brighton. In many ways, Brighton and the Earps had much in common: Midwest origins, Civil War service, time in Kansas, law officer careers, and time in the slammer (Brighton, in Kansas). Brighton held several law positions but was mostly known as a detective. In Apache County, Arizona, on June 1, 1887, he killed rustler Ike Clanton, the fellow who had precipitated the famous Tombstone shootout of 1881 with the Earp faction.[2] Later, in California, Brighton was instrumental in bringing in the tough Evans-Sontag gang of criminals.

From 1900 through his death in 1928, Brighton lived mostly in Sawtelle, often at the Soldiers' Home, where he was sometimes a law officer. Brighton was an out-going, forceful, ego-ridden fellow, often controversial, and often successful. During the years 1901 through 1907 he must have encountered James, Virgil, Nicholas, Newton, even Wyatt, dozens of times. Ten minutes of their conversation, or a paragraph summary, could contain some gems of frontier lore. Brighton's family lived in Sawtelle (he remarried there), and when he died in 1928, he was buried at the Soldiers' Home cemetery, next to his wife Mary who had preceded him in death in 1918, and just a few hundred yards southwest of Earp patriarch Nicholas's grave.[3]

The Wardwell case, which disturbed many Angelenos, was another unusual Sawtelle story with an Earp connection. General David K. Wardwell, with a solid Civil War record, settled in Arizona in 1880 where he became postmaster at Fort Huachuca. He was later in Tombstone, a member of the Territorial Legislature, a justice of the peace, and well known and respected. Virgil, as a U. S. Deputy Marshal, and Wyatt, as a Pima County deputy sheriff, crossed paths with Wardwell often.

Wardwell and wife moved to California; then in 1906 he was admitted to the Soldiers' Home; they also maintained a cottage in Sawtelle. There it was learned that Mrs. Wardwell had leprosy, probably contracted while

General Wardwell trying to protect his leper wife from authorities.
San Francisco Examiner, September 6, 1908.

caring for her diseased brother while they lived in Mexico. The word "leprosy" got the attention of health officials, and news stories were carried about the Wardwells from the *Sacramento Union* to the *New York Times* and many papers in between.

While she was hospitalized in Los Angeles, General Wardwell abducted her, and they fled to Arizona. They were quickly quarantined outside of Tombstone, where General Wardwell died in mid-1908. Southern Pacific was forced by the Arizona Territory health authorities to transport her back to Sawtelle. Mrs. Wardwell was returned to Sawtelle, but was soon found wandering the streets of Los Angeles. She was locked in the county hospital, placed in jail, chained to a bedpost, then died in the hospital in early December 1908. Phrases like "missing fingers," "insane leper," and "dethroned her reason" were part of her legacy.[4]

Another Cochise County fellow that James and Virgil may have met up and had a reunion with in greater Sawtelle was George Thiel. He lived mostly in Tombstone and nearby Fairbank and for years drove a stage between those points. He was a Civil War veteran with naval service, and he entered the Soldiers' Home in 1904, dying there in June 1907. Joe Stinson was another Southwest figure of note, a saloonkeeper of Santa Fe who had been in at least ten gunfights. Stinson, debauched and lead-loaded, entered the Soldiers' Home on a $10 pension in 1895 and died there in 1902.[5]

One of the more famous residents of the Soldiers' Home was Captain Charles Fay Robinson. As a member of the 1st Wisconsin Cavalry, he had been a principal figure in the capture of Jefferson Davis. Captain Robinson, who later worked at the U. S. Mint in San Francisco, was a close associate of General O. H. LaGrange, manager of the Soldiers' Home. Robinson died at the Home in late 1903.[6]

William Bradley was another old Tombstoner well known to the Earps. He had been in mining in Contention and Tombstone from the beginning, held good mining claims, and became Cochise County Recorder as well as a probate judge. He had served in the California Column during the Civil War, was admitted to the Soldiers' Home in 1904, and came into contact with James and Virgil at that time. Bradley pretty much got to know most people at the Home, as he worked in the post office and handled the money orders. He died in 1907.[7]

After the death of Virgil in late 1905, James soon went back to business as usual, but in a few months, events unfolded which led to big trouble for him and his blind pig neighbors. In May 1906 authorities in Santa Monica and Los Angeles decided to press hard on the illegal Sawtelle operations. They sent out investigators and issued warnings. Decoration Day was approaching, as well as pension day, when big money would be floating around the Home and in Sawtelle. In late May Constable Jacques

De La Monte and fellow officers raided Sawtelle. They closed some questionable places of business and arrested J. T. Hines and James Earp and jailed them in Los Angeles.

This flurry of activity led to much newspaper coverage in Los Angeles and Santa Monica which sheds considerable light on how these men operated. The word "boot-legger" was used and clearly explained: "These men carry flasks of whiskey secreted on their persons, generally stuck in their boot-leg, and they sell the stuff to the old soldiers by the drink." One of the major violators arrested was Tom Hines. He was a shoemaker on Fourth Street and apparently kept whiskey in an old coffee pot, and "whenever the old soldiers called in to have their shoes fixed he sold them a drink."

There were several charges against James Earp, who was identified as "conducting a card playing resort." Earp was playing poker and winning the money of the old soldiers "through the 'kitty.'" The second charge was that "he sold liquor illegally as a side issue to his gambling room." One newspaper gave a capsule history of the Earps, "a notorious family," concluding that "the father of this sextette of frontier characters is a member of the Soldiers' Home near here." The result of these arrests is not known. Those arrested could have, of course, faced a trial, but in most cases blind pig operators, gamblers, and prostitutes merely paid a fine and were released. A fine of $100 or so was insignificant when thousands of dollars of pension money was almost "in hand."

This above incident caused such a furor in greater Los Angeles and Santa Monica that there were half a dozen articles on the arrests. The *Times* of May 30 had two articles in which James was mentioned, though in one article they botched his name, referring to "N. J. Earp." This is sort of humorous, as only yards away, in the Soldiers' Home, were two fellows probably resting comfortably, Nicholas P. Earp and son Newton J. Earp. The *Times* pointed out that the Earp arrested was pushing poker playing, "but it is for selling liquor that he was arrested." In other words, blind pig stuff.

The arrests and closing of the blind pigs and the card rooms were not done at the request of the citizens. In fact, the veterans were indignant. Many of them claimed that "they want liquor sold in Sawtelle, and that if they cannot get it there they will simply have to go to Los Angeles." Some veterans had even protested to the district attorney, stating that their liberties were being taken away: "If they wanted to play poker whose business was it?"[8]

Some of the alcohol publicity in the general area was related to life at the Soldiers' Home, where from time to time a canteen had been operated. Policies and products varied, as sometimes only coffee was served; then there were periods of near-beer, and from time to time, real beer. The annual reports indicate that this was a problem, from Maine to Kansas to California. Congressmen got involved occasionally; the W. C. T. U. took positions on the matter; and there was never a clear-cut attitude towards Soldiers' Home canteens. In spite of the newspaper coverage, though, any drinking that went on in Soldiers' Home canteens was miniscule compared to what took place on the streets of Sawtelle.

During this first decade of the twentieth century, the man in charge of the Soldiers' Home was General O. H. LaGrange, a Civil War hero with the 1st Wisconsin Cavalry. LaGrange was a reasonable fellow, and he was usually at odds with the Board of Managers in Washington. He favored having the canteens; "Men Must Have Liquor from Some Source." This was a true rock-and-a-hard-place situation. Alcohol could not be sold on Home grounds, yet General LaGrange also opposed vigorously the folks who operated the Sawtelle blind pigs. It was LaGrange who frequently implored the Los Angeles Township, Santa Monica, Los Angeles County, and Sawtelle authorities to combat the blind pig onslaught, but the issue was seemingly impossible to solve.[9]

LaGrange had reason to worry about veterans going elsewhere for a bit of drink. In March 1905, Inman Lane, a Home resident, collected his pension, went into Sawtelle, "celebrated during the afternoon and by night was jubilant," and on the way back fell asleep on the railroad track near Santa Monica. A train came by, and Lane lost an arm. In the prose of the day, "the amputation was completed, the arteries were tied and the stump of an arm trimmed." Lane died at the Home in February 1910.[10] There were dozens of similar incidents of accidents, violence, missed turns, and other problems caused by busy times in the Sawtelle blind pigs. Law regarding sale of alcohol near the Home, the Sawtelle blind pigs, the pension payments—these were practically written in stone, interacted, and were synergistic, frequently leading to unfortunate results.

The statistics for the Home as the decade wore on are clearly summarized in the Pacific Branch report in mid-1908. Residents numbered 3,584, with 232 deaths the past year. Most inmates were native born, and among the foreign born the leaders were Ireland with 492 and Germany, 292. Laborers, farmers, carpenters, and miners accounted for most of the occupations; professionals included 18 lawyers, 52 physicians, 16 ministers, and 38 educators. Add to this an overlay of a few dozen administrators and several hundred employees, and we can see why the Soldiers' Home had such an important social, cultural, and economic impact on southern California in the last decade of the nineteenth century and first of the twentieth.

CHAPTER 13

The Earps Lose the Battle of Sawtelle

The "battle of Sawtelle" was not a street fight, nor a man-on-man duel with drawn revolvers. The newspapers, though, almost every time an Earp was mentioned, used words like "notorious" and "gunfighter," and peppered most stories with references to Tombstone and other examples of frontier violence. The battle, for the Earps, was to see how big a slice of the huge federal pension fund could come their way. Many were in on the game, and the Earps hoped that their decades of prowling the bonanza towns of the West, operating the card games, whorehouses, and saloons, as well as often being cloaked with authority as lawmen and justices, would give them an edge in the environment of Sawtelle, where thousands of veterans were bored and thirsty and had some spare pension money to take care of these problems.

As a reminder of what was at stake, in the fiscal year 1908, which had ended a few months previously, $567,985 was distributed to Home veterans, most receiving between $6 and $20 a month. This was a lot of money, and certain operators in Sawtelle determined that it shouldn't go further than the card rooms and blind pigs of Fourth Street.[1]

James knew that he could count on Nicholas, and to a lesser extent Newton, "on the inside," to steer traffic towards his Fourth Street venue. For a year or so Virgil had lent his presence and his name towards the Sawtelle purse, but then he had moved on to Nevada, leaving James to head the Earp interests. Virgil's death in 1905 was not only a blow to the Earp family, but meant that there would be no return to Sawtelle for him.

Hospital Building, Soldier's Home, Cal.

Soldiers' Home Hospital (Sawtelle), built ca. 1889 and where Nicholas Earp died in February 1907. *David D. de Haas, MD, collection.*

Shortly after this was when James was arrested as drunk and disorderly in downtown Los Angeles. The following year, in May 1906, he was arrested in a major raid on Sawtelle blind pigs.

Further serious problems loomed. Inside the Home, father Nicholas was deteriorating. The old fellow had been born in North Carolina in 1818 and was almost ninety years old. The letters to the Pioneer Society in San Bernardino had lessened, as did visits to the Home from his old contacts in Colton and San Bernardino. He was placed in the Home hospital. Judge Earp was "near death."[2]

The end came for Nicholas Porter Earp on February 12, when "arterial sclerosis" proved too much for the father of the Earp boys. There were quite a few obituaries or at least death notices for Nicholas P. Earp, especially in the press of California and Arizona. A typical report appeared in the *Santa Monica Outlook* of February 14, stating that he was considered an "esteemed exemplary member by his associates both in barrack and later in the hospital." And, being polite and not mentioning blind pigs, the *Outlook* mentioned that "one son, James Earp, lives in Sawtelle, near

FRONTIER JUSTICE PASSES.

Veteran of Two Wars Dies at the Soldiers' Home—Father of Noted Sons.

SOLDIERS' HOME, Feb. 13.—"Old Judge" Earp, frontier justice and father of the noted "Earp boys," who have figured prominently in the Southwest, and especially in Arizona and New Mexico, died in the Home hospital yesterday.

Nicholas P. Earp, who was a native of Kentucky, served during the Mexican War as sergeant in Capt. W. B. Stepps's company of Illinois Mounted Volunteers. At the close of the war he settled in Iowa and was elected justice of the peace in the then not over-populous Marion county.

When the Civil War was begun, he, at the

"Father of the noted Earp Boys." The penciled entry seen here in Nick's obituary (John Floods personal copy) below the word "sons" was written by John Flood, Wyatt's friend. *Los Angeles Times, February 14, 1907, David D. de Haas, MD, Collection.*

NICHOLAS P. EARP,
frontier Justice, dead at the Soldiers'
Home.

This image of Nick
accompanied the obituary.

the home." Too bad that of Wyatt, they wrote, "another, Nathan, is in the Searchlight mining district."[3]

The interment ceremony of Nicholas P. Earp took place in the Home cemetery on February 16, 1907. The grave and stone are in Section 13, Row A, Site 18. This is a frequently visited location, either by those familiar with the career of Justice Earp, or by the more general public, knowing that he was connected with those Tombstone Earps. One of the last administrative acts regarding Nicholas Earp occurred in April 1908, when his widow, Annie Earp, began receiving a pension because of his Mexican War service. This was Nick's "new" (and much younger) wife of 1893, who was not even living with Nick in 1900 when he had moved to Redlands to be with the family of daughter Adelia.[4]

This, Nick's original headstone, was replaced in the early 2000s. *David D. de Haas, MD, Collection.*

The death of his father was no doubt a crushing blow to James, not just the passing of the head of the clan, but pretty much dashing James's hopes for any kind of financial success in Sawtelle. Yet, Nick's death was only one of several reasons why and how the Earps lost out in the battle for the Sawtelle pension bucks.

The main determinant seems to have been that James Earp, and the Earps in general, were not top dogs in the scramble for the money of the veterans. There were a half dozen or so other individuals who would overshadow the Earp family.

◇━•━◇━•━◇━•━◇

CHAPTER 14

King of the Blind Pigs and the Sawtelle Social Club

John Dupree was a native of Germany, an artillery veteran of the Civil War, a retired miner, and one of the earliest residents of the Soldiers' Home, admitted in 1891. After Sawtelle was "founded" in 1897, Dupree was one of the first veterans to rent space in town, on Fourth Street near the Home entrance. He most likely considered James Earp an inexperienced newcomer. What Dupree was doing or supposedly selling in his space is not known, but from 1900 to 1910 he must have been arrested at least fifteen times. The charge was usually "keeping a gambling house," and he was periodically carted off to Los Angeles, appeared before a justice of the peace, and was fined. The fine, anywhere from $25 to $100, was not enough to discourage Dupree from his activity.

Dupree did well enough to buy a home in Sawtelle in 1907, and in the census of 1910, he was listed as a "landlord, rooms." His notoriety, though, was known to the Soldiers' Home management, and he was dishonorably discharged from the Home.[1] So, he continued to live in Sawtelle, continued to receive his Civil War pension, and continued to provide a "card parlor" to fellow veterans. Dupree was in for the long haul. He was readmitted to the Soldiers' Home in 1919, and for a few years served as a precinct judge in local and national elections. He died in Sawtelle in 1923, and his wife was taken care of with a widow's pension. John Dupree was one of the tough, talented ones that made it difficult for James Earp to rise to the top.[2]

A fellow who seems to have thrived at the illegal booze game was Horatio Bolster, a Connecticut Civil War veteran who was "in and out" of the Soldiers' Home. Bolster was a fat man (he was discharged in the Civil War because of obesity) and was a frequent violator of the whiskey selling laws. He was a tough fellow, often arrested for assault, and in one jury trial in 1907 was acquitted because the evidence was "of an uncertain quantity and character." He was dubbed the "Father of Blind Pigs,"[3] but mostly for comic relief rather than a good description of his role. He was kicked out of the Home several times because of his blind pig work, but was readmitted prior to 1910 and died there in 1922.[4]

Although Dupree and Bolster were some of the more successful of the illegitimate Sawtelle merchants, the king of that crowd was P. J. Flynn, known also as "Pops," whose full name was Philip J. Flynn. He was a Civil War veteran of naval service, and at the time of his death it was reported that he had been captain of the *Monitor* during the famous *Monitor-Merrimac* sea battle. There is no doubt about Flynn's naval service, but he enlisted almost half a year after the famous battle. This gives us some indication of the character of the fellow.

Flynn, a native of Maine, arrived in greater Los Angeles in 1869. Over the years he operated grocery stores in Park Station, Cienega, maybe a few

P. J. Flynn, arrested a dozen-plus times, was the undisputed "King of the (Sawtelle) Blind Pigs" era. *Los Angeles Times*, September 24, 1907.

FLYNN'S GROCERY STORE IN SAWTELLE

This modest structure would entertain thousands of thirsty veterans.
Los Angeles Evening Express, November 23, 1907.

other places. He looked for bigger action, and from 1897 through 1902 he was in charge of the Army and Navy Club, which was located in the Mondonville Roadhouse in the West Adams district. The place lacked a liquor license, and Flynn was in frequent trouble with the law over the issue, being arrested and fined several times. It was in 1902 that Flynn shifted to Sawtelle, where he bought five acres near the boundary of the Soldiers' Home.

When Flynn first moved into the area he settled on Nevada Avenue (part of the future Wilshire Boulevard). He soon realized that Fourth Street, where James Earp and the other "entertainers" were operating, was the local action place, and he purchased property there. In July 1905 Flynn put up a Fourth Street store building and enlarged his presence. He had "operational" experience, was a Civil War veteran, was aware of the potential pension money from the Soldiers' Home, and threw himself into the game.[5]

From the moment Flynn appeared on the scene, he was a major factor. Often listed as a hotel keeper, he provided gambling , gaming machines, an area for dancing, made available occasional female company, and almost always had booze on hand. All of these things were illegal, all were profitable, and Flynn forged ahead.

Flynn was constantly in the public eye, and it didn't bother him. When fined, he protested, and sometimes reluctantly paid. If he received jail time, he had an attorney on hand to protest, maybe diminish the number of days. On one occasion he was facing multiple charges in court, both in Los Angeles (for his Sawtelle doings) and in Pasadena, where he was also involved in illegal whiskey peddling.

The effrontery of the fellow can be seen in the articles of incorporation listed for the Sawtelle Social Club with P. J. Flynn as a director. In other words, the state had given its blessings to a fellow charged and convicted with half a dozen crimes regarding illegal gambling and sale of liquor. Another instance of his brass happened in October1907. . He was to be jailed, but he worked out a deal regarding a writ and bonds so that he wouldn't miss church (the newspaper headline read "DEPOSITS BONDS SO MAY ATTEND CHURCH") on Sunday.[6]

In May there was anger and bitterness, "Scandal rife in Sawtelle," as even the city attorney got involved with trying to ease a liquor license for the Sawtelle Social Club, which was headed by "its imperial potentate, Mr. Flynn." There was a botched procedure in the post office, and the intended license (or, its application) instead of being mailed to the Sawtelle Social Club ended up in the mail of the Commercial Club of Sawtelle. Nothing important happened because of this, but it is a good indication how significant P. J. Flynn's role was in Sawtelle life.

More important press coverage occurred in September 1907, when eight deputies raided the "fake social club." The officers found on hand a dozen drunken veterans; they were released. The place had a booze room as well as a dance hall. "Members" would go to a peep hole out back, where Flynn would look them over. The haul included cases of beer, some whiskey and gin, and a huge refrigerator. The officers noted two books on the shelf: *Cushings' Manual of Parliamentary Law* and *How to Mix Drinks*. Flynn was taken to jail in Los Angeles. He was called an "old violator."

This particular aspect of Flynn's activities came to an end in January 1908, when the *Herald* headlined an article "Blind Pig Social Club." This time Flynn was taken in hand and sent to the cooler for seven months.

Other than some interesting press accounts, the raid had minor impact on Flynn's career. One would think he had learned his lesson, but a few months after being released, Flynn was once again arrested on a gambling charge, and this time his wife Carrie was involved, claiming an official "conspiracy" against her Philip. Things must have settled down, as the Herald mentioned that Flynn, "favorably known to many Sawtelle and Los Angeles people, will open a restaurant in his building next week." He was preparing for a big New Year's bash.[7]

These comments, along with the issuance of a state charter for the Sawtelle Social Club, suggest that neither the city of Sawtelle nor the state of California gave one whit about the numerous criminal violations involving alcohol and gambling. Only the County of Los Angeles from time to time tried to moderate or eliminate the blind pigs and card rooms.

The career of Flynn also indicates how and why the Earps never rose to the top while grasping for the important pension bucks from the Soldiers' Home. After Nick's death, James pretty much folded his tent and left town. This was not the attitude nor action of Flynn, who intended to stay in Sawtelle as long as the pension funds kept coming.

Sawtelle, and Flynn and colleagues, would continue in their blind pig and card playing ways, but only for a few years. The city, probably out of embarrassment, passed a few ordinances, especially regarding gambling. The crackdown even extended for pool— "no pool for money." Flynn applied for permission to open a pool section, but "he is too old in the business." In the following year, General O. H. LaGrange of the Soldiers' Home worked closely with Sawtelle and Santa Monica authorities to try to eliminate or at least moderate the drinking and gambling.[8]

Because of the roles in life, and because they were both well known, and because they were business and social neighbors, Philip Flynn and James Earp must have had many interactions during the period 1902– 1907. Yet, we lack any information about how they viewed one another. They may have been serious rivals, or they may have competed to see who could best outsmart the constables and deputy sheriffs.

The Flynn saga is more complicated than the above information suggests. This fellow, arrested more than a dozen times, known throughout greater Los Angeles as a wily, successful operator of blind pigs and card rooms, was beholden to the Soldiers' Home on several fronts. He not only schemed to get the veterans' pension money, he himself, a navy veteran, was admitted to the Home on three occasions, the first time in 1903, and his last release was in 1919. The public law-breaking record, with his name in headlines in five or more newspapers, did not prevent him from access to the Home benefits, nor from receiving restaurant and hotel licenses. Such was the treatment accorded to Sawtelle's "Mr. Blind Pig."[9]

Flynn's last few years were spent near Exposition Park in Los Angeles, where he died in 1922. It was fitting for this likeable blowhard that his obituary in the *Oakland Tribune* was headed "Survivor of Famous Naval Battle Dies." Even in death he was able to con the world.[10]

The pension money at the Soldiers' Home was substantial, and the guys who ran the blind pigs in Sawtelle did what they could to tap these funds. There were a variety of ways to get into these funds, and booze was just one the routes. Another was "true love," getting married to these old guys, or at least promising them some "sensual later years," was often enough to trigger a marriage license, or some type of promissory signature. One case in 1905-06 involved Kate Gallagher, who was supposedly a widow of a veteran in both Yountville (Napa) and/or Sawtelle, but she may or may not have been married to him. Her sister living in Sawtelle may have been in on the scam. Kate wasn't certain of things, because she thinks she may have fainted during the wedding ceremony. In any case, she sure did like those monthly pension payments. She pleaded memory problems, and in late 1906 she was fined $250 for pension fraud in the Los Angeles District Court. Serious research for that era would certainly uncover a few dozen similar fraud cases that involved marriage, or some type of financial relationship. [11]

CHAPTER 15

◈—▪◦▪—◦——◦—▪◦▪—◈

The Evolution of Sawtelle

The entire scene around Sawtelle as well as the Soldiers' Home would shift between 1907 and 1917, when Sawtelle was annexed to Los Angeles. In the early days the pensions were limited to disabled veterans. Then, in 1890, those who were incapable of labor were added to the list of eligibles. Old age became another qualifier in 1907, which pretty much meant that anyone with service would probably qualify. In the early 1900s there were over a million veterans on the pension rolls. By early 1907, the Pacific Branch at Sawtelle had almost 4,000 veterans on hand.[1]

Further shifts came in that year with the McCumber Bill, which raised the amount of the pensions. In some cases, this meant an increase of $5.00 a month, substantial when added to something like James Earp's pension of $17.00. The impacts of these changes were starkly reported in the *Los Angeles Herald*: "The McCumber law raising the pensions of the soldiers has enabled many of them to live away from the home and not be compelled to be under its military restraint."[2]

There was an oddity about pensions. Would anyone oppose an increase? The answer was yes, but those who felt that way were reluctant to express the thought. Without doubt, the Home residents would encourage, even clap at the news of a pension raise. But Home officials were probably not favorable to increases. Police Captain Root, in charge of the Home law enforcement, was interviewed, and to him, a pension increase meant more trouble. More money meant more Sawtelle blind pig action, more buying trips to Santa Monica and Los Angeles. Or, as phrased in the *Express*, "More Whiskey is Carried into Sawtelle."[3]

Cheryl Wilkinson in her publications used the name "Soldiers' City" when referring to Sawtelle, implying that because the community was adjacent to the Soldiers' Home, the veterans had a major impact on all aspects of community life; many of the residents and merchants were also veterans, some of them closely tied in with privileges at the Soldiers' Home. However, this would rapidly change by 1917. Veterans had a bit more money: they could afford more extended furloughs, and many thought in terms of doings in Los Angeles, Santa Monica, and other locales, not necessarily Sawtelle.[4]

Newton Earp figured in these changing ways. The *Santa Monica Outlook* headlined an article, "CAN SUPPORT THEMSELVES." Dozens of veterans were honorably discharged from the Home, claiming they were now able to maintain themselves on the outside. Newton was one of these veterans, and he headed to northern California to live with relatives. This entire loosening of conditions at the Soldiers' Home had no great impact on Home operations, but it did mean that the world of the veterans was now expanding beyond the borders of the Home grounds and the nearby community of Sawtelle.[5]

These new situations—pension changes and eventual annexation of Sawtelle to Los Angeles—meant the coming of the end of the blind pig era in Sawtelle. The "community" was becoming broader than Sawtelle for the veterans, and soon Los Angeles authorities (district attorneys and police department) would be in complete charge of law enforcement. The former city officials of Sawtelle had been only lukewarm about the blind pig and card room operations, because the pension fund flow was desirable, and many of the providers of the illegal operations were themselves veterans.

One of the puzzling aspects of the community of Sawtelle that we have considered is the standing in the region of the Rev. Stephen H. Taft and his second wife, Etta. When Sawtelle was founded, Rev. Taft was appointed the administrator of this unincorporated slice of land. Taft had a decent national reputation, had been a Presbyterian minister for decades, and had headed a college in Iowa. He was vigorously anti-alcohol, and wife Etta for years was an officer in Santa Monica and Sawtelle of several prohibitionist organizations. They both were active in the clampdowns on all sorts of vice.[6]

A Temperance Institute was organized in Sawtelle in August 1904, with twenty-one founding members, in which the Taft couple figured prominently. Some merchants and a few clergymen were in the mix, but the list of charter members does not show the name of any Soldiers' Home resident.[7]

In the 1906-07 national report of the Woman's Christian Temperance Union, Mrs. Taft was praised for her work near the Soldiers' Home, with the specific claim of having put out the "blind pigs." When the Rev. Taft died in April 1918 he was referred to as the founder of Sawtelle and was remembered as a leader who had crushed the blind pig operators. By his first wife, Taft had a son, Frederick H. Taft, who for years served as city attorney of Santa Monica, then became a Judge of the Superior Court. He was as inept as his father with dealing with the alcohol goings-on near the Soldiers' Home.

The Taft family later published a biography of Rev. Taft, An *Empire Builder of the Middle West*. Only a few pages concern his time in Sawtelle, and there is no mention of the community's reputation as a whiskey-drinking center of Los Angeles County, but they do point out that Rev. Taft was a staunch member of the Prohibition Movement and was in the forefront of any anti-saloon effort. A chapter in the book is entitled "A Lifetime Fight Against the Liquor Evil." When he completed his brick business block in Sawtelle, Rev. Taft set aside space for permanent offices of the W. C. T. U. In a flattering summary in the *Who's Who on the Pacific Coast* in 1913, Taft was praised as "first Pres. L. A. Co., anti-Saloon League. Address: Sawtelle Cal." There is considerable irony in these words.

The Rev. Taft was like a duck out of water. In June of 1907 he protested that there should be no further smoking in the Sawtelle Commercial Club. This absurd recommendation even upset his friends and neighbors. The Club frequently held "smokers," popular entertainment events for their group. Yet, the following month he was praised as the "Grand Old Man" in the prohibition cause, with his photo in the newspaper. Taft, the supposed community leader, was leading nobody. Folks smoked; folks drank.[8]

In 1919, in *American Biography and Genealogy*, a detailed presentation was made of the career of Mr. Taft. The worst stuff in the nation was "licensed poison drink traffic," and to stamp it out "is the central and highest purpose of his life."[9] What we have presented in these pages about the tremendous activity of operators of blind pigs, gambling rooms, and houses of ill fame suggests that the praise for the work of Rev. Taft, his wife, and his son was considerably overblown.

It will have been noticed by now that we have seldom mentioned women during the first decades of the existence of the Soldiers' Home. Women were not welcome at the Home, unless they were there as tourists, guests, or as speakers at a convention or similar gathering. This was not just a Home for old veterans; it was a collection of old men who didn't want women in any role of responsibility.

A major change came early in 1910 when it was decided to hire women as cooks and waitresses in the various kitchens and dining halls throughout the Home. Structural changes had to be made on the upper floor of the main dining halls, and carpenters and other tradesmen were necessary to remodel the areas for female occupancy.[10]

And, in June and July, when the female work force was installed, all hell broke loose. For days there were arguments, missed meals, and hard feelings. A *Los Angeles Herald* article opened with this sentence: "Several hundred decrepit old veterans of the United States Soldiers' Home did without their noon-day meal today: the dining halls were deserted and the hospital attendants had to turn to and serve food to the helpless patients because twenty-six new girl waiters went on strike."[11]

There were a variety of issues here. The waitresses didn't want to wheel in the trucks of food from the kitchens; the veterans were upset because they no longer had the jobs; and anyway, they didn't want women around. Some girls quit, a few others were shifted to work in the Home laundry, and other arrangements were made regarding the working conditions. In spite of the controversy and the grumbling, women from this point forward would be part of the Soldiers' Home environment.

The entire "working women" situation is bizarre when considered from a twenty-first century point of view. California, known today for its progressive stances, its pioneering in what would be major efforts in gender and minority movements, in the early 1900s was a backwater.

The federal government, the operator of many of the Soldiers' Homes, had no anti-female position regarding employment. Throughout the country, most veteran facilities gradually added women to the staff. For example, in Iowa in 1901, women were the majority of cooks and waitresses, and the soldiers "had better service." In the report of the Michigan veterans home for 1908, the women waited on the tables, and the service was much improved. The South Dakota report, also for 1908, indicated that the women serving as cooks and waitresses were much faster and provided better service in the dining halls.[12]

Only in the Pacific Branch, the Sawtelle-Santa Monica-Los Angeles veterans home, was a group of grumpy old men resistant to change and reluctant to admit that women and girls were capable of providing satisfactory work.[13]

CHAPTER 16

Santa Monica Accepts Its Destiny: Tombstone/Wild West Connections

Throughout these pages appear many comments about Santa Monica situations, its relationship to Los Angeles and to the Soldiers' Home, and some historical events and personalities that figure up to the period of 1910, when we leave our thoughts. We should, though, present a bit of the chronological structure to the Santa Monica saga.

Because of its location, Santa Monica was plagued (or blessed) by the condition so common to certain of the world's maritime landscapes—smuggling. Places like Cornwall and the Florida Keys have hundreds of years of experiences and a long literary tradition describing the details. Where you have a coast, and a government, you have taxes, and then you have locals devising hundreds of schemes to smuggle products to avoid the taxes.

The government of Spain, later that of Mexico, usually had prohibitions, and, if not, taxes on foreign goods. In Southern California, the triangle from San Pedro to Catalina Island to the Santa Monica Mountains was notorious for decades for smuggling into the Los Angeles area such items as hides, tallow, and alcohol. Ships would "come in the night," especially off Catalina and Malibu, and unload goods. The Alcalde Papers, the records of the governing body in Los Angeles, contain very few accounts or lists of fines and taxes regarding smuggling. The reason was that too many "good people" were often involved. The leading Los Angeles merchant, Abel Stearns, had warehouses at San Pedro, and was often accused of smuggling. He was usually not guilty, but was accused by other merchants with less talent.[1]

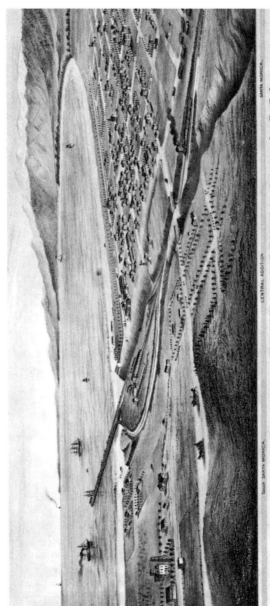

This view of Santa Monica in 1877 was only a few years after its founding. *Library of Congress.*

This didn't change when California fell under United States control. In 1847, the military governor, General R. B. Mason, reported that smuggling was widespread and hard to control because of the numerous bays and inlets. From San Diego up to Santa Barbara there was much smuggling, and even though there was a collector at Los Angeles, many "have escaped payment of duties."[2]

In the coming decades, port authorities devised effective systems, but there were occasional breaches. A major one occurred in 1894. A steamer from British Columbia landed a load of coal at the Santa Monica wharf. From the steamer, cans of opium made their way up to Santa Monica Canyon, before port authorities arrested the perpetrators. This event and subsequent trials were well publicized. However, the teeth of the law seemed not too tough. One of those found guilty, Gus Allgren, two years later applied for and received a saloon license for Santa Monica Canyon.[3]

The place called Santa Monica got on the map in 1875 when ballyhoo led to the selling of lots at the townsite. This was not a legal entity, but it was a start. Future O.K. Corral Earp attorney to be, Tom Fitch, pitched lots, and there were many bidders. Harris Newmark of Los Angeles bid in the first lot at $300, and others followed his lead.[4] However, a townsite is a real estate consideration. It was only in 1886 that Santa Monica was incorporated as a town of the sixth class. This was upgraded in 1902 as a city of the fifth class. The final "recognition" came in in 1907, after several annexations, when it was incorporated under a freeholders' charter. By this time the population was pushing towards 8,000.[5]

One of the unusual oddities in the history of Santa Monica is the role of the Vawter family. Williamson Dunn Vawter was an Indiana fellow who was apparently bored with life in the Midwest. He was a pioneer, a member of the Indiana Colony, which moved West, and in 1874-1875 was one of the original founders of what would soon be named Pasadena. He and his sons purchased one of the original Pasadena-area tracts, apparently settling in for the good life in Southern California.

Yet, almost within minutes, the goal post moved. In 1875 the Vawter family was one of the first purchasers of lots in the Santa Monica townsite. They were not only early on the scene, but in the following decades the Vawters were among the leading merchants and financiers in the area.

Vawter was a pioneer in two Southern
California tourist destinations, Pasadena and
Santa Monica. Ingersoll, *Santa Monica,* 1908.

The father and sons pretty much dominated the real estate market, and
were founders of the first bank in town as well as the Santa Monica Mill
& Lumber Company.

What makes this tale weird is that by 1900, when Americans thought
of tourism and Southern California, that usually meant either Pasadena
or Santa Monica. The two places had very little in common (other than
great climate), but the Vawter family had the unusual circumstance of
having pioneered in both communities.[6]

Once the lots started selling in the new community of Santa Monica
in 1875, and until 1910, the end of our coverage here, there was no single
purpose expressed, or acted upon, for this new entity. There were several
big aims, and they were flops. The great idea was that Santa Monica would
be an industrial center, the needed port for Los Angeles; she was beaten
in this rivalry by a city to the south, San Pedro.

A related dream was that Santa Monica (because of its port hopes)
would evolve into a major Western railroad hub, maybe even rivaling

Chicago. As absurd as these thoughts may now seem, there was a logic here. There was indeed a wharf and railroad at Santa Monica. Furthermore, two of the nation's leading financiers and political powers had placed their hopes on Santa Monica. Senator John Percival Jones possessed a tremendous, deserved reputation. He had been in politics for years, was a major railroad developer, was enormously wealthy from Nevada mining, and had been one of the founders of Santa Monica. With him, and pushing as hard as he could, was Collis P. Huntington, whose Southern Pacific Railroad was already in Santa Monica. Huntington, and the Southern Pacific, were not known for losing battles.

The port episode, when we are discussing Santa Monica and San Pedro, was one of the key events in the development of Los Angeles. The giants of the south were involved. The mighty Santa Monica faction of Colonel Baker, Arcadia Bandini de Baker, and Senator John Percival Jones were coupled with Collis P. Huntington and his powerful Southern Pacific Railroad, which already had erected a massive wharf at Santa Monica. However, the opposition, in favor of San Pedro, was up to the task. Harrison Gray Otis and his *Los Angeles Times* beat the drum constantly for San Pedro, and most Los Angeles merchants also preferred San Pedro, the traditional port. These merchants were organized by George Parsons, the leading figure in the Chamber of Commerce, which spearheaded the San Pedro assault.

Many factors came into play to end these dreams; the big collapse came in 1896 when San Pedro got the port nod over Santa Monica. The other dream, of being a railroad hub, took longer to dim. From 1895 through 1915 there were more than twenty attempts to create railroad companies, either with Santa Monica as part of the name, or at least part of the network. These were mostly paper efforts as the financing was not there for railroads once it was realized that most freight would be going elsewhere, namely San Pedro.

Although it is tempting to think that Santa Monica then turned to its beaches, and tourism, for some economic vitality, there were other possibilities that local merchants and political figures considered. What about fishing? There was an ocean there, and a wharf, probably lots of fish. This activity only became marginal. Certain locals bragged of the whitefish, mackerel, bonita, lobsters, crawfish, and the industries that would accompany fishing: fish trap manufacturing, boat building, fish packing, making of fish oil, and so forth. This would be another case where San Pedro came out the winner. Because of the more rugged shoreline, and the marine connections with Catalina Island, San Pedro developed into a major fishing zone, with dozens of companies, hundreds of employees, in an important business which lasted well into the twentieth century.[7]

Why not gold mining? From the golden sands of Nome down to Cabo San Lucas at the tip of Baja California, thousands of miles, alluvial gold can be found in the beach sands. This is a geological and geographical certainty. The problem, of course, is the quantity of gold on any given beach. Gold exists, all along the Southern California beaches, so state the reports of the State Mineralogist.

In the early years of Santa Monica's existence, gold was a periodic consideration. The first effort seems to have been in late 1880, when the Santa Monica Beach Mining District was organized at a meeting of miners at their camp on the beach. Nothing much came of the effort. In the early 1890s the Pacific Beach Mining & Dredging company was started, south of Santa Monica, to work the gray and black sands. Supposedly a hundred shafts had been sunk, some up to twenty feet deep.[8] That's a lot of sand, but apparently not much gold was found. In December 1895 the company directors had a meeting near Ballona, with "experts" on hand, and pan and shovel were used, and "several shining colors were seen." The Los Angeles Herald headed the article "FREE GOLD AT BALLONA." The precious metal was "scattered for miles along the beach." No doubt. The amount, though, would not justify further development.[9]

Even as late as 1904, when the Santa Monica Gold Mining and Development Company was organized, a few locals had not given up, hoping that Santa Monica might still rival the success at Nome. The beaches of Santa Monica would be important, but not for the inadequate amount of gold contained.

Well, if all these economic strategies are not good, why not try farming? There were many farms in and around Santa Monica and the Santa Monica Mountains. Sure, a little irrigation will be required, but we can arrange that. And, only a mile or so to the east, where Sawtelle would emerge, there were hundreds of acres of barley. Farming could be the answer. In a publication on Santa Monica for 1906, it was pointed out that in 1904 thousands of acres devoted to lima beans yielded 150,000 sacks at 80 pounds to the sack. This might be the solution. Furthermore, we can then set up a canning industry. Two crops a year, farming and canning, employing hundreds of people—an economic juggernaut![10]

All of these things— port development, railroad building, fishing, mining, farming, and canning—were thoughts along the way for Santa Monica devotees to pave the path for economic viability. None of them worked out.

No need to feel sorry for Santa Monica; not everything was a clunker. One of the things consistently praised about Santa Monica by the newspapers of San Francisco and Los Angeles was its emergence as a sporting center. Even the failure of the fishing industry was not total. Sport fishing gradually came to notice, and this led to considerable local interest and evolved into a noticeable tourist industry. This involved boats, equipment of various types, shops to provide items, and quite a few employees. This would be a steady part of the Santa Monica personality for a few decades.

In 1888-1889 the moguls Baker and Jones backed the Santa Monica Casino on Third Street. This would have several reincarnations in the coming decades, but immediately became essential for many Southern Californian events. The lawn tennis tournaments held there, at first local events, soon became regional and national in scope and coverage. Eventually, famous European figures were also participants in these events. Dances, balls, all types of organizational celebrations were held at the Casino. This became a leading Los Angeles area entertainment venue.[11]

If one built a long list of the Who's Who in Los Angeles for this era, chances are that their names would appear as participants or onlookers at sporting or entertainment events in Santa Monica. For example, in 1902, *The Capital* of Los Angeles mentioned that Abbot Kinney was on hand, and "Mrs. Arcadia de Baker was an interested spectator of the tennis games on several occasions." Names of politicians, financiers, clergymen— most would be mentioned as having been to some Santa Monica doings.[12]

George Parsons, that great Tombstoner diarist, by this time was a key figure in the Los Angeles Chamber of Commerce, and never stopped his midnight jottings. From 1900 to 1910 he was in Santa Monica dozens of times, some for business, but mostly for pleasure. Parsons was well-connected with some of the leading Pasadena personalities, such as the Fremonts, Bannings, and Pattons. In 1903 alone he recorded six Santa Monica visits, where he would meet his Pasadena contacts. On August 7, he attended a lawn tennis tournament with the Pasadena ladies, "had a gala day, fish dinner." He returned to Santa Monica the following day, for "skillful tennis."[13]

The entertainment and sporting pages of California newspapers gave heavy coverage to these Santa Monica events, because the people and teams involved were important in their fields. These were usually not Santa Monica events, but were often contests or demonstrations from regional, statewide, or national interest that took place in Santa Monica. The Polo Grounds, in addition to a fine schedule of polo events, also featured horse racing. There were also cricket, baseball, and other team sports in and around Santa Monica. And, auto racing became a major feature of the Santa Monica scene. In July 1909, for example, more than 50,000 spectators were on hand in Santa Monica for auto speed trials and races.

Now, these successful sporting and entertainment doings were 100 percent related to what eventually solved the Santa Monica identity search—the Pacific Ocean. One could do all or most of these things elsewhere (Indio, Riverside, Whittier), but what Santa Monica could offer, in addition to its excellent Mediterranean climate, were beautiful sandy beaches and an ocean breeze. As the years passed, the place-name "Santa Monica" was associated with these topics of entertainment and pleasure. Other locations would have their "place in the sun," such as Ocean Park, Venice, Redondo, and Catalina, but Santa Monica was the coastal pioneer in most of these activities, and to utter the name was usually to indicate those miles of Pacific shore.

From the beginning, Santa Monica knew it had rivals for views and uses of the Pacific Ocean. Certainly, as the years passed, Venice, Ocean Park, Redondo, and Long Beach would tout their alluring beaches. But Santa Monica feared not these competitors; they had what the others lacked: mountains and canyons. Hiking, camping, and picnicking in the

The Arcadia Hotel is featured in this beach scene of 1908. *Library of Congress.*

mountains and canyons of Santa Monica could be done, sometimes only yards from the Pacific Ocean. Those unfortunates who went elsewhere (Redondo, Long Beach, etc.) would be "amidst barley fields and alfalfa flats, and the uninteresting objects of sparsely settled farming districts."[14]

The Arcadia Hotel was the flagship of the Santa Monica-Pacific Ocean relationship. Built in 1886-87, and named for Arcadia Bandini de Baker, the grande dame of local society, the complex would be a major tourist attraction for two decades. Its offerings of bath, plunge, beach, fishing, wharf, mountain hikes, ballroom, 150 furnished rooms, lecture halls, and concert venues were known throughout the West. The Arcadia would have rivals, but the Arcadia set the standard.[15] Much of the information presented in our work here concerns the Earps and other Tombstoners and Arizonans. Just to consider what this small slice of humanity thought of Santa Monica gives a measure of that community's impact. In 1885, Tucson's *Daily Star* mentioned that "Mrs. Dr. Handy and children took yesterday's train for Santa Monica in search of a cooler clime than Tucson. They will be absent a number of months."[16] Dr. John Handy was Tucson's leading physician, and by that time many merchants and mining executives headed for Santa Monica during the summer months. The *Star* of June 1892 mentioned that "Santa Monica is the natural seaside resort for Arizonans and there are many who are already enjoying the cool breezes."[17]

The *Tombstone Weekly Epitaph* ran a series of large ads in May and June 1893, praising the Santa Monica Tract, with 178 beautiful lots, bathing, hunting, fishing, "Location Unsurpassed!" The real estate office was in Los Angeles, but you could contact S. C. Bagg, of Tombstone; Bagg was the newspaper owner-editor. In the summer of 1894, George Parsons, walking the beach at Santa Monica, spotted several good friends: Dr. George Goodfellow, sister and daughter. In the following years, Dr. Goodfellow would make Santa Monica summers a must. In early 1895, Dr. Goodfellow accompanied E. B. Gage to Santa Monica for his health; Gage, head of the Grand Central Mining Company, had been Tombstone's leading businessman.[18]

It was on another trip to the Santa Monica beach by George Parsons, in 1903, that he had a memorable reunion with Wyatt Earp, who at that

Dr. George E. Goodfellow, surgeon to the gunfighters, repairer of Earp body parts in Arizona. *Lee Silva Collection.*

S. C. Bagg, bottom line, Tombstone editor, and "in the loop" with the Santa Monica tourist promotions. *Tombstone Weekly Epitaph,* July 30, 1893.

SANTA · MONICA

TRACT.

BATHING! HUNTING! FISHING!

Own a Home by the Sea Shore Within the City Limits of Santa Monica.

178 BEAUTIFUL LEVEL LOTS } **$100 Per Lot.**
$25 DOWN
$10 PER MONTH Without Interest

FINE SOIL !
    FINE WATER PIPED!
        LOCATION UNSURPASSED!
            SANTA FE STATION ON TRACT!
                STREET CARS RUN TO THIS TRACT!

3 COTTAGES GIVEN AWAY. 3

For Further Particulars and Circulars, Address

HANNA & WEBB
204 South Spring St. Los Angeles Ca
Or **S C. BAGG** Tombstone, A. T.

time was featured negatively in a Los Angeles news account. Parsons defended Wyatt in a newspaper confutation, for which he was thanked by Wyatt.

Aside from this type of travel to the seashore by hundreds of individuals, there were important seasonal excursions, with special prices. In June 1896 the Southern Pacific offered rates of $31 from Benson to Santa Monica "To enjoy the cool salt water breeze." The Tucson papers in 1898 listed the dozens of Santa Monica beach and hotel features, coolest sea breezes, "Quickest Reached." The Flagstaff papers in 1900 listed the dates of various excursions and the cost, but by this time Santa Monica was only one of a series that included Redondo, Long Beach, and San Diego.

A further kind of travel that involved thousands was the group or organizational trip, which meant fraternal organizations, church groups, veteran societies, or youth groups. For example, in June 1905, the Knights of Columbus of Bisbee would go to Santa Monica on the electric line. A literary program was scheduled at the Santa Monica auditorium, with a plunge exclusively for members, followed by some band music at the Arcadia Hotel.[19]

These few examples of how some Arizonans took advantage of the Santa Monica offerings indicate how widespread the interest was in the Pacific Coast. Get a measure of this interest in places like Phoenix, Globe, Florence, Prescott, and other Arizona locations, then add to this amount the hundreds of communities in Nevada, New Mexico, and Utah who longed for the Pacific beaches during the hot summer months, and we can see how and why the Santa Monica identity search found its niche.

From the 1920s onward, a substantial number of Japanese settled in this area of Sawtelle, and several publications of both Sawtelle and West Los Angeles cover these developments. What is not generally realized is that a certain Japanese influence was already in place in the early 1900s, both in Santa Monica and Sawtelle.[20]

Since Santa Monica's founding in 1875, and through our coverage here, 1910, the person of Arcadia Bandini de Baker was either encouraging, sometimes pulling levers, and in most cases participating in Santa Monica's development. A daughter of one of the state's foremost rancho families, she had been married to the leading Los Angeles merchant, Abel Stearns. She later married Robert Baker, a major financier and owner of rancho lands along the Pacific Ocean. When Baker and Senator Jones planned and executed the birth of Santa Monica, it was with her encouragement. She was indeed part of the trio when lands were set aside for the new Soldiers' Home.

When the Casino opened in 1888 (founded by Baker and Jones), she was at the formal opening, welcoming the guests. Over the years she donated considerable land for local churches and other establishments, as well as land for the well-known Red Cars of the Pacific Electric route. After the death of her husband in 1894, she continued to be involved in major projects with Senator Jones; one of these was the founding of the Santa Monica Land & Water Company. At her death in 1912, Arcadia Bandini de Baker was one of the largest landowners in Southern California. Known as the "godmother of Santa Monica," in October 1987, a bronze bust would be fashioned in her honor and revealed to the public, in Palisades Park, land she had donated to the city of Santa Monica. Its plaque reads "Dedicated to Arcadia Bandini de Baker; 1827–1912; for her love and devotion to Santa Monica and generous contributions of land to benefit the people and the government of the city; by the city of Santa Monica; Bandini family and friends; Santa Monica Historical Society; Masahito Sanae Sculptor; October 18, 1987."[21]

That Arcadia Bandini de Baker was influential was obvious from what followed. Her nephew, Juan Jose Carrillo, was mayor of Santa Monica in the 1890s, and his son, Leo Carrillo, was an important movie and television personality (including as the Cisco Kids' "Pancho") into the 1950s, and a conservationist for whom the beautiful Leo Carrillo State Park and Beach near Malibu would be named. He was also very close friends with famed western artist and Earp family acquaintance Victor Clyde Forsythe.[22] The Bandini influence was major, not only in the Santa Monica region, but also in Pasadena, where her brother Arturo Bandini was in the thick of things business and social.

How the Soldiers' Home fits in with this economic and cultural evolution has been mentioned in several ways in the preceding pages. Santa Monica was founded in 1875, the Soldiers' Home a decade later.

The Home (and its veterans and pension dollars), only a few miles inland, had a major impact on the economic life and development of early Santa Monica. However, by the late 1890s, when the community of Sawtelle came into being, and with the increased transportation links among Los Angeles, the Home, Sawtelle, and Santa Monica, the Home gradually diminished as a focus of attention for Santa Monica. The City of Santa Monica had found its economic base ("groove") on the beaches of the Pacific Ocean.

◇━━◍━◇━━━◇━◍━━◇

CHAPTER 17

The Earps Retreat

For this first decade of the twentieth century, we should summarize how the five male Earps figured in this Sawtelle venture. Wyatt was the least involved. He visited James in Sawtelle and in Los Angeles a few times. The two had been involved in operations in half a dozen mining camps, were very close, and no doubt both of them figured that Wyatt's occasional presence in Sawtelle would not hurt business. However, after Wyatt's saloon try in Tonopah, he forever after stayed away from operating a gaming or drinking place. That does not mean he stayed away from those environments. Most of Wyatt's time from 1904 until 1929 was spent working a variety of copper and gold claims in the California/Arizona border desert, near the Whipple Mountains, and living seasonally in his bordering homes and campsites in Calzona, Vidal, and Vidal Junction, California, and Parker, Arizona, not far from where the small town of Earp, California, named in his honor, would evolve in the early 1930s, during the cooler months; and in Los Angeles during the hot summer months. Sawtelle was never a focus for him.[1]

In regard to Virgil's role, for a time in 1903-04 he seems to have been convinced that the Sawtelle pension flow deserved his attention, and the V. W. EARP tokens indicate more than a casual interest. Yet, by the end of 1904 he was off to Goldfield, Nevada, as a less than active deputy sheriff, where he died in late 1905. Virgil had been vitally interested in the Sawtelle blind pig possibilities, but the interest was short-lived.[2]

Father Nicholas was most likely the cause of the move to Sawtelle by the Earps. He and James had to have had that conversation, because shortly after James moved from San Francisco to Sawtelle, Nick was enrolled in the Soldiers' Home. "Justice Earp" was probably one of the best known of the thousand-plus veterans in the Home, and his forceful, out-going manner must have been important in shifting clientele towards the Fourth Street card room of son James. Nick's death early in 1907 left a gaping hole in the Earp Sawtelle influence.

Newton, half-brother to the well-known Earp brothers, was born in Kentucky in 1837 and had a stalwart Civil War career, serving for many years, being wounded in action, and rising to sergeant in the 4th Iowa Cavalry. He can best be identified as a bit apart from most members of the Earp family. He was later chief of police in Garden City, Kansas, and eventually moved to California. However, Newton and saloons were not a good mix. He and his family were of a religious bent,[3] a characteristic not often mentioned about the Earps. He did enroll in the Soldiers' Home in 1902 with father Nick, and although there is no concrete evidence that Newton in any way participated in James's illicit alcohol schemes, Newton was one of the higher status veterans of the Sawtelle area, and his Earp name was certainly not a negative so far as Earp brothers' fortunes were concerned.

One of the unusual aspects of Newton's life was that he spent some time in three Civil War Soldiers' Homes: Fort Dodge (State), Sawtelle (National), and Napa (State). After his departure from Sawtelle in 1909 he moved to northern California, working as a carpenter and a home builder. He frequently lived with daughter Alice, when he wasn't serving periods in the Soldiers' Home in Napa. He died in Sacramento on December 18, 1928.[4]

James, the leader of the Earp efforts at Sawtelle, seems to have been hit hard by the deaths of Virgil in 1905 and Nicholas in 1907. His name doesn't surface in any of the usual Sawtelle accounts after this time, and he apparently headed directly to San Bernardino County. He was listed as a laborer in the voter's register of 1908, and in the coming years usually lived near his sister Adelia. Her husband Bill Edwards was a carpenter, and the family lived in several San Bernardino communities in this era. The Edwards family had a reunion in 1911 in East Highlands, and James Earp was in attendance. In the next year's voter's register he was listed as a farmer. This makes one wonder what type of farm work would be done by a seventy-year-old veteran with a useless shoulder. By 1917 he was listed as retired. His only income was most likely his small Civil War pension.[5]

Bartender, whoremaster, jailbird, and blind pig operator, James Cooksey Earp may have surprised a few folks when they learned of his new role in life. In 1922, the election officials for San Bernardino No. 4 Precinct were listed; James C. Earp was one of the clerks.[6]

Such respectability and community participation were not to last. In 1924, Edward Johnson of San Bernardino filed an affidavit with the veterans' pension office, stating that James Earp lived in a small building on his property, had had a stroke the previous year, had difficulty walking, and in general could not take care of his own needs.

Shortly after this, James moved to Los Angeles, to the home of Allie Earp's (Virgil's wife) grandniece, Hildreth Halliwell. Allie also lived in the Halliwell home. Hildreth's mother had lived with Virgil and Allie as a young woman after first arriving in Vanderbilt, California, from Kansas. She would meet her husband (Hildreth's father) there. In Hildreth's reminiscences she mentions that although she took care of James for more than a year (his last), he didn't pass on any fascinating family tales or memorable stories of his Western experiences. While she described Wyatt as very hushed, passive, and nontalkative about his Wild West experiences, never speaking about Tombstone, James would at times open up. He died in the Halliwell home (as Allie subsequently would after living there from the time of Virgil's death in 1905 until her own in 1947) on January 25, 1926. His remains were taken to San Bernardino. After a Methodist ceremony presided over by the Rev. W. C. Loomis, James Earp was buried in Mountain View Cemetery, which would later also become the final resting place of sister Adelia and her husband Bill Edwards, as well as that of Allie. James's wife Bessie (January 1887), and mother Virginia (January 1893), had already been buried in the Pioneer Cemetery, just a few miles directly south of there, well over thirty years earlier.[7]

In order to place this Earp and Sawtelle episode in some sort of Western perspective, we need to consider the tremendous amount of geography they covered, usually in the company of other Earps. This was the end of the line for joint family activity and for their Western wanderings. From this point on, only Wyatt would be left out there trying to make a buck.

◈—◦—◦—◦—◈

CHAPTER 18

In Perspective:
A Family on the Move

The Earps were not an important family. However, one would look far, indeed, to find a family that had covered as much ground and had gotten involved in so many of the occupational activities of the West that were considered exciting, exotic, challenging, and sometimes remunerative. They were never top dogs, but in a few of the places, such as Tombstone, San Bernardino County, and Nome, they were rubbing elbows with the folks in charge. Also, in the several dozens of places that had some Earp "stamp," more than one Earp had been present.

Just a listing of their law positions is amazing. Nick was a constable and provost marshal in Illinois, Iowa, Missouri, and California. Wyatt wore badges in Missouri, Kansas, Arizona, Idaho, and Nevada. Virgil was a constable, deputy sheriff, chief of police, and deputy U. S. marshal in Arizona, California, and Nevada. Morgan had been a law officer in Montana and Arizona. Even James and Warren had served as deputies on occasion in Kansas and Arizona. Newton had been the first chief of police in Garden City, Kansas.

In the nineteenth century, military service was a reasonably high-status activity. Father Nicholas had served in the Mexican War, and during the Civil War did his best in several Iowa communities to raise troops for the Union cause. His attitude and actions had an impact on his sons, as James, Newton, and Virgil had years of service in Iowa and Illinois regiments, James and Newton both being wounded in action.

It would be too challenging to list the saloons, card parlors, and whore houses that had some connection with the Earp family. There were several dozen, at least, from Peoria to Fort Worth to Tombstone to Coeur d'Alene to Nome to San Bernardino to Tonopah, Dulzura, California,[1] and on and on. The facilities varied, from Virgil serving as a bartender in Peoria to James playing faro in a small room in Calico, to Wyatt and James having a tent saloon in Idaho, to Wyatt and James running the important Dexter Saloon in Nome.

Aside from this, we know of ancillary activity, such as Wyatt hauling saloon gear from San Diego over the desert to the new mining community at Harqua Hala, Arizona, Virgil backing race horses at San Luis Obispo, Wyatt refereeing a championship fight in San Francisco, James escaping from jail in Montana, Warren getting killed in an Arizona saloon fight, and father Nicholas pushing to get himself named Indian agent in San Bernardino County. Wyatt had a stable of horses in San Francisco, owned properties in San Diego, while at the same time running gambling games in Baja California.

An important ingredient in this complicated traipsing around is that it was seldom an individual Earp involved. Tombstone, Colton, and San Bernardino involved most of the family. There was constant visiting, such as Virgil going to see Wyatt in San Diego, or Virgil's wife dropping in on Los Angeles relatives. Even in distant Nome, not only was James part of the scene with Wyatt, but Josie's brother, Nathan Marcus, also had a hand in the saloon operations. The Idaho saloon operation was Wyatt, James, Warren, and to keep Colton honest, Nicholas and Virgil were the law in the town.[2]

This, then, brings us to the turn of the century, and Sawtelle brought together the remaining members of the Earp family to have one final sling at their Western bonanza. The new community was wide open (no legal structure), only feet away from the Soldiers' Home where over a thousand veterans each month received a pension, with almost nowhere to spend it. Good old soldiers Nicholas and Newton would be residents of the Home, while in nearby Sawtelle, James would set up shop, with some encouragement from Virgil and Wyatt. That seems to have been the intended scenario.

In 1906 the local newspaper, the *Sentinel*, published a small pamphlet extolling the greatness of the community. The "best days are yet to come," and the place was "one of the neatest, healthiest and most pleasantly located little cities in the state." Sawtelle was celebrating its recent vote in favor of cityhood. This was the same year that there were over a hundred arrests for blind pig operations, and the same year that the name of James Earp was publicized in three metropolitan newspapers as a violator of the gambling and liquor laws.[3]

Things didn't evolve well enough for the word *bonanza* to apply for the Earps. James ran a blind pig, had a card room for the boys, but although the money was there, others, such as P. J. Flynn ("King of the Blind Pigs"), Horatio Bolster, and John Dupree seemed better positioned and experienced in the ways of working with and around the law. The deaths of Virgil and Nicholas put a damper on things, and the changing ways of pension payments, as well as cityhood for Sawtelle, spelled the decline of the wide-open blind pig era for Sawtelle.

The Earp family's last big team effort, an attempt to grab the Sawtelle pension purse, was a (borrasca) bust.

Epilogue

Times certainly changed, especially in the first part of the twentieth century. The Prohibition Movement, sparked by a vigorous religious push, by 1900 had interested many parts of the country in a morality attitude that determined that alcohol was one of mankind's great evils. Other parts of society joined in these efforts after 1900, when forces such as the anti-saloon drives gained momentum across the United States. By the time that the Volstead Act, and the 18th Amendment of 1919, were made law in 1920, the culmination of this attempt to outlaw alcohol from American society was now fulfilled.[1] We all know how this ended, as the upheaval in American society and its aftermath concluded that alcohol, and whatever its associations, would be part of the future. The great Prohibition Movement was important, but it was not to be the America way. With the demise of prohibition in 1933, with the repeal of the 18th Amendment, came the demise of the blind pig, and all its proprietors and enablers.

Santa Monica went on to what in retrospect seems to have been its destiny, a medium-sized Pacific Coast center that was a leading resort mecca and symbol of what was important in American aspirations. Los Angeles, by the early 1900s, was already on its way to becoming a leading North American transportation and commercial entrepot.

The Soldiers' Home, although it increased in size and function, gradually lost its significance in the grand scheme of things as a dozen or more institutions and municipalities in Southern California jockeyed the Home into being just one of the many organizations in the region. Sawtelle, by the 1920s, had for the most part ceased to exist, not only by becoming a part of the city of Los Angeles, but by being swallowed into phrases like "the west side" and "West Los Angeles." Following World War I, a whole new large crop of veterans with injuries, diseases, and disability required medical attention and rehabilitation. In 1921, Congress created the "Veterans Bureau," combining all veterans' programs, and in 1927 the Wadsworth Hospital, replacing the old 1889 hospital and its 1905 hospital annex,[2] opened on the Soldiers' Home campus. The Veterans Administration (VA) was formed in 1930 by President Hoover with the merging of the Veterans Bureau, the National Home, and the Pension Bureau. In the late 1930s a new Wadsworth Hospital was erected, and the modern present-day Wadsworth Hospital, the largest of the VA's medical facilities, now known as the West Los Angeles (Wadsworth) VA Medical Center, opened in 1977. The Soldiers' Home, and Sawtelle, became submerged in that huge giant, Los Angeles, and most recently, the Home integrated into the West Los Angeles Veterans Affairs (VA)/Medical Center complex, which is now also home of the UCLA Bruins off-campus Jackie Robinson Baseball Stadium complex.[3]

The Earps had made their play. They took their frontier, gambling, and saloon experiences and skills, and believed they had an opening for a final flourish in the new community of Sawtelle, where veterans with their steady pension money would participate in some faro, poker, and illegal drinking. They showed up in numbers, with father Nicholas and Newton in the Soldiers' Home, James in nearby Sawtelle, a period of activity by Virgil, and occasional visits by Wyatt to put an Earp stamp on things. They put up a good show, but Sawtelle wasn't the gold mine (bonanza) they had planned.

Virgil passed on at age sixty-two in Goldfield, Nevada, on October 19, 1905, and was buried in River View Cemetery, near the homes of his daughter Nellie Jane, and first wife Ellen Rijsdam Eaton, in Portland, Oregon. Nicholas ended his days at age ninety-three on February 12, 1907, and was placed in a grave at the Home (now Los Angeles National Cemetery). James retired to, and later died in, Los Angeles, on January 25, 1926, at age eighty-four, , and was buried in Mountain View Cemetery, San Bernardino. Newton, a bit lonely in Sawtelle, headed north to relatives in Sacramento, where he died on December 18, 1928, at age ninety-one, and is buried not too far from his daughter Alice Earp Wells, in the East

James at rest in Mountain View Cemetery, San Bernardino, California. He is buried next to his sister Adelia and sister-in-law Allie Earp. His mother Virginia and wife Bessie, who proceeded him in death, are buried a few miles south of this location in the Pioneer Cemetery. *David D. de Haas, MD, Collection.*

Lawn Memorial Park Cemetery.[4] Wyatt, the last of the crew, and never a major believer in the Sawtelle effort, died less than a month later, at age eighty, in Los Angeles on January 13, 1929. After significant funeral ceremonies involving show business personalities such as actors William S. Hart and Tom Mix as pallbearers, politicians, the writers Jimmy Mitchell and Wilson Mizner, and the Western figures Tombstone Mayor John Clum, diarist George Parsons, and lawyer William Hunsaker,[5] he was subsequently buried south of San Francisco, in Colma, California at the Hills of Eternity Memorial Park. He was buried next to where his wife Josephine ("Sadie"), whom he preceded in death by nearly sixteen years, later would be, in her Marcus family plot.[6]

One might think that the Earp story ended here, but it did not. Although already well-known and quite famous in his own lifetime as a "gun fighter"[7] and relating to his 1870s Dodge City and Wichita, Kansas, Cowtown years, 1881 Tombstone, Arizona O.K. Corral Gunfight and following 1882 "Vendetta Ride," 1896 Sharkey-Fitzsimmons heavyweight boxing debacle, and subsequent events in Alaska, Nevada, Arizona, Southern California, oil interests, gambling, horse racing (especially with Tombstone colleague, and 1881–1882 Oriental Saloon owner, Lou Rickabaugh), as well as his association with so many other famous and influential individuals of his time;[8] Wyatt's fame would begin to catapult just before his death with the 1927 publication of Walter Noble Burns's book *Tombstone: An Iliad of the Southwest,* where he was branded "The Lion of Tombstone," and even much more so just afterwards with the 1931 publication of Stuart Lake's influential book *Wyatt Earp: Frontier Marshal.* The ensuing plethora of television shows and movies made from these books involving Wyatt, Virgil, Morgan, and James Earp, as well as their other family members, and friends, including western icons Bat Masterson, Doc Holliday, Bill Tilghman, and Luke Short accelerated the process; and it didn't hurt that some of Hollywood's biggest stars (one a future two-term president of the United States)[9] portrayed Wyatt,[10] Doc,[11] and the Earp brothers in various iterations.

The Wyatt Earp legend would skyrocket even further in 1955 with the premiere of the first adult western television series, *The Life and Legend of Wyatt Earp,*[12] starring Hugh O'Brian as Wyatt, and the show's catchy (characterizing Wyatt "Brave, Courageous, and Bold") theme song. So much so that Wyatt would make national news yet once again on July 7, 1957, when his 300-pound monument was discovered stolen, by treasure hunters. And when the town of Tombstone, Arizona, was accused of being in on the theft, for reburial there in its Boothill Cemetery (a few citizens there had actually threatened to do so prior to the incident), the national news outlets went even more berserk. The monument was consequently dumped by the hapless thieves, and recovered by authorities in mid-October 1957, after the manhunt and widespread nationwide publicity the act generated, and a financial reward offered by actor Hugh O'Brian. This tombstone was not immediately replaced due to the damage it sustained and the fear that it would be promptly stolen once again due to the popularity of Wyatt Earp and the television series. The current monument was placed by historian Truman Rex Fisher on December 16, 1996.[13]

In the 1990s, two competing major Hollywood productions with all-star casts once again inspired intense interest in Wyatt and the Earp family: *Tombstone* (1993) starring Kurt Russell as Wyatt Earp, Val Kilmer as Doc Holliday, Sam Elliott as Virgil Earp, Bill Paxton as Morgan Earp, Dana Delaney as Josephine Earp, and Michael Biehn as John Ringo; and *Wyatt Earp* starring Kevin Costner as Wyatt, Dennis Quaid as Doc, David Andrews as James Earp, Michael Madsen as Virgil Earp, Jim Caviezal as Warren, and Gene Hackman as father Nicholas Earp. The popularity of the *Tombstone* movie instigated bountiful ensuing literature and internet discussion boards; and western/Tombstone groups blossomed. Currently innumerable Facebook pages have dominated the day and continued the fascination with all things Wyatt and Earp. The Earps are now mostly remembered as important frontier lawmen, major players in the sporting world, and by certain contemporary historians, as essential historical figures to study, in some detail, for modern-day society to comprehend its current epidemic of firearm related, and other violence.[14]

Some of the fellows. *West Coast Magazine*, February, 1912.

A Memorial Day event at the Home in the early 1900s. *Postcard view.*

LOS ANGELES NATIONAL CEMETERY

950 South Sepulveda Boulevard
Los Angeles, California 90049

Phone: (310) 268-4675
Fax: (310) 268-3257

This is a handout for the Los Angeles National Cemetery, the current name for the Soldiers' Home grave facility.

⟨◇━●━◇━━◇━●━◇⟩

Some of the Other Soldiers

Tens of thousands of veterans were connected with the Pacific Branch, the Soldiers' Home at Sawtelle, and for many it was their final stop. With such numbers, from a variety of locations and occupations, it is relatively easy to pinpoint some famous or at least unusual individuals. Our look, though, has been primarily at some of the happenings in the first decade of the twentieth century, and many of the folks that made greater Sawtelle such an interesting place at that time have received attention in the previous pages.

What follows are additional entries, most from the same period, of veterans or personalities who came from near and far and who deserve a few comments. Most of these veterans likely knew many of the fellows involved in the events highlighted in this book, and chances are they may be a grave or so distant from Nicholas Earp, P. J. Flynn, or Horatio Bolster. The following individuals give an additional view of the type of folks who selected the Soldiers' Home for their final years and resting place. The basic documentation for these people is their sheet, or file, in the National Archives. A few sources have been added, either for interest or possible future research.

THOMAS J. ANDERSON Anderson was one of the Home's notables. He was an attorney in Iowa at the outbreak of the Civil War, joined the 40th Iowa Infantry, and ended as a captain. He subsequently held major political and administrative positions. In 1889 President Cleveland appointed Anderson an associate justice of the Supreme Court of the Territory of

Utah, where he continued to serve after Utah was admitted to statehood in 1896. Declining health led to his admission to the Soldiers' Home in mid-1908, and he died in the Home hospital in the spring of 1910. Anderson is buried in Section 17, Row A, No. 7.[1]

STRICKLAND AUBRIGHT (or, Albright) Heading West was a main theme in Aubright's life. He was born in Pennsylvania, became a physician, and served four years with Ohio infantry and artillery units, rising to the rank of major. He settled in New Mexico, became a leading physician in Albuquerque, and also worked as a surgeon with the Santa Fe Railway. He served as mayor of Albuquerque in the late 1890s. Around the turn of the century he retired to San Bernardino, but age and ill health caught up with him. He moved into the Soldiers' Home in 1902, dying there in October 1906.[2]

EDWIN BAILEY Bailey was one of the more publicized veterans of the Home, for years hailed as their oldest resident. He was a native of Bath, England, arrived in the United States in 1822, and supposedly saw service in the US Navy during the 1830s. He saw naval action at the Battle of Mobile during the Civil War. He was usually referred to as "Captain Bailey," though this rank may be suspect. His enlistment in New York City in 1863 lists him as a seaman. Bailey moved to southern California in 1871, as he had daughters in San Diego and San Bernardino. He also had a wife, but she divorced him and married the poet Edwin Markham. Bailey had a long stay at the Home, arriving there in 1890. He died there in February of 1912, and is buried in Section 21, Row B, N. 10.[3]

ENOS B. BAILEY A native of St. Johns, Michigan, Bailey started the Civil War as a private in the 3rd Michigan Cavalry and at the end was a captain in the 10th Michigan Cavalry. He then worked as a painter until the early 1880s, when he moved to Los Angeles. He was admitted to the Home in 1892 and almost at once began working with the undertaker.

Balloon Route station, one of the few remaining (now in disrepair as can be seen) structures of the Old Soldiers' Home Earp era. *Wikipedia Commons.*

The Chapel, National Soldiers' Home, Cal.

Soldiers' Home Chapel. One of only few remaining original structures which was there when the Earps were. Please compare to photos on page 38 (chapel on left) and page 157 (modern day chapel in disrepair) as well as Gary Zaboly dustjacket artwork. It is said that Nicholas Earp had his funeral services in this Chapel after his death (as most veterans who died in the Soldiers' Home did) in 1907, just prior to his burial in the nearby cemetery. *David D. de Haas, MD, collection.*

Within a few years Captain Bailey headed that unit. When interviewed in 1905, Bailey had already prepared 1,619 veterans either for burial or to be sent elsewhere for interment. He pointed out that the Home averaged eighteen deaths a month, with November and December being the highest. Bailey died on May 13, 1915, and was placed in Section 26, Row F, No. 3.[4]

WILLIAM TRUE BENNETT This fellow had the types of careers that leave folks practically unbelieving. He was born in Calhoun County, Michigan, in 1836, and by 1857 he was in Australia, where he opened a photography studio in Brisbane. He was getting a good start in his profession when the American Civil War erupted. He returned to Michigan and joined the 1st Michigan Colored Infantry and was soon its commanding officer. After a few years of solid service, he moved to the 22rd Connecticut Infantry and was promoted to colonel. He was breveted a brigadier general in 1865 and ended his service in the following year.

Bennett returned to Australia and in the following decades was a leading figure in the worlds of photography and art. He had projects and studios from Sydney to Perth. He developed an interest and some talent in gold mining and gave lectures on mining in Colorado and England. Time and the busy life led to Bennett's going to the Soldiers' Home in 1899, which in the coming years he left from time to time. He died there in March of 1910 and is buried in Section 16.[5]

PHILIP J. BOYLE This, or O'Boyle, was his name, with substantial contradictory evidence. He was born in the 1870s and was a veteran of the Spanish-American War with service in the Philippines. He was a town resident in March of 1907, living in an apartment in the Brown Block in Sawtelle, owned by Dr. J. Brown, a dentist. O'Boyle didn't pay his rent, so Dr. Brown began ejectment proceedings against him. O'Boyle picked up a handy iron bar and clobbered Dr. Brown on the head. Dr. Brown, in typical dental reaction, whipped out a revolver and fired at O'Boyle. The dentist was not a good marksman, and the opponents settled their business, so neither was arrested. The *Los Angeles Times* of March 29, 1907, headed the article as: "Gas Pipe vs. Pistol."[6]

JOHN E. CAMPBELL This Pennsylvania native moved to Arizona Territory, and modestly listed himself as a "farmer." Campbell must be considered one of the most unusual, daring figures in American military and law enforcement history. What he did in one decade's deeds was enough for a dozen men. When McClintock's Troop B of the Rough Riders went from Arizona to Cuba in 1898, one of their stalwarts was Sergeant John E. Campbell, who was praised for his work by Roosevelt. With that campaign over, back in Arizona, Campbell had a hand in organizing a unit for the Philippine campaigns. He would be a first sergeant in the 34th Regiment of U. S. Volunteers, where he figured in several campaigns in Ilocos Norte. After his return to Arizona Territory, Campbell served as an officer in the Arizona National Guard, in charge of the Tempe Company. Subsequent to this, Campbell served a stint as a sergeant with the Arizona Rangers. His body wore out, and in 1908 he was admitted to the Soldiers' Home. While in the hospital, he "wandered," fell from a second-story window, broke his collarbone, and had head and other injuries. Campbell died at the Home on September 16, 1910, and was returned to Arizona Territory for burial in Tempe.

WILLIAM T. COLLINS Canadian-born Collins was a major in Berdan's Sharpshooters of Civil War fame. Severe wounds had led to amputation of his left leg. He later graduated from Georgetown University Medical School and had successful practices in North Dakota and Montana. He also served in the legislatures of both states. Dr. Collins was one of the best-known veterans nationally, being adjutant-general of the G. A. R. He moved to Santa Monica around 1900. He was never a member of the Home. When he died in October of 1906, the family carried out his wishes for burial. At the family's request, permission was received from Washington for him to be buried among his Civil War comrades. This was done with elaborate ceremonies at the Home on October 3.[7]

Front view of the aging dilapidated chapel in 2019, one of the few remaining structures of the Soldiers' Home. Compare to prior photo on page 154 where Chapel is shown at about the time the Earps were there. Photo taken May 31, 2019, by Mary de Haas. *David D. de Haas, MD, Collection.*

RILEY (RYLAND) DARNELL This Chicago merchant was one of the veterans of the Home who came from a wealthy background. He had served as a 1st sergeant in an Indiana infantry regiment, and later moved to Chicago. Within a few decades he owned at least a dozen men's furnishings stores, mostly in Chicago's Loop. However, his career was "spotty," as his love for the racetrack caused multiple problems. Several times he went "missing," as debts caught up with him. Darnell moved to the Los Angeles area after 1900 and was admitted to the Home in 1906. He worked as a hospital orderly, but was always trying to have his pension increased, as he thought he deserved it. The "Old Haberdasher" died at the Home in March 1913, with his pension accumulation of $13.00 being sent to his widow in Chicago. He is in Section 22, Row K, No. 11.[8]

CHARLES A. DUDLEY The well-documented life of this Buffalo Soldier indicates a career in many states and territories. Born a slave in 1843 North Carolina, Dudley served three years in the Civil War with a Massachusetts cavalry regiment. Later he did the unusual by serving in two well-known Negro frontier units, the 10th U. S. Cavalry and the 24th U. S. Infantry. He was in Texas, Colorado, Utah, New Mexico, and Arizona. After retirement he worked for years at the Commercial Hotel in Flagstaff. Poor health made him shift to the Soldiers' Home, arriving at Sawtelle in September 1908. He died there in May 1910 and is buried in Section 17, Row A., No. 10.[9]

LULA BELLE DURKEE Miss Durkee, a nurse, is one of the few women in the Los Angeles National Cemetery. She was born in Michigan in 1867, received a nursing diploma in 1894, and practiced as a nurse in Detroit until the Spanish-American War. Her service in the Army Nurse Corps began in 1898, and in mid-1901 she went to the Philippines. After her military service she returned to Michigan and for years was at Harper Hospital in Detroit. In 1928 she received a military pension and was categorized as an invalid. Somewhere along the way she moved to California and was a registered voter in San Bernardino in 1950, and in Los Angeles in 1954. She died in Los Angeles in July of 1954; her burial is in Plot 252, Row E, No. 4.

GEORGE H. ELDRIDGE   Sergeant Eldridge had an unusual military career, serving in the Civil War with a Michigan regiment that was part of the Iron Brigade. After the war his farming career was short-lived, as he joined the 6th U. S. Cavalry and was in several Texas Indian campaigns. He was one of the few soldiers awarded two Medals of Honor. His most noteworthy deeds were performed along the Wichita River in Texas in 1870, in the campaign against the Kiowa and Comanche forces led by Chief Kicking Bird. He settled in the Ft. Grant area near Tucson, where in addition to ranching he also served as a justice of the peace. He was admitted to the Soldiers' Home in 1907 and was soon appointed to several leadership positions. Eldridge died at the Home in 1918 and is buried in Section 12, Row A, No. 5.[10]

FREDERICK ELSER   German-born Elser entered the 15th Connecticut Infantry as a private in the Civil War and finished as a lieutenant. He was a musician, moved West, and for some years was bandmaster of the Los Angeles City Band. Elser in retirement moved to the Soldiers' Home, where in 1891 he organized the Home Band, which usually had between fifteen and twenty members. Because of his long connection with Los Angeles, and because of his many performances at the Home and around Southern California, Elser was one of the better-known people of the region. He retired in 1906, died at the Home in 1913, and is buried in Section 14.

FATHER and SON (EVANS) There were probably not many of these combinations to be found in the Soldiers' Homes across the nation. William M. Evans served in the Civil War in a Missouri unit, then for years operated a farm near Fresno. He entered the Soldiers' Home in March 1907. His son John D. joined the 6th California Infantry in 1898, aiming no doubt for some action in the Philippines. What he got was guard duty in Benicia and Santa Cruz. However, things were not going well, and he was admitted to the Soldiers' Home in June, just months after his father's admission. John was suffering from severe pulmonary problems. His father was at the bedside on July 28, 1907, as his son died. The father would die in the Home in 1915, so their graves are several sections apart.[11]

FREDERICK FACKNER This fellow served in a New York infantry regiment during the Civil War, then operated as a merchant in Phoenix for decades. He arrived at the Home in 1896 and became well-known locally for his valuable collections. He frequently displayed them to friends and journalists, and this was impressive stuff: some 700 gold and silver coins, 3,000 copper coins, and many other pieces from throughout the ancient world. Maybe he received too much publicity. It was found that he had several wives, and he had made fraudulent claims on his pension application. This fellow, who was filthy rich, lied to prevent a wife from getting one-half of his pension. Fackner had other troubles, but the Home administrators had enough and discharged him in 1904. He served a brief term in San Quentin. He moved to South Pasadena, where in July 1909 he died after a fall from a stepladder. Several relatives from New York arrived on the scene, not only to push aside the claiming "wives," but most likely to help inventory the coin collection.[12]

MARION FANNER After a few years' service in the Illinois infantry during the Civil War, Fanner headed to the Phoenix area where for years he was involved in mining. He was admitted to the Soldiers' Home in 1902. According to the *Arizona Republican* of October 10, 1905, Fanner was an inoffensive man, but was frequently drunk and often in the justice and police courts. He would get work as a cook or ranch hand until his next pension check came in, then "enter upon another prolonged debauch." In July 1905, Fanner was given a furlough from the Soldiers' Home and he headed east towards Phoenix, probably trying to revive some mining project. In October travelers found a badly decomposed body between

Salome and Phoenix. The coroner's conclusion was that it was an accidental death. Rumor had it that Fanner had money and headed east in the company of another man. Could this have been murder? A man who knew Fanner thought not: "he would not have left a place where liquor is sold as long as he had a cent."[13]

MANUEL FRANCISCO GARCIA Born near Santa Barbara in 1841, Garcia was of a family from the Azores Islands. He was raised in the Santa Barbara and Ventura area, then in 1864 became a member of the 1st Battalion, Native California Cavalry, which spent most of their time in Arizona campaigns. He served through 1866, married the next year, and in the following years was a resident of Santa Barbara, Ventura, and Carpentaria. He was frequently listed as a barber. Garcia entered the Soldiers' Home in 1901 and lived there until 1924; he then lived with relatives in Los Angeles and Ventura. Garcia died on January 10, 1940, and was buried in Section 72 in the cemetery at the Soldiers' Home. He was probably the last living member of the Native California Cavalry.[14]

MICHAEL HALPIN A native of Ireland, Halpin entered British service with the 14th Light Dragoons. In the mid-1850s, while stationed at Gibraltar, Halpin noticed an American frigate in the harbor. He decided it was "too temptatious, so I suddenly took it in me head to give her Royal Majesty the slip and come to America." The New World suited him just fine, and in 1858 he joined the 2nd U. S. Infantry Regiment, serving throughout the Civil War. He later moved to California, and for years was a railroader, living in Needles.

Halpin moved to the Soldiers' Home in 1891 but left in 1895. He returned in 1897 and would become one of the best known of all veterans in the Sawtelle vicinity. Sergeant Halpin became head of the honor guard, the "firing squad" that was the colorful part of burial ceremonies. Sergeant Halpin and his men were featured in dozens of parades and gatherings, not only at the Home and in Sawtelle but also in other locations in Southern California. He died in late April 1907, and the *Times* of

April 30 devoted a full column to his interesting career. Then, under a new leadership in the burial detail, Sergeant Halpin was placed in Section 13, Row 6, No. 18.[15]

HERMANN E. HASSE. Born in Wisconsin of German parents, Hasse was sent back to Europe to study medicine, at Leipzig and Prague. He served during the Civil War, finishing as a major and chief surgeon of the 24th Wisconsin Infantry. He practiced medicine in Milwaukee for a few years, then headed to Los Angeles. In 1888, at the founding of the Soldiers' Home, Hasse became Chief Surgeon, a post he held until 1905. During these years he headed one of the largest medical facilities in the West and was praised as a surgeon as well as an administrator. Dr. Hasse was also a well-known national botanist, and he wrote on lichens and other botanical subjects for scientific magazines in the United States and Europe. Much of his field work was in the Santa Monica Mountains, on Catalina Island, and in the Arizona deserts. After his retirement in 1905 he practiced in Los Angeles and Santa Monica, with offices on Wilshire Blvd., near the Soldiers' Home. He died in 1915.[16]

CHICKEN DICK (HARTMAN) Andrew Hartman served as a musician during the Civil War with an Ohio infantry regiment. In later years he lived in Cochise County, Arizona, near Bisbee, where he kept a chicken farm. He did not shrink from publicity, as he was involved in several legal cases, and he also presented President Theodore Roosevelt with a bear, which ended up in the Washington Zoo. He was also known as one of the local Knights of the Green Cloth, which meant that he had to sell many a chicken to keep up with his gambling debts. He was admitted to the Soldiers' Home at Sawtelle in 1904, but never adjusted to the place. In 1909 he was dropped from the rolls, for having extended his furlough too many days. He was in poor health for years and died in Bisbee in August of 1917.[17]

WILLIAM W. HAVENS This clergyman probably didn't enjoy the Soldiers' Home, nor the Sawtelle environment. After serving with the 21st New York Cavalry he served in churches in Minnesota and South Dakota, then became field agent in South Dakota for the Anti-Saloon League. Rev. Havens moved to Albuquerque in 1904 and among other things became superintendent of the Arizona and New Mexico Anti-Saloon League, giving speeches and raising funds in both regions. Poor health forced his move to the Home late in 1909; he died there in 1914, and was buried in Section 25, Row 9, No. 7. Because of his deteriorating mental health, he was probably spared the frequent news of the Fourth Street booze consumption. In one of the oddities of veteran family life, his wife moved to the Soldiers' Home in Iowa, where she died in 1930.[18]

WILLIAM H. HEISTAND Heistand became a well-known local figure, mostly because he was a publicity hound, and a scoundrel. He was born in Louisiana, served in infantry and cavalry units in the Civil War, and may have been an attorney and/or a district judge. He was admitted to the Soldiers' Home in 1900 and died there in February 1912. In one of his escapades, in mid-1904, he took a furlough and moved to Santa Barbara, where he convinced a merchant that he was a wealthy widower with a large Louisiana estate. Heistand boarded with the family, put out much "smooth talk," told them he would leave his estate to them, even gave a "little bequest of $2,000 for spending money," which would, of course, come later. He left after some weeks, promising to return, and handed Mr. C. D. Lyons some "valuable" mining stock. Mr. Lyons soon learned the worth of Heistand's estate and mining stock. Heistand, even in December 1909, was able to convince newspapers in Utah and California that he should now be addressed as Baron Karl Frederik Heistand, having just inherited a title and $60,000 from a rich Bavarian uncle. It must have been tough sharing a bunk bed near Heistand at the Soldiers' Home.[19]

DAVID L. HUGHES This famous Rough Rider had the makings of a fantastic life. His father Samuel was a Welsh immigrant to Tucson who married young Atanacia Santa Cruz. Samuel became a leading Tucson merchant, and his brother Louis became Territorial Governor. When the Spanish-American War erupted, young David was working in the Bisbee copper mines. He became a Rough Rider, and when Roosevelt and crew charged up San Juan Hill, Sergeant Hughes was carrying the colors. The success, the glory, and the medals were also accompanied with a severe head wound which pretty much disabled him forever. He was admitted to the Soldiers' Home in 1919. When the movie *The Rough Riders* was made in 1927, Hughes spent a few weeks as a consultant at the original training camp in San Antonio. Hughes, one of the stalwarts of the Rough Riders, died at the Soldiers' Home in July 1935 and is buried in Section 58, Row G, No. 27.[20]

GEORGE HUTCHINS (HUTCHINSON)   Buffalo Soldiers is the term usually applied to members of four Negro or Colored cavalry and infantry regiments with wide service on the Western frontier. Hutchins, born a slave in Kentucky in 1841, was a member of the 116th Regiment, Colored Infantry, in the Civil War. He was wounded in action and was discharged in 1865. He moved to Louisiana and Texas and served in both the 9th and 10th U. S. Cavalry Regiments, mostly in Texas, New Mexico, and Colorado. After military service he worked as a blacksmith at Ft. Bliss. The Hutchins family eventually settled in Los Angeles, where he died in 1936. His family opted for burial in the Los Angeles National Cemetery. There are more than 100 Buffalo Soldiers buried here, the former cemetery of the Soldiers' Home.[21]

JEREMIAH "LIVER-EATING" JOHNSON   Jeremiah or John Johnston (later, Johnson), was a New Jersey native who is known for a dozen or so roles on the frontier, including Civil War service in Colorado and Missouri. In the following decades he was a scout, trapper, and prospector, as well as serving as a law officer in Colorado and Montana. His wife, a member of the Flathead people, was killed by a Crow hunting party, and Johnson became well-known for his revenge mission against the Crows.

Johnson's last position was as town marshal of Deer Lodge, Montana. Soon age and a downhill slide led him to the Soldiers' Home in Sawtelle in December 1899, where he died on January 21, 1900.

His few weeks of life at Sawtelle were followed by more than seventy years in a grave in Section 5. Then, in 1974, Liver-Eating Johnson became one of the few veterans who ever left the grounds. Following a campaign by students in Wyoming, Montana, and California, federal authorities granted permission to transfer Johnson's remains to a cemetery in Cody, Wyoming, where he was reburied with full ceremony. The career of this unusual frontier figure was highlighted in 1972 in the popular film, *Jeremiah Johnson*, starring Robert Redford.

ROBERT JOHNSON   Born in Virginia in 1866 to an ex-slave, Johnson became a Buffalo Soldier in 1887, joining the 10th Cavalry. He was in several Apache campaigns, served five years in Montana, then was in Cuba for the charge up San Juan Hill during the Spanish-American War. Johnson was a 1st sergeant and was an outstanding pistol shot, participating several times in the U. S. Cavalry national competitions. He retired to his Virginia farm in 1913, but was called back in 1918 as an officer, to aid in training recruits. Sometime around 1940 Johnson landed in San Francisco, and in 1943 was admitted to Letterman Hospital there. He died in January of 1946, and as he had planned, he was buried in the Los Angeles National Cemetery; he is in Plot 189, RWC.[22]

O. H. LAGRANGE   Oscar Hugh LaGrange was a Wisconsin lawyer who ended the Civil War as a general, participating in Sherman's March through Georgia. He later served as superintendent of the U. S. Mint in San Francisco and in the 1890s was the fire commissioner of New York City. In 1899 he was appointed governor of the Soldiers' Home and served into 1908, the years of the focus of this saga. The "LaGrange era" should rank high if we compare his work to that of other Home administrators, and with heads of similar facilities throughout the country. He was a reasonable, efficient administrator, but was saddled with the unfortunate blind pig situation in Sawtelle, which though only yards removed, was not in his legal domain. General LaGrange spent his last years as a lawyer in New York City, dying there in 1915.[23]

BENJAMIN F. LEEDS This New York City native was referred to as Captain Leeds, an obvious inflation of his Civil War rank; he was a naval seaman. After his naval service he headed for the West, and became fairly well known as "Captain Leeds" when for years he was the operator of the lighthouse on Alcatraz Island. He was admitted to the Soldiers' Home in 1904, but after a year there he moved into the town of Sawtelle.

When Leeds died in August 1906, another additional distinction was revealed for him: "State's Heaviest Man Dies At Sawtelle." By this time he weighed more than 350 pounds. Leeds was cremated, and following his wishes his remains were placed in the National Cemetery at the Home.[24]

ROBERT LONG Long served a few years in the Civil War, ending in 1866, with the California Cavalry; apparently, he lived in or near Sacramento. At the time he moved to the Soldiers' Home in 1904, he was listed as a resident of Arizona, somewhere near Prescott. His importance here is related to a letter he wrote to a friend, which appeared in the *Prescott Daily Courier* of October 14, 1904, shortly after his admission: "He says he does not like the place very well as it is inhabited by 'a lot of quarrelsome old men' who have not a bit of humor in their composition, and who just sit around and growl at everyone and everything." This was apparently not an exaggeration, as he left the Home in 1908, "at his own request."

IRA A. LUCAS This native of Philadelphia was listed as a "free black inhabitant" in the census of 1850. In 1864, in Brooklyn, he enlisted in the U. S. Navy and saw service all along the Atlantic Coast as well as in New Orleans. He was mustered out in 1867 for a spinal injury and heart disease. By the mid-1870s he was in California, working as a barber and as a waiter in Santa Barbara. The family was listed as "mulatto." He later worked as a barber in Long Beach and Santa Monica. Lucas was admitted to the Soldiers' Home in 1897. After a few years he "went on furlough" and moved into a small cabin near Utah Avenue. He was found dead in his cabin in January 1909.

Several of the Lucas sons had their share in the limelight. One was "Sunny" Lucas, high priest of the Limitless Life Cult, with followers from Denver to San Diego to Santa Barbara. His son Winthrop, at the beginning of the Spanish-American War, tried to enlist. The mustering officer "did not want him because of his color." He did later serve in the U. S. Army with the 24th Infantry Regiment, a Black unit. After his service, Lucas worked for years in Los Angeles as an auto mechanic.[25]

MICHAEL MOONEY Born in Ireland, Mooney was living in New York when he joined the U. S. Navy in 1862, and he served for more than a year. After the war, Mooney moved West where for years he was a fireman in San Francisco. Mooney's name is enshrined in many accounts and publications, as he was a participant in the famous *Monitor-Merrimac* naval battle. He may not have been a "Master" or "First Class Fireman," but he was Michael Mooney, one of several "Coal Heavers." Mooney, admitted to the Home in September 1898, was one of the most admired veterans. He died in July 1911 and is buried in Section 20, Row D.[26]

BUSH PAIN A few years' service in the Missouri cavalry during the Civil war was followed by years in mining, mostly in and around Deadwood. In 1895, Pain was admitted to the Soldiers' Home in California, but discharged soon. The Pain trail then leads to headaches galore for Soldiers' Homes across the country. He was at the Leavenworth Branch, then shifted to the Danville Branch in Illinois. He then spent periods at the State Home in Colorado, then at the State Home in Nebraska, then back to the Danville Branch in 1900. He was back at Sawtelle in 1903, but discharged in 1904, so he went to the Central Branch at Dayton, then spent a year at the Mountain Branch in Tennessee. He was readmitted to the Pacific Branch in July 1906 and died there on February 3, 1907.

Some of his stays were ended "at own request," and at other times he was discharged. His departure each time was probably welcomed by those in charge.[27]

UMBRELLA MAN (PATTEN) Robert W. Patten was a New York native who headed westward; he served in a Wisconsin regiment during the Civil War. He later settled in the Pacific Northwest, becoming a longtime houseboat dweller near Seattle. The Seattle reputation for rain, and his houseboat way of life, made him very conscious of the weather, and from time to time he sported various umbrella headgear. He became the subject of newspaper articles, and soon even cartoonists joined in the fun. It may be that Umbrella Man's visage was the most well-known of any resident of greater Seattle.

Umbrella Man was in the Soldiers' Home for half of 1897, then returned for a permanent stay early in 1911. He died there on April 19, 1913, and his grave is in Section 23, Row B, No. 5.[28]

SURE-SHOT JOHNNY (PETRIE) Exaggerations are common with this fellow, because he had such an unusual career. He was an Illinois fellow, serving in several of that state's regiments during the Civil War. His full name was John R. Petrie, and his subsequent career was mostly as a lawman in Dakota Territory and Montana. He was a constable, deputy sheriff, town marshal, and Deputy U. S. Marshal under Seth Bullock in South Dakota. He tracked down murderers, rustlers, you name it; some accounts mention hundreds of lawbreakers brought to bay. His spectacular career caused him to be the model for the lawman in a novel of 1907, *Langford of the Three Bars*. This great career didn't lead to much bread on the table, and he was admitted, penniless, to the Soldiers' Home in 1910. The *New York Herald* headed this news with "HERO OF NOVEL IN POVERTY." Sure-Shot Johnny remained in the Home until his death in September of 1921. He is buried in Section 42, Row I, No. 5.[29]

HERMAN E. REINHARDT The fellow had one helluva career, although stating that he served in the Mexican War was a bit of a stretch. He arrived from Germany in 1850, and within months was in the U. S. Artillery, taking his discharge in San Diego in 1851. During the Civil War he served in the 1st Washington Territory Infantry and later participated in several Western Indian campaigns. In civilian life he worked as a baker. He may have been a hard man to satisfy, as he was admitted to Soldiers' Homes in both Dayton and Leavenworth before he "got comfortable" in greater Sawtelle. The end was not pleasant, as in September 1905 he ran across the tracks, trying to board a Santa Monica car, but was hit by a car coming from the opposite direction.[30]

ELEAZER T. ROOT Root served in an Illinois infantry regiment in the Civil War and subsequently lived in Chicago. In retirement he lived for a few years in the Soldiers' Home in Leavenworth, then in the early 1900s he shifted to the Pacific Branch in Sawtelle. Late in 1906 Root was appointed head of the ten-man police force at the Home. This was not an easy job, mostly due to the large numbers of tipsy veterans returning from Sawtelle, Santa Monica, or Los Angeles. Things got out of hand in September 1908 when a few guards were accused of knocking around the old vets, "who may have had a drink or two." Root admitted his men had gone over the line, and apparently, he had tried to calm his men and the veterans. However, it was decided to clean house and fire all the guards. Root figured his days were over at the Home and he resigned, moved to San Diego, and died there in 1914.[31]

CONFEDERATE and UNION (RUSH) James F. Rush was born in Mississippi in 1842, and in 1862 was drafted into service in the 7th Mississippi Infantry. He was in several engagements; then near Nashville early in 1865 he was taken prisoner. He changed sides and enlisted in the 5th U. S. Infantry and served into 1866. Rush moved West, worked for a stage line for years, then herded cattle in Texas. He entered the Soldiers' Home in 1893 but left after a few years; in 1900 he was working as a mine laborer in Globe, Arizona. He returned to the Home, where he was employed in the gardens. In 1906 he married a widow, but probably remained in the Home, where he was still living in 1910.[32] He died in Los Angeles on April 28, 1918, and is buried in Plot 36, Row E, No. 14.

RUSSELL BROTHERS Henry and John Russell were at the Soldiers' Home for a few years without recognizing each other. Natives of Southampton, Connecticut, Henry had enlisted in a Massachusetts regiment, and John joined the U. S. Navy. Later they both moved West and had no contact for over forty years. Henry was admitted to the Home in 1894 and later moved into a Sawtelle cottage. John, an engineer, lived in Santa Ana until 1900, when he moved into the Home, where for some years he worked as a nurse in the hospital. A chance encounter in 1903, because of the same family name, led to Henry pulling out the family Bible, where their names were inscribed.

The brothers spent their remaining years in the area, John dying in 1911, Henry in 1913. Henry's grave is in Section 23, John's in Section 20, much closer than they had been during that forty-year gap.[33]

LOUIS C. SCHILLING (SHILLING) If a Hall of Fame for con men existed, Schilling would get prominent space. This German-born, Texas-raised fellow served about a year in the Ohio 7th Cavalry Regiment in the Civil War. His later years were sprinkled with fist fights in the streets of Washington, D. C., shooting at imagined smugglers before he was fired as a government inspector near El Paso, getting at least three divorces under weird circumstances, and causing an international incident with Mexico because of false assassination claims. This is all small potatoes compared to his major claims —he was the sole survivor of the Fall of the Alamo (his parents hid him in a box); he was the major scout and guide for John C. Fremont on his expeditions; he was the adopted stepson of Kit Carson, and was an intimate of Davy Crockett and Jim Bowie. Schilling was in Soldiers' Homes at Danville, Napa, and Sawtelle off and on between 1914 and 1919. He died and was buried at Sawtelle in 1920; he is in Section 40, Row D, No. 12. His absurd claims to fame were published (accepting their authenticity) by the *New York Times, the New York Herald, Grizzly Bear, Overland Monthly,* and other newspapers and magazines.[34]

WASHINGTON L. SIBLEY This fellow served a few years in the Civil War in a Connecticut infantry regiment, and by the turn of the century was working in Los Angeles as a carpenter. He is noteworthy because of arrests and assaults—his and others. He was robbed several times, arrested off and on, sometimes in Sawtelle, sometimes in the Santa Monica Canyon, was accused of several crimes, and accused others of theft and assault. A scrapbook could be compiled on his encounters with the constables and the justice courts.

One night in 1906, after a poker session with John Dupree in Sawtelle, Sibley claimed that near the Home, highwaymen threw him down and "robbed him of 35 cents, a plug of tobacco and a bottle of whisky." In March 1907 he was arrested for running a blind pig in Sawtelle, "although only a gallon of whisky was found on the premises." These are just a few incidents in the rough-and-tumble life of Washington L. Sibley. He left the Home "at own request" late in 1910 and was killed "accidentally" by a fractured skull in the Santa Monica Canyon in June of 1913. Those wishing to pay homage to this hard case may visit his grave in Section 23, Row E, No. 7.[35]

JAMES SMITH There were more than thirty veterans of this name at the Soldiers' Home. This Smith was born in Ireland around 1815, and according to several sources, had served in the British Army and was present at the Battle of Balaklava during the Crimean War. He moved to the United States and during the Civil War was in the 40th New York Infantry. He later lived in Oakland County and was admitted to the Soldiers' Home in 1891. At the time of his death in September 1912, newspapers declared that the "Hero of Balaklava Dies at Soldiers' Home." His personnel file contains this note regarding his service records: "mislaid & lost." He may have told a good story over the years; or, he may have been a hero.[36]

SHOTGUN SMITH William A. Smith served in an Ohio regiment during the Civil War, then headed to Arizona Territory, prospecting and mining in Graham and Pima Counties. His nickname comes from an incident near Pantano in 1867, when Smith and three companions held off a band of Apaches. His companions were killed, but Smith and his two double-barreled shotguns were too much for the attackers.

Smith had several successful mining properties in three Arizona counties. He moved into the Soldiers' Home in 1895, but checked out in 1903, going back to prospecting and mining. He returned to Sawtelle in 1915 and died there in November 1918. Shotgun's grave is in Section 36, Row D, No. 14.[37]

CLARK B. STOCKING A member of the 5th Infantry, the California Column, that went to Arizona during the Civil War, Stocking had a career filled with Indian engagements, mining, frontier banditry, scouting, and law enforcement that took books and articles to summarize; these have been written. He was in Wyoming, Nevada, New Mexico, and Arizona in a variety of frontier occupations, including that of bullions guard. His first experience with the Soldiers' Home was in 1898, but the lure of prospecting and mining pulled him back to Arizona periodically. After a final spell in the Soldiers' Home in 1918, Stocking checked out, made further wanderings in Arizona and California, and died in Los Angeles in early June 1934.[38]

JOB B. STOCKTON He was one of the more high-profile veterans of the Home. This native of Ohio became a prominent figure in Leavenworth, Kansas, where the Stockton Hall was a major institution. He organized the 1st Kansas Volunteer Infantry for the Civil War, and for much of this time Captain Stockton was part of the President's Guard. After the war he moved to Southern California and developed farm property at Gardena. He was admitted to the Home in 1902 and died there in April 1910. He had an unfortunate legal tangle in 1906 when he brought suit against his wife. He had deeded valuable Gardena property to her, but she was not to record them until after his death. The *Los Angeles Herald* of January 18, 1906, reported that "she at once put the deed on record."[39]

THOMAS J. THORP Thorp was a colonel in the 1st New York Dragoons and at the end of war was a general, having served at the Battle of the Wilderness and other major encounters. In later years he lived in Michigan, then in Corvallis, Oregon, where he had a substantial farm. Thorp retired to the Soldiers' Home in 1909, but things there were too quiet for him. While still a resident of the Home, Thorp and a son took and worked a homestead of forty acres near Malibu and he was described as a "vigorous and able man." He still had time to serve as the Soldiers' Home postmaster. General Thorp eventually returned to Corvallis, where he died in July 1915.[40]

BUTTERMILK JOE (TRUMBULL) Joseph Trumbull became one of the better-known veterans of the Home. He had served in an Illinois infantry regiment and after the war moved to the Rawlins, Wyoming, area, working mostly as a baker. He was admitted to the Home in 1892 and kept a small ranch nearby. He received permission from the Home governor to operate a buttermilk business on the Home grounds. There he not only provided buttermilk, but often entertained the veterans with violin music. Buttermilk Joe died at the Home in March 1907. As he requested, his violin was placed in his grave with him. This is in Section 13, Row B, No. 10.[41]

SLAP JACK BILL (WEABER) Born in Philadelphia in 1842, Andrew J. Weaber (or, Weaher) served several years in a Pennsylvania regiment during the Civil War, then headed West. He joined the 8th U. S. Cavalry, and during an Apache campaign in the Black Mountains in 1868, did major service in scouting and fighting and was awarded the Medal of Honor. Weaber lived in the Phoenix area for more than forty years, but was always hampered by his poor eyesight.

Weaber was admitted to the Soldiers' Home in 1910, totally blind. Within weeks he was operated on in the hospital and was able to see again. Within a few days the other eye was similarly treated, and sight was restored. The *Arizona Republican* of July 16, 1910, reported on these marvels from Sawtelle and quoted Weaber as saying "he can see now nearly as well as when he was a boy." Weaber moved back to Phoenix, but returned to the Soldiers' Home in 1918-19 for further treatment. He died in Phoenix in 1920. He was well-known, one of the oldest pioneers, and was usually referred to as "Slap Jack Bill."

Slap Jack Bill's experiences as a medical patient at the Soldiers' Home illustrate one of the many reasons that veterans from near and far would consider spending some time in Sawtelle.

OSBORNE WILLSON Willson graduated from an Ohio dental school and served on General Grant's staff during several Civil War campaigns; he was also a participant in the capture of Vicksburg. Later, Dr. Willson moved to Aurora, Illinois, where he kept dental offices for almost fifty years. Willson was known nationally for patents regarding chloroform and inhalers. For years he was chairman of the Illinois State Board of Dental Examiners as well as president of the Illinois Dental Society.

The Willson family moved to Los Angeles, where son Osborne was an attorney. Dr. Willson was admitted to the Soldiers' Home in 1906 and died there in 1922. His widow Mary died in the same year. She had also been in the Union Army, as a commissioned nurse.[42]

EDWARD W. WILSON Methodist minister Wilson was appointed chaplain at the Soldiers' Home about 1906, but was never very popular. He had no military service, was over-bearing, decided what should be in the library, and in general was disliked by all. Hearings and investigations were held in 1912 about administrative practices at the Home, and the Rev. Wilson did not earn high marks. One account, published in a Utah newspaper, claimed that Wilson did not permit women the right to preach in the chapel "because he was opposed to anybody who came in to make a row." Wilson termed suffragettes "Hen Hussies," and when one woman was speaking in the chapel, he "compelled her to leave the platform." In an ironic name situation, in August 1913 Rev. Wilson was dumped as chaplain in a notice from President Wilson to the governor of the Soldiers' Home.[43]

The Sawtelle Battle Earp Reserve Troops

The Earps were not unknown in greater Los Angeles and Sawtelle when they made their move, and they had what could be considered efficient reserve, backup, or support troops. What follows are some of the family's friends and acquaintances, not necessarily all friendly, from their Tombstone and other days, who were in Southern California, in and around our time frame. The authors do not in any way claim that this is a complete list, nor that any of the following individuals participated in, or were consulted during, the "Battle of Sawtelle." These friends and famous personalities were in the general area at the time and more than likely had some interactions with the Earp brothers in one form or another.

Most of these folks, when in town, often stayed at Bilicke's Hollenbeck Hotel, and more than likely contacted George Parsons. Many of these people received brief notations in the detailed Parsons diaries over the years. Some of these individuals are well known, and most of those with Arizona connections have biographical details in Bailey and Chaput, *Cochise County Stalwarts* (2000), or Bailey, *Tombstone, Arizona* (2010), the best work on that mining camp. We have added a few sources for some of the lesser known people.[1]

Lucky Baldwin, investor, gambler, scoundrel, and Wyatt's friend;
in his "office" doing business. *Los Angeles County Arboretum*.

LUCKY BALDWIN   Elias Jackson "Lucky" Baldwin was a Western
mining mogul who became a national horse racing figure and "made the
papers" for high finance, courtroom shootings, sex scandals, and so forth.
Saloons, card rooms, racetracks, and boxing bouts were the meeting places
for Lucky and the Earps, especially Wyatt and James. They rubbed shoul-
ders (and tried to fleece customers) in San Diego, San Francisco, Nome,
and Los Angeles. Much of Lucky's last two decades were in Southern
California, where he had considerable contact with Wyatt and wife Josie.
Lucky died in 1909, leaving a mixed legacy of debauchery and interesting
accomplishments. The latter include the city of Arcadia, and the basis of
Santa Anita, a world-famous racetrack.[2]

BILICKE FAMILY Carl Gustavus Bilicke was a German immigrant who
by the 1850s had been a merchant in California, Oregon, and Idaho. Son
Albert was born in San Francisco in 1861. The Bilickes were in business
in Florence and Globe in the 1870s and became Tombstone pioneers,

arriving in 1879. Their Cosmopolitan Hotel would become Tombstone's largest and finest. The Bilickes were part of the community's higher status group, which included Clum, Gage, Vickers, and similar folks. Their well-known backing of the law and order crowd, especially the Earps, appears in all Tombstone accounts. By the mid-1890s the Bilickes had shifted to Los Angeles and took controlling interest in the Hollenbeck Hotel. This would become a focal point for Tombstoners, and several of the Earps frequently stayed at the Hollenbeck. Albert Bilicke became a prominent man in the California hotel business and was often listed as a "capitalist." In 1906 he built the luxurious Alexandria Hotel in downtown Los Angeles, just a few blocks from the Hollenbeck. It was constructed to become, and advertised as, a "fireproof hotel," after Albert Bilicke had witnessed his fathers' Tombstone hotels destroyed in the devasting fires of the 1880s. The Alexandria still stands today. The good life ended early for Albert and his wife Gladys. They were on the *Lusitania*, going on a trip to Europe in May 1915, when the ship was sunk by a German torpedo. Although Gladys did survive, Albert perished. This infamous event is one in a chain that dragged the United States into World War 1.[3]

L. W. BLINN Blinn, who became a leading lumber dealer in the Southwest, opened a business on Tombstone's Toughnut Street in 1880. He was a community leader, almost became mayor in 1882, and by 1888 had major interests in Maricopa County with Dr. Goodfellow and other Tombstoners. He gradually shifted his interests to California, and he was a frequent visitor in Los Angeles with George Parsons and other Arizona figures. Blinn's interests and connections were so widespread that he either owned or operated lumber works in forty California locations, mostly in Los Angeles and San Bernardino counties. He died in Los Angeles in 1928 and is buried in the Hollywood Forever Cemetery.

Wyatt Earp and John Clum on
the golden sands of Nome, 1900.
Don Chaput collection.

JOHN CLUM Born in New York State in 1851, Clum was in the West
in the early 1870s and served for a time as Apache agent at the San Car-
los Indian Reservation in Arizona. He then operated the *Arizona Citizen*
newspaper for a few years, but quickly opted for Tombstone in 1880, where
he founded the *Tombstone Epitaph*. His career can be easily followed in the
standard accounts, as he served as mayor of Tombstone, and was a backer
of the Earps and the town faction in the troubles of 1881-82. Clum later
held a variety of newspaper and administrative positions and for years
was a U. S. Postal Inspector. He spent some years in Alaska in this role,
even visiting in Nome with Tombstoners Wyatt Earp and George Parsons.
A very close friend and confidant of Wyatt's, he spoke with him the night
before he died,[4] and he , too, was one of Wyatt Earp's pallbearers. The
last decades of Clum's life were mostly in Southern California, where he
remained in contact with Parsons and other old Tombstoners. Clum died
in Los Angeles in 1932. He would subsequently be portrayed by war hero
turned actor Audie Murphy in the 1956 movie *Walk the Proud Land*[5]

District Attorney of San Bernardino County, William Jesse Curtis. His family accompanied the Nicholas Earp wagon train (see Sarah Jane Rousseau diary, 1864) West in 1864. *Bench and Bar in Southern California,* 1909.

CURTIS FAMILY In 1864 the Curtis family of Pella, Iowa, headed across the plains towards California. Leading the wagon train was Nicholas Earp, a not over-friendly fellow who pushed the travelers mercilessly. They reached what would become San Bernardino County, California, where the Earp and Curtis families would become prominent in different ways: the Earps, in the law in Colton, as previously examined; William Jesse Curtis would become a leading attorney, head of the bar association, as well as district attorney of San Bernardino County. His son Jesse W. Curtis, after getting a law degree from the University of Michigan, would also become district attorney of San Bernardino County, and in 1926 was appointed a justice on the California Supreme Court. The families intermeshed dozens of times over the years, and probably disagreed on a hundred different issues. Yet, these were two Southern California pioneer families that had made their mark in Western history.[6]

EDWARD L. DOHENY This fellow, one of the world's leading oilmen of the early twentieth century, had his start in "extraction" by prospecting and mining in Arizona and New Mexico. Between 1878 and 1880 (before he shifted to New Mexico), he worked a gold property in the Peck District and mostly lived in Prescott. During that same era, Virgil drove a stage in the area, visited the Peck District many times, and was also a lawman (two positions) in Prescott. Some folks suggest Doheny was later at Tombstone, an event not yet proven.[7] There is no doubt, though, of his familiarity with the Earps in this era. In later years, Josie seems to have leaned on this Doheny-Earp connection and borrowed a few dollars from time to time.[8] Doheny brushed by some national scandals (Teapot Dome, for instance), and finally died in Los Angeles in 1935, far from being a pauper. In 1963 he would be immortalized by the South Orange County, California, state beach (on the land he donated) named after him, and in the Beach Boys song celebrating it, "Surfin USA," (written with legendary rock musician Chuck Berry) "All over Manhattan, and down Doheny Way, everybody's gone surfin', surfin' USA ...."[9]

FRANK C. EARLE Earle arrived in Tombstone in 1880 where he opened an assay office. For a few years he was an important figure in a community loaded with mines and mills. During the period he had many contacts with George Parsons, a mining man, and the Earp brothers, the law and order crowd. In later years Earle had important positions in Sinaloa, Sonora, and in the El Paso districts. He was a frequent visitor of Los Angeles and was in close touch with Parsons and other former Tombstoners. Earle died in El Paso in 1913.

JOHN H. FLOOD This Easterner, who became the closest confidant to Wyatt and Josephine Earp, spent the years 1903-04 at Yale's Sheffield Scientific School studying mining. He met Wyatt at the Hampden Arms rooming house in downtown L.A. in 1906,[10] and shortly thereafter accompanied the Earps on one of their many prospecting trips to the Whipple Mountains. Flood became a constant companion to Wyatt for decades, acting as personal secretary and would-be biographer. After Wyatt's death Flood continued to assist Josephine in her "paper tasks," especially in dealing with attorneys and publishers. No one knew the Earps better than loyal friend John Flood. Unfortunately, he may have been the worst writer in North America, and in his "Flood Manuscript," accepted Wyatt's accounts as Gospel.[11] Flood died on March 29, 1958, in Long Beach, California, and is buried in Ivy Hill Cemetery in Philadelphia, Pennsylvania.[12] Prior to Flood's death, tenacious Earp aficionado and researcher/historian John Gilchriese discovered a newspaper article from the 1931 *New York Times* in the Munk Collection, at the Southwest Museum, that Flood had written, proclaiming he had known Wyatt Earp and served as a secretary for him for many years. Gilchriese, who had an obsession with Wyatt, as many more still do today, undertook to learn and collect everything he could about him, having purportedly briefly met or seen Wyatt when he was a young child. He subsequently read about him in the seminal Stuart Lake and Walter Noble Burns books in the late 1920s/early 1930s, and tracked Flood down and befriended him circa 1951. The elderly and lonely Flood was more than happy to oblige him with his stories of Wyatt and the Earp family.[13] Prior to his death, Flood passed his extensive Earp collection down to Gilchriese, including many items which had once belonged to Josie and Wyatt. He had held on to every scrap of paper the Earps had given him through the years. After Gilchriese's own death, these were auctioned in 2004 and 2005, and many are now in the collection of second author de Haas; a few are used as illustrations in this book.[14]

W. B. (and ALICE CHANDLER) FORSYTHE These were the parents of renowned artist Victor Clyde Forsythe who in later years (1952) would paint his parents, uncle, and their 1880s Tombstone-Los Angeles based friends, most likely including Wyatt and Virgil. His recollections of *The Gunfight at OK Corral*, has been called by many "the closest thing we have to an actual photograph of the gunfight." W.B. and his brother-in-law Ira Chandler owned a store, "Chandler & Forsyth's Cash Store," in Tombstone, Arizona, which was initially located on Allen Street, but subsequently moved in early 1882 to Fremont next to the post office, and a few lots east of the rear entrance to the O.K. Corral. They claimed to have witnessed the famous gun battle and recorded their interpretations contemporaneously into a diary, which Clyde purportedly consulted to execute his painting. Sadly, this priceless diary has never surfaced, although second author de Haas has many of their other family personal letters and belongings in his collection. Their Tombstone store burned down in the devastating fire of May 25, 1882, and they moved back to the downtown Los Angeles area, very close to where Wyatt was living at the Hampden Arms Hotel, when he first met John Flood in 1906.[15] W.B. has recently been positively identified, believed to be for the first time in modern record,[16] by coauthor de Haas, as one of the individuals in the famous C.S. Fly "1882 Tombstone O.K. Corral Fire aftermath Photo."[17] Clyde died in 1962 and is buried next to his wife Cotta (Owen) in the San Gabriel Cemetery. Buried nearby is his close friend, and famed western artist, Frank Tenney Johnson, who was his partner in his Los Angeles Biltmore Hotel art studio and who preceded him in death.[18]

RICHARD "DICK" GIRD Gird, from New York State, was an assayer and prospector with a sound reputation in Arizona Territory before he linked up with Al and Ed Schieffelin. They then explored and patented what would become the richest silver mines in the Tombstone District. Gird was the intellectual and forceful personality of this trio. He soon took his riches to Southern California, becoming a major landowner, developer of large sugar beet interests, and also had extensive mining and milling projects in Mexico. Gird, often referred to as "The Father/Founder of Chino, California," was in and out of Los Angeles a hundred times, and although he appears in scattered mentions in the Parsons diaries, he does not appear to have had significant contact with the Earps.

DR. GEORGE E. GOODFELLOW Born in 1855 in Downieville, California, to a mine manager father, Goodfellow went East for his medical education. He practiced for a few years in Prescott, Arizona, where he first met Constable Virgil Earp. They both ended up in Tombstone, Virgil as a Deputy U. S. Marshal, Goodfellow as the best gunshot surgeon in the

West. They moved in the same circles. Dr. Goodfellow got to know Virgil intimately; he operated on Virgil's left arm after the ambush of December 1881. He also knew Morgan Earp well; Dr. Goodfellow testified to a coroner's jury in March 1881 how Morgan had died from a gunshot wound in Bob Hatch's saloon. Goodfellow became one of the best-known medical men in the West. He held major positions and was an author in the leading medical journals. He and his family considered Los Angeles as a second home. His daughter was educated and married there, and Goodfellow frequently visited with diarist George Parsons; their close association had started in Tombstone. Goodfellow opened a practice in San Francisco and was doing well, until he was wiped out in the San Francisco Earthquake of 1906. His last years were spent as a railroad physician in Mexico, where he apparently contracted beriberi. He returned to Los Angeles for treatment but died there in December 1910.[19]

BEN GOODRICH Ben and brother Briggs were Texans who became legal bigwigs in Arizona Territory. They held all kinds of county and territorial offices and were particularly keyed into the world of mining law. Ben shifted to and from Tombstone and Los Angeles and was a noted legal player in both locales. Ben was almost the first governor of the new state of Arizona, at the same time he had a strong legal practice in Los Angeles. He was, like most Tombstoners, in frequent contact with George Parsons in Los Angeles. Some may question about placing him in an Earp "Support" section, seeing that he was the personal attorney of Ike Clanton and represented him in the Spicer hearings of 1881 in Tombstone. One wonders, though, about the Goodrich and Clanton link. For example, it was brother Briggs who in 1882 tried to warn Wyatt and Morgan that the cowboys were in town looking for trouble. Ben Goodrich settled for good in Los Angeles, dying there in February 1923.

WILLLIAM S. HART Hart (1864-1946) was the most productive, successful star of Western movies from 1914 to 1925, turning out several dozen. He is included here because during a few years in the 1920s, Hart and Wyatt Earp visited frequently; they also carried on correspondence, and Hart tried to find a publisher for Wyatt's memoirs. He failed, but the Earp-Hart correspondence contains considerable information on the Earp family and their wanderings and connections in San Bernardino and Los Angeles counties, the area that interests us here. This correspondence, as well as the Hart Ranch, are under the umbrella of the Natural History Museum of Los Angeles County. Hart also at one point gifted the Earp's a bear rug of which they were quite proud and often boasted to family. [20]

HEARST FAMILY It is no negative to be associated with one of the West's leading families. Wyatt Earp's first contact with them was in early 1882, when he served as guide and bodyguard to Senator George Hearst, who was in Cochise County to inspect some mining properties. Later, in San Francisco in the 1890s, when dealing with Lucky Baldwin, and acting as bodyguard to Andrew Lawrence of the *Examiner*, Wyatt was in contact with Senator Hearst's son William Randolph Hearst, soon to be America's "big" journalist. In 1903, when Hearst was expanding his empire (San Francisco to New York) to include Los Angeles, he entered the Los Angeles market by setting up quarters in the Bilicke Building, owned by A. C. Bilicke, Wyatt's close friend from Tombstone days. All of these pivot points could not have been accidental.

Senator George Hearst, mining mogul, Wyatt's first contact with the family. *Memorial Addresses*, 1894.

HOOKER FAMILY Henry Clay Hooker's career is easy to follow, as he was a major rancher and cattleman in southern Arizona. He was a key supplier to the merchants of Tombstone, was part of the important Cochise County moguls (E. B. Gage, J. V. Vickers, John Clum, etc.), and backed the Earp faction during the troubles of 1881-82. Hooker frequently visited Los Angeles, and his children spent years in school there. Henry moved to Los Angeles, where he died in 1907. Daughter-in-law Forrestine became an author, worked on the *Los Angeles Examiner* for a time, and around 1919 interviewed Wyatt Earp for what was to be the "inside story" of the Cochise County saga now known as "The Hooker Manuscript." Apparently the "inside track" via the Hooker family wasn't enough, as the end result was a poor mishmash of almost-history.[21] The Hookers are buried in the family plot at the "Hollywood Forever" Cemetery in the Hollywood district of Los Angeles, California, not far from the Blinn family plot, and several other old Tombstoners.[22]

WILLIAM J. HUNSAKER The Hunsakers were true California pioneers, in the region before the Gold Rush; William was born in Contra Costa County in 1855. He was raised in San Diego, where he worked as a journalist and studied law. He arrived in Tombstone in 1880 as one of the many lawyers there. He remained only a year or so, but had some contact with the Earps. After practicing some years in San Diego, Hunsaker moved to Los Angeles. By the turn of the century he was the attorney for the Santa Fe Railroad, many major mining companies, and headed the Los Angeles Bar Association as well as the California Bar Association. The extensive Earp Papers have occasional mentions of Hunsaker, and after Wyatt's death in 1929 , Hunsaker handled legal problems for Josephine ("Sadie").[23] . He was a pallbearer at Wyatt's funeral. There may have been other reasons over the years for their contact as a Hunsaker brother, and other relatives, had extensive ranching operations in and around Cochise County. Hunsaker died in Los Angeles in 1933.

SOL ISRAEL Sol was born in Hamburg in 1858 and by 1880 was in Tucson. He quickly shifted to Tombstone, where as a merchant he had the largest news agency and bookstore. Sol was a "card," active in many affairs, and for some years handled the events at Schieffelin Hall. In 1888 Sol moved on, opening businesses in Arizona and northern California, finally settling in Los Angeles in the early 1900s. He had a "place" on Seventh Street where he pushed wine and beer, as well as books and stationery. It also became a meeting place for old Tombstoners such as John Clum, Wyatt Earp, George Parsons, and Billy Hattich among others. Sol's interest can be seen in his death notice in Los Angeles in 1931: "Tombstone papers please copy."

ALEXANDER J. MITCHELL He was a leading surveyor, assayer, and mining engineer in the Tombstone area during 1879-1885. He mapped the San Pedro River for mill placement, had an office in Tombstone, was close friends with Sheriff Shibell, and was especially close with lumber dealer L. W. Blinn. He left Tombstone in 1885 for Colorado, then for mining in the Yuma County area. He moved to Los Angeles in 1900, to the San Pedro harbor area, and again connected with L. W. Blinn and George Parsons. Mitchell became a leading industrialist, head of the State Bank of San Pedro, head of a yacht club, and was one of the flashier, better-known people in greater Los Angeles, where he died on August 28, 1929. Mitchell had a long, diverse career. He was born in England, worked as an engineer in Australia, arrived in Tucson in 1879, then to the Tombstone District. Not only were old Tombstoners Mitchell and Blinn connected later in Los Angeles County, but at the State Bank of San Pedro, Blinn was the president and Mitchell the largest shareholder.

GEORGE W. PARSONS Born in the District of Columbia in 1850, George had a sound education, and after a period in Florida headed to San Francisco in 1876. He worked in banking, but that field was in free fall at that time. In 1880 he headed for booming Tombstone. He was a mine laborer, then mine agent. In Tombstone he was "plugged in" with the Earps, John Clum, Dr. Goodfellow, and other town leaders. His diaries of those years are leading classics of Western history. Moving to Los Angeles in 1887,

Parsons was a founder of the Chamber of Commerce and the Los Angeles Mining & Stock Exchange, as well as a leader in desert water signpost placement, so vital for miners and travelers. Parsons was well connected, with close friendships with the Pattons, Bannings, Fremonts, and other prominent southern California figures. Parsons was also an "old Tombstoner," and his diaries have hundreds of entries regarding the Earps, Goodfellow, Clum, Sorin, Gage, and other Arizona visitors to Los Angeles. He even visited with Wyatt in Nome in 1900, and in 1903 penned a forceful letter to the *Los Angeles Herald*, emphasizing Wyatt Earp's important contributions to Western law and order. At Wyatt's funeral in January 1929 in Los Angeles, George Parsons was one of the pallbearers. Although he accomplished so much in his lifetime, a major achievement[24] is one historians have rarely recognized: his leading role in the preservation of the beautiful beaches of Santa Monica, enjoyed by so many to this day. It was his strong influence which directly led to San Pedro, rather than Santa Monica, becoming the port for the city of Los Angeles. Parsons died (and is buried) in Los Angeles on January 5, 1933.[25]

CHARLES SILENT German-born Silent was raised in Ohio, and arrived in San Francisco in 1856. He taught school, attended the University of the Pacific, then lived and practiced law in Santa Clara and San Jose. In 1878 he was appointed an Associate Justice in the Territory of Arizona. He resigned in 1880, and for a few years, out of his Tucson office, was mostly involved with legal affairs and mining investments in Tombstone. In 1885 he moved permanently to Los Angeles. He was a major force in legal and business affairs and was particularly interested in parks and gardening. His residence, Chester Place, was on many tourist lists. During his decades in the city he was usually referred to as Judge Silent.

He deserves mention here because he was always interested in Tombstone and Arizona affairs. He often visited and had business arrangements with George Parsons, who was everyone's Los Angeles contact with Tombstone doings. Judge Silent retired in 1908 and died in Los Angeles on December 14, 1918.[26]

JOHN S. VOSBURG He was one of the few who knew when to grab and run. Vosburg was a close friend and associate of Governor Anson Safford of Arizona Territory, the fellow who appointed him Adjutant-General and Territorial Auditor. They were also involved in a few mediocre mining investments. Then they met Dick Gird, who told them of the Schieffelins' prospecting. In 1878 these fellows backed financially what would become the Tombstone bonanza. Vosburg almost at once began investing in Southern California land and ranches in Los Angeles County. He became a major fruit grower and canner in the San Gabriel Valley. A favorite hobby was to visit with George Parsons in Los Angeles; he and George were on the board of the Southern California Academy of Sciences. Vosburg also made regular visits to Tombstone over the years, no doubt to praise himself for his investment prowess. Vosburg died in Los Angeles in 1931.

ENDNOTES

EPIGRAPH

1. Ben T. Traywick, *Wyatt Earp: Angel of Death* (Honolulu, HI Talei Publishers, 2007).

2. Walter Benjamin, "Thesis on the Philosophy of History," in: Arendt H, ed. Zohn H, trans. *Illuminations, Essays and Reflections* (New York: Houghton Mifflin Harcourt, 1968). Extracted from Jeffrey A. Greene, MD, PhD, "Amnesia, Adverse Events, and the Angel of History," *Annals of Internal Medicine* 171, no. 6 (Philadelphia, PA: American College of Physicians) (September 17, 2019): 434 – 435.

3. Jeffrey A. Greene, MD, PhD, "Amnesia, Adverse Events, and the Angel of History," 434 – 435. Please see also Gary L. Roberts's thought provoking "'*Suppose ... Suppose ...*': Wyatt Earp, Frontier Violence, Myth, and History," Epilogue in *A Wyatt Earp Anthology: Long May His Story Be Told*, (Denton: University of North Texas Press, 2019), especially pp. 781–785, for a germane exposition of why the study of Wyatt Earp/Earpiana specifically, and frontier violence in general, is still relevant, and even imperative, to modern-day society.

PREFACE

1. Jane Matson Lee, Mark Dworkin, H.F. Sills, "Mystery Man of the O.K. Corral Shootout," *WOLA Journal*, Spring 2004. Bob Palmquist, "Justice in Tombstone," *Wild West Magazine*, October 2015.

2. Ban on the sale of alcohol in the early 1900s.

3. The 1950 award-winning Broadway musical *Guys and Dolls*, which was subsequently made into a movie (one of my favorites) starring actors Frank Sinatra and Marlon Brando in 1955, was based upon a series of short stories by Damon Runyon. Runyon was a friend of fellow New York newspaper columnist/sportswriter, and retired frontier lawman (and Wyatt Earp confidant and staunch ally), Bat Masterson, in the early 1900s, and his Sky Masterson character (portrayed by Brando in the hit movie) was patterned after Bat. This story, which it appears was being played out across the country, just in our case with the Earps and ironically Bat Masterson, involves prohibition-era drinking, gambling, prostitution, and gangsters, in the early twentieth century, as does the one to follow....

4. Robert K. DeArment, *Broadway Bat: Gunfighter in Gotham: The New York City Years of Bat Masterson* (Honolulu, HI: Talei Publishers, 2005), 45–47. Bob Boze Bell, "Wyatt Earp in Hollywood," *True West Magazine*, October 2015.

PROLOGUE

1. Burton Devere Jr., *Bonanzas to Borrascas: The Mines of Tombstone (Arizona*, Rose Tree Museum, 2010)

CHAPTER 1

1. Nick's Mexican War service file is in the National Archives. Solid information on his Western life can be found in Nicholas R. Cataldo, *The Earp Clan: The Southern California Years* (San Bernardino, CA: Back Roads Press, 2006), and Nick Cataldo and Fred Holladay, *The Earps of San Bernardino County* (San Bernardino: City of San Bernardino Historical & Pioneer Society, 2001).

2. Lee A. Silva, *Wyatt Earp: A Biography of the Legend, Vol. I, The Cowtown Years* (Santa Ana, CA: Graphic Publishers, 2002), p 66.

3. Silva, *Wyatt Earp: A Biography of the Legend, Vol. I, The Cowtown Years*. Timothy W. Fattig, *Wyatt Earp: The Biography* (Honolulu, HI: Talei Publishers, 2002).

4. Donald Chaput, *The Earp Papers: In a Brother's Image* (Encampment, WY: Affiliated Writers of America, 1994); Donald Chaput, *Virgil Earp: Western Peace Officer* (Norman: University of Oklahoma Press, 1996); Silva, Wyatt Earp: A Biography of the Legend, Vol. I, The Cowtown Years. Fattig, *Wyatt Earp: The Biography*.

5. Chaput, *The Earp Papers: In a Brother's Image*; Chaput, *Virgil Earp: Western Peace Officer*; Silva, *Wyatt Earp: A Biography of the Legend, Vol. I, The Cowtown Years*. Cataldo, *The Earp Clan*, and Cataldo and Holladay, *The Earps of San Bernardino County*. Garner Palenske, *Wyatt Earp in San Diego: Life after Tombstone* (Santa Anna, CA: Graphic Publishers, 2011). Fattig, *Wyatt Earp: The Biography*.

6. Jack DeMattos, *The Earp Decision* (College Station, TX: Creative Publishing Company, 1989). Robert K. DeArment, *Knights of The Green Cloth: The Saga of Frontier Gamblers* (Norman: University of Oklahoma Press, 1982).

7. Silva, *Wyatt Earp: A Biography of the Legend, Vol. I, The Cowtown Years*. Fattig, *Wyatt Earp: The Biography*.

8. Roy B. Young et al., *A Wyatt Earp Anthology: Long May His Story Be Told* (Denton: University of North Texas Press, 2019).

9. Federal Census of 1870, Deer Lodge County, Montana. *The New North-West (Deer Lodge)*, March 3, March 10, 1871. *Anaconda Standard*, November 5, 1894. *Butte Miner*, November 24, 1902.

10. Federal Census of 1870, Deer Lodge County, Montana.

11. *The New North-West (Deer Lodge)*, March 3, March 10, 1871. *Anaconda Standard*, November 5, 1894. *Butte Miner*, November 24, 1902.

12. Our James Earp is not the same James C. Earp who was arrested in Arkansas in 1894 for violation of liquor laws. Please see Roy B. Young, *James Cooksey Earp Out of the Shadows: The Never Before Told Story of Wyatt Earp's Brother* (Apache, OK: Young & Sons Enterprises, 2006), 9–10.

13. Sources abound, but for this Kansas and Texas period, details and reliable material can be found in Gary Roberts, *Doc Holliday: The Life and Legend* (Hoboken, NJ: John Wiley and Sons, Inc., 2013), Paula Mitchell Marks, *And Die in the West: The Story of the O.K. Corral Gunfight* (New York: William Morrow and Company, 1989).

The extensive Ben Traywick book series (Tombstone, Arizona: Red Marie's Bookstore), Silva, *Wyatt Earp: A Biography of the Legend, Vol. I, The Cowtown Years*. Fattig, *Wyatt Earp: The Biography*, Young et al., *A Wyatt Earp Anthology: Long May His Story Be Told*. Ben T. Traywick, *Wyatt Earp: Angel of Death* (Honolulu, HI: Talei Publishers, 2007). Casey Tefertiller, *Wyatt Earp: The Life Behind the Legend* (New York: John Wiley and Sons, 1997). William B. Shillingberg, *Dodge City: The Early Years, 1872-1886* (Norman, OK: The Arthur H. Clark Company, 2009).

14. In addition to above, please see William B. Shillingberg, *Tombstone, A. T.: A History of Early Mining, Milling, and Mayhem* (Spokane: Arthur H. Clark Company, 1999). Garner Palenske, *Wyatt Earp in San Diego: Life after Tombstone* (Santa Ana, CA: Graphic Publishers, 2011). Don Chaput, "The Earp Brothers' Body Count," *NOLA Quarterly*, April–May 2000, pp. 33–39.

15. Roy B. Young, *James Cooksey Earp Out of the Shadows*. Cataldo, *The Earp Clan*, and Cataldo and Holladay, *The Earps of San Bernardino County*.

16. Earp/Tombstone literature is a mile high. In addition to the Roberts (see footnote 13), see Silva, *Wyatt Earp: A Biography of the Legend, Vol. I, The Cowtown Years*, and Silva, *Wyatt Earp: A Biography of the Legend, Vol. II, Tombstone Before the Earps* (Santa Ana, CA: Graphic Publishers, 2010); Chaput, *The Earp Papers : In a Brother's Image*, Chaput, *Virgil Earp: Western Peace Officer*; Lynn Bailey and Donald Chaput, *Cochise County Stalwarts, 2 vols.* (Tucson: Westernlore Press, 2000); Shillingberg, *Tombstone, A. T.: A History of Early Mining, Milling, and Mayhem*. Palenske, *Wyatt Earp in San Diego*. Traywick, *Wyatt Earp: Angel of Death*. Earl Chafin, *Wyatt Earp in Alaska* (Riverside, CA: The Earl Chafin Press, 1999). *Ann Kirschner, Lady at the O.K. Corral* (New York: Harper Collins Publishers, 2013).

17. Michael M. Hickey, *The Death of Warren Baxter Earp: A Closer Look* (Honolulu, HI: Talei Publishers, 2000). Fattig, *Wyatt Earp: The Biography*.

CHAPTER 2

1. In the scheme of government, the "state" is the dominant player, and the state is divided into counties. The next level down in significance is that of townships. This is where Sawtelle, and the Soldiers' Home, would find itself in a ping-pong legal environment. The Soldiers' Home would end up in Los Angeles Township, which,

although in Los Angeles County, had varying degrees of legal responsibilities. The township, with its justices of the peace and constables, was "sort of" responsible to the County of Los Angeles. On the other hand, the powers in Los Angeles County, full of their own problems, from time to time suggested (directed) that Los Angeles Township seek legal and law enforcement help from nearby jurisdictions (i.e. justices of the peace and constables in Santa Monica, Long Beach, Pasadena, etc).

2. The *Los Angeles Herald* had a dozen or so articles on this Santa Monica event; see in particular July 9, July 17, 1875. *La Cronica*, the Los Angeles Spanish-language paper, had an extensive article on July 29, 1875. Most of these dozens of articles mentioned the role of Fitch.

3. Steven Lubet, *Murder in Tombstone: The Forgotten Trial of Wyatt Earp* (New Haven, CT: Yale University Press, 2004). Alfred Turner, ed., *The O.K. Corral Inquest* (College Station, TX: The Early West, 1981).

4. Lynn R. Bailey, *A Tale of the "Unkilled": The Life, Times, and Writings of Wells W. Spicer* (Tucson, AZ: Westernlore Press, 1999). Bob Palmquist, "Justice in Tombstone," *Wild West Magazine,* October 2015. Hugh O'Neil, *Utah Historical Quarterly,* V.24 (1956), 157–64

5. Sim Moak, *The Last of the Mill Creeks and Early Life in Northern California* (Chico, CA: np, 1923), 36. "The First Through Train, Carson City, Nevada," *The Carson Daily Appeal,* May 13, 1869.

6. Silva, *Wyatt Earp: A Biography of the Legend, Vol. I, The Cowtown Years,* 672.

7. Utah, Arizona, Nevada, and California.

8. David D. de Haas, MD, "Collectors Roundup," C.T. Hayden, Tempe, Arizona, *Wild West History Association Journal,* February 2012, pp. 49-52. David D. de Haas, MD, Letter to the Editor. Follow up to "Collectors Roundup": "U.S. Senator Carl Hayden and the Graham/Tewksbury Feud," *Wild West History Association Journal,* August 2012, pp. 3-4. Earle R. Forrest, *Arizona's Dark and Bloody Ground* (Caldwell, ID: Caxton Printers, 1936). Zane Grey, *To the Last Man* (New York: Harper & Brothers, 1921).

9. *Honolulu Republican,* November 2, 1901. *Nevada Historical Society Quarterly* 20 (Winter, 1977): Notes & Documents section.

10. Good coverage on Santa Monica's founding can be found in Luther A. Ingersoll, *Santa Monica Bay Cities* (Los Angeles: L. A. Ingersoll, 1908), and Charles Sumner Warren, *History of the Santa Monica Bay Region* (Santa Monica: A. H. Cawston, 1934). Mark Boardman, *True West Magazine Blog,* "The Talents of Thomas Fitch," July 7, 2015. Steven Lubet, *Murder in Tombstone: The Forgotten Trial of Wyatt Earp* (New Haven, CT: Yale University Press, 2004), 79 – 82. San Francisco Biographies—Thomas Fitch transcribed by Donna Baker from *The Bay of San Francisco.* V. 2. 1892.

11. In the Spanish, later Mexican, regimes, huge grants of land were made to individuals. The parcels of land were referred to as ranchos, which led to decades of legislative conundrums during the early years of the American regime.

12. Pacific Branch, National Home for Disabled Volunteer Soldiers; West Los Angeles, California – Property Deed, 1888. Trevor K. Plante, "The National Home for Disabled Soldiers," *Prologue Magazine*. National Archives, 36, Spring 2004. Hearings, Committee on Military Affairs, House of Representatives: Washington: GPO, 1926, "Sale of Land." Cheryl Wilkinson, "The Soldiers' City: Sawtelle, California, 1897 – 1922," *Southern California Quarterly* 95. (Summer, 2013): 188 – 224. Cheryl Wilkinson, "The Veterans in our Midst: Disabled Union Veterans in West Los Angeles, 1888–1914" (M.A. Thesis, California State University Northridge, 2013).

13. The Jones career was long, distinguished, and somewhat controversial. Useful details of his life are in his obituary in the *Los Angeles Times*, November 28, 1912.

14. A "Californio" is a Hispanic native of California who is culturally or genetically descended from the Spanish-speaking community which existed in California since the 1600s.

15. Baker was a major figure in Southern California life. He had early been successful with merchandising mining supplies, later in sheep and cattle, and had huge real estate interests, including the Baker Block in Los Angeles. He was not a "rancho type" or Californio; he just happened to be married to one, the largest landowner in Southern California, and it was some acres of this huge patrimony on which the Soldiers' Home would be erected. Baker died on March 11, 1894. The *San Francisco Call* of December 28, 1895, mentioned that part of the Baker Estate was being settled, an amount around $350,000, which gives some idea of his status in life.

16. Extensive literature exists on this port scramble. A useful pamphlet explaining one point of view is *Santa Monica: A Protected Harbor* (Santa Monica: Press of the Outlook, 1894).

17. The role of Parsons as a Tombstone personality is well known. Yet, he had a long, varied, successful career in Los Angeles. The *San Francisco Call* of February 24, 1897, has an illustration of Parsons, along with an article regarding his appointment by the governor as vice-president for a large exposition at Omaha. There and at other venues Parsons would be promoting San Pedro, rather than Santa Monica. For a summary of the Parsons career see Lynn Bailey and Don Chaput, *Cochise County Stalwarts* (Tucson: Westernlore Press, 2000), Volume 2, pp. 57-61.

18. Trevor K. Plante, "The National Home for Disabled Soldiers," *Prologue Magazine* 36 National Archives, (Spring 2004). Hearings, *Committee on Military Affairs*, House of Representatives: Washington: GPO, 1926, "Sale of Land." Cheryl Wilkinson, "The Soldiers' City: Sawtelle, California, 1897–1922," *Southern California Quarterly* 95 (Summer, 2013): 188 – 224. Cheryl Wilkinson, "The Veterans in our Midst: Disabled Union Veterans in West Los Angeles, 1888 – 1914" (M.A. Thesis, California State University Northridge, 2013).

19. The Soldiers' Home files are in the HABS Collection (Historic American Buildings Survey) in the Library of Congress.

20. Primary documents on the land planning, indentures, number of acres, and other details for this institution are included in Robert S. Sherins, *Wadsworth Veterans Hospital ... Sawtelle Veterans Soldiers' Home* (Los Angeles: UCLA School of Medicine, 2012).

21. Details of these and many other mining transactions are in the Cochise County Recorder files, under Mines; Deeds; Locations. Throughout the spring of 1880, Tucson's *Arizona Daily Star* printed a "Mining Notice" by E. J. Winders, warning folks of ownership changes, names of mines, and so forth. In the notice he mentions the concerned parties, including the Earp brothers, Comstock, Senator Jones, and others. The specific mines appear on Frank S. Ingoldsby, *Map of the Tombstone Mining District* (San Francisco: H. S. Croker & Co., 1881).

22. Fattig, *Wyatt Earp: The Biography*, 440.

CHAPTER 3

1. Throughout this work we relied heavily on the solid work of Cheryl Lynn Wilkinson, "The Veterans in our Midst: Disabled Union Veterans in West Los Angeles, 1888-1914," M. A. Thesis, California State University, Northridge, 2013, and her "The Soldiers' City: Sawtelle, California, 1897-1922," *Southern California Quarterly* 95 (Summer, 2013): 188-244. However, she didn't have our strong interest in arrests, booze, card playing, suicides, and general mayhem. *Los Angeles Times*, September 3, 1889. *Los Angeles Herald*, October 4, 1889

2. The Jones and Gillis family are well covered in Ingersoll, *Santa Monica Bay Cities*, 1908. The best primary materials on these fellows is the Incorporation Files, Seaver Center, Natural History Museum, Los Angeles. These show the type and extent of their participation, especially in land, water, and merchant life in and around Santa Monica. The *Los Angeles Herald* of September 11, 1896, mentioned the incorporation, which turned out to be a family affair; directors included Robert Gillis, Fanny L. Gillis, Robert F. Jones, and Maria T. Jones.

3. Barrett was a well-known California personality. An illustration of him, in military uniform, appears in the *Los Angeles Herald* of May 18, 1905, when he was appointed Adjutant General of California.

4. William E. Sawtelle was not as deserving of fame as it seems; the town was given his name only because the first choice wasn't available. He shows up in the census of Los Angeles in 1910 as a banker, but prior to 1920 he moved to San Diego, where he died in 1934.

5. The basics of Taft's life appear in a work by his son, Fred H. Taft, *An Empire Builder of the Middle West* (Los Angeles: Parker, Stone & Baird Co., 1929), but this doesn't contain much about our topic here, illegal booze.

6. *The San Francisco Call*, December 22, 1900.

7. *The San Francisco Call* of February 19, 1895, mentioned that Bulla had introduced

the bill. In its final form it was headed "Intoxicating Liquors-Soldiers' Home," and was approved on March 26, 1895.

8. *Santa Monica Outlook*, March 31, 1898.

9. These conditions are well explained in Wilkinson, "The Veterans in Our Midst," 2013.

10. William W. Bunce file, Sawtelle, National Archives, U. S. National Homes for Disabled Volunteer Soldiers; this is a typical file, a one-page summary of Military, Domestic, and Home History, including details of his death, and any property inventoried at that time, as well as a mention of survivors or relatives. *Veteran Enterprise*, December 17, 1904.

11. Just because one can't find a Sawtelle directory doesn't mean that none existed. The same with Santa Monica. One must persevere. These local directories may, or may not, appear under "Los Angeles" or "Los Angeles County." A most useful one for our purposes is *Directory of the Santa Monica Bay District* (1907) available at the Santa Monica Public Library. This includes the residents of Santa Monica, Ocean Park, Sawtelle, and Palms.

12. Population for all of the Soldiers' Homes is given in most of the annual reports. Local newspapers also carried this information, as it was of interest and merchants liked it. Much of this information, for all Homes, appeared in the *Leavenworth Times*. For a specific local example, see *Los Angeles Herald,* September 3, 1907; this issue gave the current number as 3,860, pointing out that 2,000 lived in the Home, while the remainder were on furloughs. Many of the "on furloughs" were actually residents of Sawtelle, a few yards distant from the Home. One of the more detailed was the report of 1902, carried out on August 7-10. Discipline, menus, water supply, entertainment, hospital care, parades, jail, food variety, building repairs, and dozens of other topics are covered: *Annual Reports of the War Department, Volume VIII, Miscellaneous Reports* (Washington: GPO, 1902).

13. *The Evening Express*, April 16, 1907.

CHAPTER 4

1. The "open checkbook" offer of Rindge comes through in the *Los Angeles Times*, March 5, 1900. As a major figure in Southern California, considerable space is devoted to him in Ingersoll, *Santa Monica Bay Cities,* 1908.

2. *Los Angeles Times*, March 5, 1900.

3. *Los Angeles Times*, April 10, 1900.

4. *Annual Reports of the War Department,* June 30, 1902, Vol. III, Miscellaneous Reports (Washington: GPO, 1902), 106–118.

5. This episode was dramatic, and newspaper coverage included illustrations as well as many biographical details of Smith, who apparently had a controversial administrative record; *San Francisco Call*, September 29, 1898, *Los Angeles Herald*, September 29, 1898.

6. Most California newspapers gave daily coverage to this presidential visit; the *Los Angeles Herald* of May 6, 1901, included the timetable of the coming visit, and the *San Francisco Call* of May 13, 1901, listed the local sites on the McKinley agenda. There are thousands of photographic views of the McKinley days in Southern California, scattered in all the major archives and libraries.

7. *Chicago Tribune,* May 10, 1901.

8. Cataldo, *The Earp Clan,* and Cataldo and Holladay, *The Earps of San Bernardino County.*

9. There are dossiers for Nicholas, James, Virgil, and Newton Earp in the Military Records Section, National Archives. In addition, there are the one-page summaries of Nicholas and Newton in the Sawtelle files, U. S National Home for Disabled Volunteer Soldiers. The Newton career is a bit trickier to follow, though, as he spent time in three Homes: the Kansas State Home in Fort Dodge, the National Home in Sawtelle, and the California State Home in Napa.

10. Nicholas P. Earp was listed as one of the Californians who had just received a pension increase; *San Francisco Call,* January 21, 1902.

11. James Earp file, National Archives, indicates that from 1901 to 1902, the Civil War pension check for him was shifted from San Francisco to Sawtelle. It should be stressed here that Sawtelle in this sense does not mean the Soldiers' Home. James was never a member of the Soldiers' Home; he lived yards away, in the community of Sawtelle.

12. A clipping in our possession of 1896 reports a dispatch from San Francisco, with this opening sentence: "Riley Grannan narrowly missed being killed by a wild Arizona dead shot, Jim Earp." From time to time, because of the Earp name, James was credited with considerable firearms smarts. Jack DeMattos, *The Earp Decision* (College Station, TX: Creative Publishing Company/The Early West, 1989).

13. His pension raise to $17.00 was listed in the *San Francisco Chronicle* of November 23, 1902, and around that time James was already established in Sawtelle.

14. *San Francisco Call,* January 21, 1902.

15. These admission dates are on their one-page summary sheets, mentioned earlier.

16. There can be no confusion here, as the *San Francisco Examiner* of May 25, 1900, under an article entitled "FOR NOME," lists "J. C. Earp, Mrs. J. C. Earp."

17. Plans and the progress of the Wilshire Boulevard project, as well as a map, appear in the *Los Angeles Herald,* April 14, 1906.

CHAPTER 5

1. The founder of this newspaper was A. A. Bynon, but Susie Pearson Miller took charge early on and controlled the content and did most of the writing and editing for a decade.

2. *Republican Journal,* Belfast, Maine, May 15, 1902.

3. The *Leavenworth Times*, November 16, 1905. The *Leavenworth Times* deserves some comment here. Kansas had one of the larger, more successful of the Soldiers' Homes. For over a decade, this newspaper carried a Veterans Page, with interesting, unusual, or important news from Soldiers' Homes across the country. We haven't done any testing, but feel that this newspaper gave better coverage of veteran's news than any other publication in the country. The incident is another of the strange ways in which geography gets confusing. True, Russell eventually went before a court in Los Angeles, but immediately after the stabbing he was first "quickly seized" and taken to Santa Monica. One can envision various lawmen, attorneys, justices, and judges pondering where to send this fellow: *Los Angeles Herald*, November 2, 1905.

4. The *Los Angeles Herald*, August 17, 1905.

5. The *Los Angeles Herald* of April 6, 1903, referred to James, as he had been visited by brother Wyatt.

6. In the *Los Angeles Herald* of August 26, 1902, Nicholas was listed as a resident of the Home, and was one of the Democratic delegates.

7. These paragraphs are based on the Voting Registers, maintained by each county in California. We used the collection of the California State Library in Sacramento.

8. This notice was picked up from the local newspaper and was reprinted in the *Leavenworth Weekly Times* on March 2, 1905. Extreme hospital cases would be the only ones admitted.

9. *Ogden Evening Transcript*, November 18, 1911.

10. *Los Angeles Times,* April 14, 1904.

11. This incident was also reported in the *Leavenworth Times*, August 7, 1904.

12. Walter Vandercook, one-page summary, Soldiers' Home files. A dozen or so articles about Vandercook appeared in the local press. The *Los Angeles Herald* of June 22, 1905, contains phrases "Mystery Deepens," and "Police Officers Puzzled."

13. *Los Angeles Herald*, October 9, October 14, 1909.

14. Trogden made such a fuss by waving that pistol at the anarchists that the *San Francisco Call* of October 11, 1908, devoted most of a page to the topic, along with a large illustration of a wide-eyed Trogden.

15. *Los Angeles Herald*, June 19, 1901.

16. *Los Angeles Times*, April 3, 1906.

17. *Los Angeles Times*, October 12, 1904.

18. *Los Angeles Herald*, June 20, 1905.

19. Many details of the Milne case appeared in the *Los Angeles Herald*, January 14, 1902.

20. The unusual circumstances of these cottages led to an explanation in *National Tribune* (Washington, D.C.), March 22, 1906, discussing how certain of the veterans were now enabled to live in nearby Sawtelle.

21. *Los Angeles Herald*, June 2, 1904. When veterans are named throughout these pages, assume that we have also consulted their one-page summary, National Archives, Soldiers' Home.

22. *Los Angeles Herald*, March 10, 1909, *Arizona Republican*, March 15, 1909.

23. *Oakland Tribune*, June 22, 1909.

24. *Los Angeles Herald*, June 27, 1904.

25. *Los Angeles Herald*, March 25, 1906.

26. *Los Angeles Times*, June 29, 1904.

27. In re Estate of Doolittle, 153 Cal. 29 (1908).

28. *Los Angeles Herald*, April 3, 1904, *San Bernardino Sun*, April 7, 1904.

29. Oregon *Daily Capital Journal,* June 19, 1909.

CHAPTER 6

1. For Schultz, *Los Angeles Herald,* July 9, 1904; for Mitchell, *ibid.,* June 17, 1905.

2. Constable Charles Lederer was himself a veteran, and from 1906 until his death in October 1926 was in the Soldiers' Homes for three different periods.

3. *Los Angeles Herald* of June 11, 1906.

4. Details of this encounter are in the *Los Angeles Herald* of June 13, 1906, and *Santa Monica Outlook*, June 11, 1906.

5. *Los Angeles Times*, March 25, 1905.

6. *Los Angeles Times*, March 15, 1904.

7. Gustave got a few paragraphs, even an illustration, in a feature of the Sawtelle "dens" in the *Los Angeles Times* of March 15, 1904.

8. *Los Angeles Herald*, October 31, 1905.

9. *Santa Monica Outlook*, October 25, 1904. Dr. Chapman was one of the "big guns," Superintendent of the Anti-Saloon League, and in 1904 alone preached dozens of times in greater Los Angeles on the evils of alcohol, tobacco, card playing, etc.

10. *Los Angeles Times,* May 21, 1906.

11. *San Bernardino Sun*, June 24, 1906. Kellogg was a veteran who was "known to the police" in the area. In 1905 he was arrested on a battery charge in Santa Monica; *Los Angeles Herald*, August 23, 1905.

12. *Oakland Tribune*, December 13, 1907.

13. The National Archives, Soldiers' Home files on veterans who were in trouble with civil authorities seldom included details of the various transgressions. Often, words like "was discharged" are left without explanation, but more details were usually included in the newspaper accounts. The Gilbert case was mentioned in the *Leavenworth Times*, February 4, 1909. For Moore case, see *Los Angeles Herald*, September 23, 1906.

14. The Gerant case generated quite a few news reports; *Los Angeles Herald*, August 20, 21, and September 9 of 1902 are just a few. The National Archives, Soldiers' Home

file, indicates that Lasher left the Home "at own request" in April 1910; he died in Los Angeles in 1916 and is buried in the Home cemetery.

15. Being sent to San Quentin gives us a view of the seriousness of the incident; *Los Angeles Herald* of June 28, 29, contain many details.

16. *Los Angeles Herald*, December 5, 1907.

17. This unusual event was even covered in the *Oakland Tribune,* July 13, 1914.

18. *Salt Lake Telegram,* August 18, 1915. The unusual nature of the article comes through in its heading: "Ban on Soldiers Canteen Hastens Death, Says Loud."

19. Canteens, coffee clubs, and similar activities were frequently recommended by the anti-alcohol groups, with seldom any interest on the part of either the veterans or the Home administrators. The word "canteen" had several meanings. To some outsiders, it meant soft drinks, or "soft beer," while to others it meant beer, but in limited quantities. These differences were explained by General LaGrange, the Soldiers' Home governor, in an interview with the *Santa Monica Outlook*, March 18, 1907.

20. *Los Angeles Herald*, February 24, 1907.

21. *Los Angeles Evening Express*, May 23, 1906.

CHAPTER 7

1. Details on these internal Home officers appear in most of the annual reports for all of the nation's veteran facilities.

2. *Los Angeles Times*, September 17, 1905.

3. The evolution of the townships was quite a quagmire of complications, as some names were partially maintained, and so forth. And, in transition from one to another, various lawmen had joint responsibilities and authority. Some understanding of the region can be found in *Official Boundaries of Congressional Districts* (Los Angeles: Board of Supervisors, 1912).

4. *Los Angeles Herald*, January 31, 1909.

5. Rita K.W. Ackerman, *O.K. Corral Postscript: The Death of Ike Clanton* (Honolulu, HI: Talei Publishers, 2006). Ben T. Traywick, *The Clantons of Tombstone* (Tombstone, AZ: Red Marie's Bookstore, 1996), 159–175.

6. Careers of all can be followed in the voting registers, the local newspapers, and in the National Archives, Soldiers' Home files.

7. *Santa Monica Outlook*, December 29, 1905.

8. *Los Angeles Times*, December 9, 1909.

9. *Los Angeles Evening Express*, December 21, 1907.

10. *Los Angeles Evening Express,* December 21, 1907.

11. In 1907, Bolster was seen giving whiskey to a veteran, but he claimed that he and the veteran "had simply been exchanging drinks"; *Los Angeles Times*, March 22, 1907.

12. In some quarters this joint jail was referred to as a "sub-county jail." Details of this Sawtelle arrangement are in the *San Jose Mercury News,* February 21, 1907.

13. *Santa Monica Outlook*, April 9, 1907.

14. Details of the robbery, and the various authorities involved, are in *Los Angeles Herald*, September 14, 1902.

15. Details of the Caswell detective couple are in *Los Angeles Times*, May 10, June 7, 1907.

16. *Los Angeles Times*, December 30, 1907.

17. *Los Angeles Times*, April 23, 1909.

CHAPTER 8

1. *Leavenworth Times*, November 22, 1907.

2. *Oshkosh Northwestern*, October 27, 1894.

3. *Arizona Republican,* January 14, 1913.

4. *California Journal of the Assembly*, February 2, 1911. This particular quote was from a speech indicating the evil impact on women and children of the blind pigs in Sawtelle.

5. *Los Angeles Herald*, April 6, 1903.

6. The most useful maps for our topic are those of the Sanborn Insurance Agency. We used the maps of the Los Angeles Public Library, but the entire collection is available online through the Library of Congress. The maps of Fourth Street adjacent to the Soldiers' Home reveal business places named "gaming," "barber," "restaurant," and so forth, and this was the environment of James Earp and other entertainment providers. Fourth Street is currently named Sawtelle Boulevard and at its intersection with Ohio Avenue serves as a rear entrance to the modern West Los Angeles Veteran Affairs (VA) Medical Center. David and Mary de Haas personal research visit on 5/31/2019. "VA – West Los Angeles Campus Index" – map.

7. Cataldo, *The Earp Clan*, and Cataldo and Holladay, *The Earps of San Bernardino County*.

8. *Tombstone Weekly Epitaph,* Monday March 23 and 27, 1882. Copy of funeral notice in Lee A. Silva archives/David D. de Haas, MD collection.

9. As an example of this, the *Daily Arizona Silver Belt* of Globe, throughout 1907, ran ads for the Hollenbeck Hotel, owned by A. C. Bilicke, "HEADQUARTERS FOR ARIZONANS." Traywick, *Wyatt Earp: Angel of Death*. Don Chaput, *"Buckskin Frank" Leslie* (Tucson, AZ: Westernlore Press, 1999). Ben T. Traywick, *Tombstone's "Buckskin Frank": Nashville Franklyn Leslie* (Tombstone, AZ: Red Marie's Publisher's, 2013). Jack DeMattos and Chuck Parsons, *They Called Him Buckskin Frank: The Life and Adventures of Nashville Franklyn Leslie* (Denton: University of North Texas Press, 2018). *The Tombstone Epitaph*, Roy B. Young (lead article), "The Cosmopolitan Touch: The Bilickes – Hoteliers in Tombstone," March 2020. The authors wish to thank *Tombstone Epitaph* editor Mark Boardman for expeditiously furnishing them a prepublication copy of this article, just two days prior to the due date for final edits to this book.

10. Frank Waters, *The Earp Brothers of Tombstone*, p. 45, 46, 63, 64. Of note is that Waters Earp book is only tenuously accepted by Earp historians, although this time-lime and information appears to be solid here, and consistent with the known facts regarding the Nicholas Earp party wagon train of 1876 – 1877. Waters was decidedly "anti-Earp" and his works reflect such and have been shown to be tainted with primary sources ... altered. Please see S.J. Reidhead, *Travesty*. Don Chaput, *Virgil Earp*, pp. 23 – 26. *The Sterling Kansas Bulletin*, May 24, 1877.

11. This incident and the Adelia Earp Memoirs have also always been only tenuously accepted by Earp historians. It was used in Chaput, *Virgil Earp: Western Peace Officer*, and by Earl Chafin in his Adelia Earp-Edwards, *Wild West Remembrances* (Riverside: Earl Chafin Press, 1998). It can also be found in the writings of Nick Cataldo, well known San Bernardino historian, and those of many other respected Earp historians (Tim Fattig, Roy Young, etc.). See also original David Cruickshanks letters in the personal collection of coauthor David D. de Haas, MD; and Scott Dyke and Bob Palmquist, "Adelia Earp's Dubious Memoir," *Wild West Magazine*, October 2016.

12. George Parsons 1903 Diary, Arizona Historical Society. Parsons, from Los Angeles, was a frequent visitor to the beaches and tennis areas of Santa Monica.

13. There are interesting news notes and ads regarding Wyatt's efforts in the *Tonopah Bonanza* for 1902. The issue of May 29 contains an ad for "THE NORTHERN," Wyatt Earp, prop., "A Gentleman's Resort." Ann Kirschner, *Lady at the O.K. Corral*, New York, N.Y.: Harper Collins Publishers, 2013.

14. All of these Arizona events are covered in several different chapters in Donald Chaput, *Empire of Sand* (Santa Ana: Graphic Publishers, 2015).

15. John's Western Gallery and William B. Shillingberg, "Wyatt Earp, Tombstone & the West (Parts I, II, and III)," John D. Gilchriese Collection Auction Catalogues. San Francisco, California: John's Western Gallery, 2004/2005. Gilchriese had also tracked down and had multiple extensive interviews with Virgil Earp's wife Allie in her later years. See Hildreth Halliwell, September 21, 1971 interview recordings (with Al Turner and Bill Oster) in Valley Center, California; Tucson, Arizona: University of Arizona, 1971.

CHAPTER 9

1. Some of the material which follows is drawn from Chaput, *Virgil Earp: Western Peace Officer* (Norman: University of Oklahoma Press, 1996). Hildreth Halliwell, September 21, 1971, interview recordings with Al Turner and Bill Oster in Valley Center, California; Tucson, Arizona: University of Arizona, 1971; copies in collection of David D. de Haas, MD.

2. Hal V. Dunn, "Virgil Earp and the Mystery of his Sawtelle Token," *Token and Medal Society Journal* 37 (October 1997): 160-68.

3. Hildreth Halliwell, September 21, 1971, interview recordings with Al Turner and Bill Oster in Valley Center, California; Tucson, Arizona: University of Arizona, 1971; copies in collection of David D. de Haas, MD. Halliwell was Allie Earp's grand-niece with whom Allie lived from the time of her husband Virgil Earp's death in 1905 until her own death in 1947. Halliwell was born in Virgil and Allie Earp's home in Prescott, Arizona. Virgil's brother James spent the last year of his life living with Halliwell too, and also died in her home.

4. National Archives, Soldiers' Home file for Seaver. An article entitled "Barney and His Driver" appeared in the *Santa Monica Outlook*, October 25, 1904. *Railroad & Street Journal*, October 20, 1906.

5. *Los Angeles Times*, March 16, 1907.

6. Hal V. Dunn, "Virgil Earp and the Mystery of his Sawtelle Token," *Token and Medal Society Journal* 37 (October 1997): 160-68.

7. Prescott *Weekly Journal-Miner*, June 1902.

8. Prescott *Weekly Journal-Miner*, August 1902.

9. Prescott *Weekly Journal-Miner*, October 29, 1902.

10. See also Adelia Earp/George Parsons, Adelia Earp Memoirs; Chaput, *Virgil Earp: Western Peace Officer*; Earl Chafin, Adelia Earp-Edwards, *Wild West Remembrances* (Riverside: Earl Chafin Press, 1998). The George W. Parsons Collection at the Arizona Historical Society, consisting primarily of his diaries and correspondence, has as a focus greater Tombstone and Los Angeles, where for fifty years he was involved with many of the key personalities of those locations. Lynn Bailey and Donald Chaput, *Cochise County Stalwarts* (2 vols) (Tucson: Westernlore Press, 2000).

11. Obverse and reverse views of these tokens can be viewed on several internet sites and here in the photo section.

CHAPTER 10

1. *Report of the City Auditor of the City of Los Angeles* (Los Angeles: City of Los Angeles, 1905), Exhibit A.

2. The multiple roles of Constable George Brown are discussed in *Los Angeles Herald,* February 22 and March 22, 1901.

3. The *Los Angeles Herald* of April 14, 1905, carried an article entitled "Local Saloons Well Regulated," which was pretty much the accepted thinking.

4. *Southern California Practitioner* 23 (1908:, 256.

5. *Los Angeles Herald*, May 15, 1905.

6. The Vusich case is examined in detail, with several photographs added, in *Los Angeles Times*, November 20, 1906.

7. In early February 1903 the *Los Angeles Herald* carried ads for Carrie, referring to her as the "Kansas Saloon Smasher." Her visit to cribtown and other aspects of

this less than successful visit are in Fran Grace, *Carrie A. Nation: Retelling the Life* (Bloomington: Indiana University Press, 2001).

8. The City Auditor's report for 1903-04 gave some details on the Coffee Club Association, where folks could "read, rest and amuse themselves away from any harmful influence." The *Los Angeles Herald* of September 10, 1905, gave considerable space to "Second Anniversary of Coffee Club Formation."

9. *Los Angeles Times*, June 3, 1905.

10. *The Pacific*, December 6, 1911.

11. *Los Angeles Herald*, December 28, 1903.

12. John A. Main, *The Booze Route* (Los Angeles: Commercial Printing Co., 1907). Main was identified on the title page as of "Alhambra," a Los Angeles County community trying to join Pasadena in its fight against alcohol.

13. Fattig, *Wyatt Earp: The Biography*, 733.

14. *Los Angeles Times*, September 28, 1911. Fattig, *Wyatt Earp*, 733.

15. *Vestkusten*, July 27, 1911.

16. *Tonopah Daily Bonanza*, July 24, 1911.

CHAPTER 11

1. *San Bernardino Sun,* April 14, 1904.

2. *Los Angeles Times*, December 8, 1904.

3. The city of San Bernardino passed a tighter liquor ordinance in 1905, yet even in 1908 was complaining of a few blind pigs as well as some gambling; *Los Angeles Herald,* October 3, 1905, *San Bernardino Sun*, September 25, 1908. Donald Chaput, *Virgil Earp: Western Peace Officer*, 1996.

4. *Los Angeles Herald,* September 5, 1904.

5. These comments are mostly drawn from Chaput, *Virgil Earp: Western Peace Officer*, 1996. Donald Chaput, *Empire of Sand* (Santa Ana, CA: Graphic Publishers, 2015).

6. *Reno Evening Gazette,* March 1, 1905.

7. *Bisbee Daily Review,* November 1, 1905, *Weekly Arizona Journal-Miner*, November 1, 1905, *Los Angeles Herald*, October 29, 1905.

CHAPTER 12

1. *Bakersfield Mountain Echo*, December 6, 1905.

2. Ben T Traywick, *The Clantons of Tombstone* (Tombstone, AZ: Red Marie's Bookstore, 1996), Chapter 11.

3. There is quite a literature on Brighton regarding his lawman and detective days in Arizona and California, and the local press also frequently commented on his doings. Some of the details of his years at the Soldiers' Home and nearby Sawtelle are in National Archives, Soldiers' Home file. Rita K.W. Ackerman, *O.K. Corral Postscript: Death of Ike Clanton* (Honolulu, HI: Talei Publishers, 2006). Mary and David D. de

Haas, MD, research visit 5/31/2019. Jim Groom, Troy Kelley, and David de Haas research visit 2005.

4. National Archives, Soldiers' Home file. The records indicate that he left the Home in 1908 "at own request," a sad phrase to disguise the departure to abscond with his persecuted wife. *San Francisco Examiner*, September 6, 1908.

5. There is a summary of Stinson in Bill O'Neal, *Encyclopedia of Western Gunfighters* (Norman: University of Oklahoma Press, 1979).

6. *Los Angeles Times*, September 20, 1903.

7. National Archives, Soldiers' Home file.

8. This particular raid was one of the most dramatic in the Sawtelle blind pig saga. The three major newspapers carried many of the details: *Los Angeles Times*, May 30 (several articles), *Santa Monica Outlook,* May 29, and the *Los Angeles Herald,* May 30, 1906.

9. *Santa Monica Outlook,* March 18, 1907.

10. National Archives, Soldiers' Home file. At his death his personal effects were appraised at $2.20, but were finally sold for $3.00. Details of the incident are in *Santa Monica Outlook,* March 16, 1905.

CHAPTER 13

1. *West Coast Magazine*, November 1908.

2. *Los Angeles Times,* February 3, 1907.

3. Other useful obituaries appeared in the *San Bernardino Sun*, February 15, 1907, and the *Los Angeles Times* of February 14, 1907, also contained a photograph.

4. His service in the Mexican War is documented in his National Archives file, as are his various pension records. The National Archives, Soldiers' Home file contains admission and death details, as well as location of his grave. Nick Cataldo, *The Earp Clan*, and Cataldo and Holladay, *The Earps of San Bernardino County.*

CHAPTER 14

1. There is a long, sort of meaningless article in the *Los Angeles Herald* of February 17, 1906, where Dupree (spelled Du Prez) explains that poker is a scientific game; this came after he was arrested for gambling.

2. National Archives, Soldiers' Home file. Dupree was one of the troublemakers mentioned by Wilkinson in her thesis, "The Veterans in our Midst," but her interests were in administration and legal aspects of the Home, not in skullduggery or blind pigs.

3. *Los Angeles Times*, March 22, 1907.

4. National Archives, Soldiers' Home file. Bolster was given press coverage a few times a year, mostly when arrested, or causing trouble while in jail.

5. *Los Angeles Times*, July 27, 1905.

6. *Los Angeles Financier,* April 15, 1907. *Los Angeles Herald,* October 5, 1907.

7. *Los Angeles Herald,* December 28, 1908.

8. Santa Monica *Outlook,* January 23, 1907.

9. National Archives, Soldiers' Home file. The Flynn career was dynamic, and the Sawtelle blind pig era was just one of Flynn's interests and projects over many decades in Southern California. One would need file drawers to accumulate documentation on this fellow. He was constant press fodder, enjoyed controversies, always seemed to be ahead of the game, was an outright crook, and seemed to have friends galore. His career can best be followed in his military and pension records, voting and real estate files, the Southern California newspapers, and in the many justice court records.

10. *Oakland Tribune,* June 29, 1922.

11. National Archives, Soldiers' Home, John Gallagher file. This weird case generated quite a bit of publicity in California, dealing with a few women, one or more soldiers being defrauded, jail time for women, and so forth. A few of the detailed articles are *Los Angeles Times*, December 21, 1906, and *Los Angeles Herald*, June 22, 1907.

CHAPTER 15

1. This is well summarized, with statistics, in Claire Prechtel-Kluskens, "A Reasonable Degree of Promptitude" [Civil War pension policies], *Prologue* 42 (Spring, 2010): 1-16.

2. *Los Angeles Herald,* September 3, 1907. Senator Porter James McCumber of North Dakota was in the forefront of these veteran benefits.

3. *Los Angeles Evening Express*, October 17, 1907.

4. Wilkinson, *Southern California Quarterly* 95 (Summer 2013): 188-224.

5. *Santa Monica Outlook*, April 13, 1909.

6. The Taft case is indeed bizarre. Here we have a couple, thoroughly dedicated to anti-alcohol, yet blind pigs, arrests, confusion, and controversy abound about booze during their years in Sawtelle.

7. Mrs. Taft became the vice-president; *Los Angeles Times*, August 3, 1904. The Tafts were mentioned frequently and favorably in the *Santa Monica Outlook* and the *Veteran-Enterprise* of Sawtelle, mostly in connection with their prohibition activities.

8. *Los Angeles Evening Express*, June 17, July 22, 1907.

9. Robert J. Burdette, ed., *American Biography and Genealogy: California Edition*, 2 vols. (Chicago: Lewis Publishing Co., 1919), I, 838-39

10. *The Los Angeles Times* of April 17, 1910, headed an article, "WOMEN REPLACE VETERANS."

11. *Los Angeles Herald*, July 2, 1910.

12. After 1900, most of the annual reports of the Soldiers' Homes across the nation frequently had comments about the number of women employed, and their various types of duties.

13. These amazing statistics, and philosophy, are apparent in the annual reports of the Soldiers' Home from 1900 through 1920, quite a contrast with California's reputation these days as a forefront of liberal thinking and a bastion of feminine advancement causes.

CHAPTER 16

1. The Alcalde Papers are in the Seaver Center, Natural History Museum, Los Angeles.

2. This was in a Treasury Department report of 1849, in *Message of the President of the United States*, Senate, 31st Cong., 1st Sess., Rep. Com. No. 18, of 1850.

3. The *Los Angeles Herald* covered this incident in many issues during 1894-1895. The most detailed article, September 15, 1894, also carries an illustration of the arrest of the smugglers.

4. W. W. Robinson, *Santa Monica: A Calendar of Events in the Making of a City* (Los Angeles: Title Insurance & Title Co., 1969).

5. Santa Monica directories carry statistics, advertisements, and names of individuals. Even more useful are the many Pacific Coast and Los Angeles directories of the late 1800s, which usually published a Santa Monica section.

6. Vawter information abounds in many Pasadena and Santa Monica accounts, local biographical publications, and land and business records. His obituary is in the *Los Angeles Times*, July 12, 1894.

7. Much of the material in this chapter is based on thousands of records in Articles of Incorporation, Seaver Center, Natural History Museum, Los Angeles. Each file contains place of business, purpose, financing, names of directors, and so forth. The Santa Monica entries are indeed diverse, including churches, laundries, banks, barbershops, ethnic organizations, etc.

8. *Thirteenth Report of the State Mineralogist* (Sacramento: State Printer, 1896), 204.

9. *Los Angeles Herald,* December 16, 1895.

10. The great farming potential was highlighted in a 24-page pamphlet, *Santa Monica* (Los Angeles: Kingsley, Coles & Collins, c. 1906).

11. The Casino was a steady topic in Santa Monica and Los Angeles newspapers. The *Los Angeles Herald* of August 18, 1888, has construction and opening event details.

12. *The Capital*, Los Angeles, August 9, 1902.

13. George Parsons Diary, 1903, Arizona Historical Society.

14. *Santa Monica Outlook*, April 21, 1894.

15. A leading magazine of the era, *Land of Sunshine*, throughout 1899 carried full-page ads featuring Santa Monica, most of the page devoted to the Hotel Arcadia.

16. *Tucson Daily Star,* July 7, 1885.

17. *Tucson Daily Star,* June 3,1892.

18. The Parsons, Gage, and Goodfellow material is from Donald Chaput, *Dr. George Goodfellow: Physician to the Gunfighters* (Tucson: Westernlore Press, 1996). The Tucson

Arizona Daily Star of January 5, 1896, mentioned that the ill E. B. Gage had gone to Santa Monica, specifically to be under the care of "Tucson's great surgeon, Dr. Goodfellow."

19. *Bisbee Daily Review*, May 31, 1905.

20. For example, a Japanese tea house was opened on Arcadia Beach (*Santa Monica Outlook*, June 13, 1902, ad), and a Japanese nursery was in business at this same time (*Santa Monica Outlook*, February 9, 1903, ad).

21. A few of the standard, detailed obituaries are the *Los Angeles Times,* September 16, 1912, and *Oakland Tribune.* September 16, 1912. She and her brother, Arturo Bandini, were of a family of wealth and landed interests, and following their deaths there were considerable legal squabbles regarding inheritors. In the publicity of these legal affairs, interesting family history surfaced.

22. David D. de Haas, MD collection of personal photos and Forsythe family items/letters. Please see Appendix 2.

CHAPTER 17

1. Donald Chaput, *The Earp Papers: In a Brother's Image.* Cataldo, *The Earp Clan*, and Cataldo and Holladay, *The Earps of San Bernardino County.* Fattig, *Wyatt Earp: The Biography.* Kirschner, *Lady at the O.K. Corral.* Donald Chaput, *Empire of Sand* (Santa Ana, CA: Graphic Publishers, 2015).

2. Donald Chaput, *Virgil Earp: Western Peace Officer* (Norman: University of Oklahoma Press, 1996).

3. S.J. Reidhead, *Travesty: The Story of Frank Waters and The Earp Brothers of Tombstone* (Roswell, NM: Jinglebob Press, 2005), 54. Gary L. Roberts, "Allie's Story: Mrs. Virgil Earp and the "Tombstone Travesty," *WOLA Journal*, Fall 1999; reproduced in Roy B. Young, et al., *A Wyatt Earp Anthology: Long May His Story Be Told*, 692.

4. National Archives, Soldiers' Home file; in this collection, information on Newton can be found for all three of the Homes. The National Archives also has a file on Newton's Civil War service. One of these documents lists a Civil War wound, whereas most of the biographical published material on him has no mention of this.

5. There are entries for James in many of the Voting Registers of San Bernardino County, as well as in the census of 1910 and 1920. The reunion is mentioned in *San Bernardino Sun*, June 21, 1911. Cataldo, *The Earp Clan*, and Cataldo and Holladay, *The Earps of San Bernardino County.* Roy B. Young, *James Cooksey Earp: Out of the Shadows* (Apache, OK: Young and Sons Enterprises, 2006).

6. *San Bernardino Sun,* August 15, 1922.

7. Some of these details are in Chaput, *The Earp Papers.* The burial details are from *San Bernardino Sun*, January 29, 1926. Cataldo, *The Earp Clan.* Cataldo and Holladay,

The Earps of San Bernardino County. Roy B. Young, *James Cooksey Earp: Out of the Shadows* (Apache, OK: Young and Sons Enterprises, 2006). Hildreth Halliwell, September 21, 1971, interview recordings (with Al Turner and Bill Oster) in Valley Center, California; Tucson, Arizona: University of Arizona, 1971; copies in collection of David D. de Haas, MD.

CHAPTER 18

1. In March 1908, a "gold find" in Dulzura, California, an area of about 25 miles southeast of San Diego, and ten miles north of the border with Mexico, led to national newspaper coverage of "the next El Dorado," and depletion of mining supplies in the San Diego area by the "rush" which ensued. Also prominent national mention of the arrival of Wyatt Earp, "the famous gun fighter and prospector." Wyatt would claim that the prospects for the area had "Goldfield beat (by) a mile." Of course, this in time would turn out to be proven incorrect. *New York Times*, March 13, 1908; *The Sacramento Star*, March 13, 1908, page 1; *Stockton Daily Evening Record*, March 13, 1908; *Evansville Press* (Evansville, Indiana), March 20, 1909; *Pittsburgh Post-Gazette*, March 14, 1908.

2. Much of this information appears in Chaput, *The Earp Papers*, 1996, and Chaput, *Virgil Earp*, 1996, and Bailey and Chaput, *Cochise County Stalwarts*, 2000. The two massive tomes by Lee A. Silva contain hundreds of Earp events, often with full documentation; his Volume I is especially useful for the Dodge City and Texas activities. Much of the Earp family doings will be found in Roberts, *Doc Holliday*, 2013, and Chuck Hornung, *Wyatt Earp's Cow-boy Campaign* (Jefferson, NC: McFarland & Co., 2016). Fattig, *Wyatt Earp: The Biography*. Cataldo, *The Earp Clan*. Cataldo and Holladay, *The Earps of San Bernardino County*. Garner Palenske, *Wyatt Earp in San Diego* (Santa Ana, CA: Graphic Publishers, 2011).

3. Henry Schultz, *Sawtelle, California* (Sawtelle: L. D. Loomis and S. Cole, c. 1906). This is a 15-page pamphlet, and we are only familiar with the copy at Los Angeles Public Library.

EPILOGUE

1. The 18th Amendment was ratified on January 16, 1919, and established prohibition in the United States. The National Prohibition Act, also known as the Volstead Act, was enacted to carry out and enforce the intent of the 18th amendment, prohibiting the sale of alcohol. The 18th Amendment would be repealed by the 21st Amendment on December 5, 1933.

2. *Los Angeles Herald*, January 2, 1905. Nicholas Earp died in this same hospital in 1907 (see his obituaries and hospital photo). In the *Annual Report, Secretary of War* (Washington: GPO, 1905, IV, 246.) – it was stated that as of June 30, 1905 the hospital had the capacity for 373 patients and convalescent quarters for 60. The daily

average number of patients in the hospital was 291 and in the convalescent quarters 32. The main diseases were alimentary system (6.16 %), circulatory system (5.63 %), respiratory (5.16 %), genitourinary (3.71 %), and nervous system (3.16%). Average age of death was 66.2 years as opposed to 67 years in 1904. The total number of members buried in the Home cemetery were 1621 with a cemetery capacity of 5000 graves. The average number of hospital employees in 1905 was 107 members, 95 civilians, and 13 female nurses. The report also mentions that at the facility the tuberculosis cases are "kept in same ward with other patients."

3. Much of this is well summarized in Wilkinson, *Southern California Quarterly*, Summer 2013, pp. 188-224. Detailed information, as well as documents, are in Sherins, Wadsworth Veterans Hospital, 2012.

4. Jim and Lynda Groom collection of Alice Earp Wells handwritten letters; copies in David D. de Haas, MD collection courtesy of Jim and Lynda Groom.

5. Fattig, *Wyatt Earp: The Biography*, 741–747.

6. Donald Chaput, *Virgil Earp: Western Peace Officer* (Norman: University of Oklahoma Press, 1996). Kirschner, *Lady at the O.K. Corral*. Chaput, *The Earp Papers: In a Brother's Image*. Letter from Congregation Sherith Israel Synagogue, San Francisco, of March 29, 1956, to Earp historian/researcher/collector John Gilchriese (Glendale, California, at the time) enabling him to relocate the grave of Wyatt Earp in Colma, California, as well as original photos of Gilchriese's first visit there in early 1956, before Wyatt's headstone was stolen; courtesy of the Jim and Lynda Groom collection, Grass Valley, California. Current modern-day monument was designed and placed by Earp historian Truman Fisher on December 16, 1996. His personal copy of the "Wyatt + Josie Earp Monument rubbing" of December 16, 1996, is in the collection of coauthor David D. de Haas, MD. For photos and further discussion, please see the *Wild West Collectors* Facebook page of September 17, 2019. Please also see Truman Rex Fisher, "Wyatt Earp's Multitudinous Tombstones," *True West Magazine*, April 1997, pp. 26 – 29.

7. *Bakersfield Morning Echo*, December 5, 1905. *Los Angeles Times*, February 14, 1907. *Grand Forks Herald*, North Dakota, November 2, 1905, p. 52. Fame of Wyatt and Virgil (and brothers) mentioned four times in this one article alone. *The Spokesman Review*, Spokane, Washington, September 13, 1884. A February 2020 search of Newspapers.com for mentions of Wyatt Earp AFTER the famous gunfight of 1881 – 1882, and BEFORE his 1929 death (and many obituaries), reveals 3,747 different mentions of Wyatt Earp in the newspapers of the United States and Canada. In other words, Wyatt, and the Earp family, had considerable local, regional, statewide, and international coverage from 1881 through 1929. Please see also the handwritten letters of Joe E. Milner in the collection of second author David D. de Haas, MD. Milner was the grandson of famed Custer scout "California Joe" and met and had long discussions with Wyatt on a few occasions. He had some very interesting

observations. Milner also personally knew many other famous Wild West characters and his father and grandfather were with Wild Bill Hickok in Deadwood at the time of his murder.

8. Edward Doheny, William S. Hart, Tom Mix, William Randolph Hearst, Lucky Baldwin, Wilson Mizner, Jack London, Bat Masterson, Tex Rickard, Doc Holliday, and "Wild Bill" Hickok, to name a few. Bailey and Chaput, *Cochise County Stalwarts*, vol. 2, p 81, 2000.

9. Ronald Reagan – 1953's "Law and Order." 40th President of the United States; 1981 – 1989.

10. Bert Lindley (1923), Randolph Scott (1939), Richard Dix (1942), Henry Fonda (1946), Will Geer (1950), Joel McCrea (1955), Hugh O'Brian (1955 – 1961), Burt Lancaster (1957), James Stewart (1964), James Garner (1967, 1988), Kurt Russell (1993), Kevin Costner (1994), Val Kilmer (2012).

11. Cesar Romero, Victor Mature, Stacy Keach, Jason Robards, Kirk Douglas, Val Kilmer, Dennis Quaid, etc.

12. The series ran for six seasons between 1955 and 1961.

13. Truman Rex Fisher, "Wyatt Earp's Multitudinous Tombstones," *True West Magazine*, April 1997, pp. 26–29. Please see also, footnote # 6.

14. Gary L. Roberts, "'Suppose ... Suppose ...': Wyatt Earp, Frontier Violence, Myth, and History," Epilogue in Young, Roberts, et al., *A Wyatt Earp Anthology: Long May His Story Be Told*, especially pp. 781–785.

APPENDIX I

1. *Salt Lake Herald Republican*, April 14, 1910.

2. Obituary in *Abilene Weekly Reflector*, October 18, 1906.

3. *Leavenworth Weekly Times*, April 22, 1909.

4. *Los Angeles Herald*, July 5, 1905.

5. The unusual Bennett career can be followed in many Michigan sources as well as biographical and photographical sources in Australia.

6. The US Census of 1910 shows Philip J. O'Boyle as an inmate of the Soldiers' Home, "on furlough."

7. *Los Angeles Times*, October 4, 1906.

8. *Chicago Tribune*, March 25, 1913.

9. *Coconino Sun* (Flagstaff), April 15, 1905; *Williams News* (Arizona), September 28, 1907.

10. *Los Angeles Herald*, October 2, 1910, contains a photo and many details.

11. *Los Angeles Herald*, July 30, 1907.

12. *Los Angeles Herald*, July 31, 1909; *Sacramento Daily Union*, July 31, 1909.

13. *Arizona Republican*, October 10, 1905; *Los Angeles Herald*, October 15, 1905.

14. Article in *Los Angeles Times*, January 12, 1940.

15. Some details in "Fighting Mike," *Los Angeles Times*, April 30, 1907.

16. *Southern California Practitioner* 20 (1905): 486.

17. *Bisbee Daily Review*, August 24, 1917.

18. *Coconino Sun* (Flagstaff), October 15, 1909.

19. *San Francisco Call*, December 16, 1909; *Morning Press* (Santa Barbara), July 12, 1904.

20. *Coconino Sun* (Flagstaff), April 12, 1918; *Los Angeles Times*, July 25, 1935.

21. *Los Angeles Times*, April 22, 2007.

22. A detailed article on Johnson's military career appeared in *New York Age*, December 11, 1943.

23. LaGrange held a bundle of important administrative posts following his Civil War career. For years he lived in San Francisco, where he had been appointed superintendent of the U. S. Mint in 1869; Alonzo Phelps, *Contemporary Biography of Representative Californians* (San Francisco: A. L. Bancroft & Co., 1881), 39-41.

24. *Los Angeles Evening Express*, August 15, 1906.

25. *San Francisco Call*, July 8, 1898.

26. *San Francisco Chronicle*, July 15, 1911.

27. *Leavenworth Weekly Times*, February 21, 1907.

28. There is considerable information on Patten in Seattle sources. Interestingly, the *Leavenworth Times* of May 7, 1913, carries his obituary without mentioning the "umbrella" connection.

29. *Los Angeles Times*, November 13, 1910. New York Herald, November 14, 1910.

30. *Los Angeles Herald*, September 17, 1905.

31. *Oxnard Courier*, August 23, 1907, *Sacramento Union*, September 6, 1908.

32. *Los Angeles Herald*, January 7, 1906.

33. *Los Angeles Herald*, December 2, 1903.

34. *New York Times*, April 9, 1920; *San Francisco Examiner*, October 13, 1912.

35. *Los Angeles Evening Express*, March 16, 1906, March 21, 1907.

36. *Oakland Tribune*, September 11, 1912.

37. Some details appear in *Evening News* (San Jose), November 23, 1907.

38. *Copper Era* (Clifton, AZ), October 11, 1906.

39. *Bakersfield Mountain Echo*, April 22, 1910.

40. *Weekly Gazette-Times* (Corvallis), March 1, 1912; Oregonian (Portland), February 1, 1916.

41. *Los Angeles Times*, March 16, 1907.

42. This unusual family is covered well in the obituary in *Los Angeles Times*, April 25, 1922.

43. *Los Angeles Herald*, December 4, 1912. *Santa Ana Register*, November 29, 1912.

214 ENDNOTES

APPENDIX II

1. Also see Lee A. Silva, *Wyatt Earp: A Biography of the Legend, Vol. I, The Cowtown Years*, and Silva, *Wyatt Earp: A Biography of the Legend, Vol. II, Tombstone Before the Earps*. Fattig, *Wyatt Earp: The Biography*. Chaput, *The Earp Papers: In a Brother's Image*. Donald Chaput, *Virgil Earp: Western Peace Officer* (Norman: University of Oklahoma Press, 1996). William B. Shillingberg, *Tombstone, A. T.: A History of Early Mining, Milling, and Mayhem*. Gary Roberts, *Doc Holliday: The Life and Legend* (Hoboken, NJ: John Wiley and Sons, 2013).

2. Important Baldwin Papers are in the Los Angeles County Arboretum in Arcadia as well as in the Arcadia Public Library. Hildreth Halliwell, September 21, 1971 interview recordings (with Al Turner and Bill Oster) in Valley Center, California; Tucson, Arizona: University of Arizona, 1971. Ann Kirschner, *Lady at the O.K. Corral: The True Story of Josephine Marcus Earp* (New York: Harper Collins Publishers, 2013).

3. Lynn Bailey and Donald Chaput, *Cochise County Stalwarts* (2 vols) (Tucson: Westernlore Press, 2000).

4. *Arizona Historical Review* 4 (Jan 1932).

5. Gary Ledoux, *Nantan: The Life and Times of John P. Clum*, 2 vols. (Victoria, BC: Trafford Publishing, 2007/2008).

6. William Jess Curtis was killed in an auto accident on October 13, 1926. Justice Jesse W. Curtis lived to the age of 95; there is a detailed obituary and a photo in *San Bernardino County Sun*, October 6, 1960. Nicholas R. Cataldo, *The Earp Clan: The Southern California Years* (San Bernardino, Calif.: Back Roads Press, 2006), and Nick Cataldo and Fred Holladay, *The Earps of San Bernardino County* (San Bernardino: City of San Bernardino Historical & Pioneer Society, 2001). See also Sarah Jane Rousseau, *Rousseau diary*, 1864.

7. John's Western Gallery and William B. Shillingberg, *Wyatt Earp, Tombstone & the West (Parts I, II, and III)*, John D. Gilchriese Collection Auction Catalogues (San Francisco, CA: John's Western Gallery, 2004/2005). Kirschner, *Lady at the O.K. Corral*, 171.

8. Kirschner, *Lady at the O.K. Corral*, 171.

9. For more about the Teapot Dome scandal, please see David D. de Haas, *Albert B. Fall and His Teapot Dome Scandal* in *The Wild West History Association Journal*: February 2012, pp 4 – 5.

10. John's Western Gallery and William B. Shillingberg, *Wyatt Earp, Tombstone & the West (Parts I, II, and III)*, John D. Gilchriese Collection Auction Catalogues. San Francisco, California: John's Western Gallery, 2004/2005.

11. Lee A. Silva, *Wyatt Earp: A Biography of the Legend, Vol. I, The Cowtown Years*, 7-10.

12. Truman Rex Fisher research archives/John H. Flood files; in the collection of co-author David D. de Haas, MD. Roy Young, *Cochise County Cowboy War* (Apache, Oklahoma: Young & Sons Enterprises, 1999), p. 47.

13. John D. Gilchriese, Wyatt Earp's Diagrams. United States Marshals Foundation.

14. John's Western Gallery and William B. Shillingberg, *Wyatt Earp, Tombstone & the West (Parts I, II, and III)*, John D. Gilchriese Collection Auction Catalogues, San Francisco, California: John's Western Gallery, 2004/2005, pp. 1 – 15 (part I). The appropriately named "A Flood of Earp Materials," with biographical data and illustrations, appeared in the *Tombstone Epitaph: National Edition*, October 2017. John Henry Flood, Jr. (edited by Don Taylor), *Wyatt Earp* (Tombstone, Arizona: Old West research & Publishing, 2011). Gary L. Roberts. " *'Suppose ... Suppose...': Wyatt Earp, Frontier Violence, Myth, and History*," Epilogue in Roy B. Young, Gary L. Roberts, et al., *A Wyatt Earp Anthology: Long May His Story Be Told*, 767, 768, 789/790 (footnote 33).

15. See David D. de Haas, "Clyde Forsythe Painted California Deserts; and One Little Vacant Lot in Tombstone," *Wild West Magazine*, October 2013, 1-2, 22-23, and the readily available, documented and illustrated expanded version online, "Victory Clyde Forsythe—Art of the West," HistoryNet. com. See also Clyde Forsythe personal family letters/photos/artwork/possessions in the collection of coauthor David D. de Haas. Ed Ainsworth, *The Cowboy in Art* (Cleveland, OH: The World Publishing Company, 1968). Ed Ainsworth, *Painters of the Desert* (Palm Desert, CA: *Desert Magazine*, 1960), 26 – 32.

16. November 2015 Facebook/e-mail survey of preeminent Tombstone researchers; David D. de Haas, MD.

17. *Wild West Magazine*, April 2016. Please see also *Wild West Magazine* website online version, HistoryNet. com.

18. October 13, 2013, research visit, Mary and David D. de Haas.

19. Don Chaput, *Dr. Goodfellow: Physician to the Gunfighters, Scholar, and Bon Vivant* (Tucson, AZ: Westernlore Press, 1996). Lynn Bailey and Donald Chaput, *Cochise County Stalwarts*, 2 vols. (Tucson: Westernlore Press, 2000).

20. Coauthor Don Chaput is the curator emeritus of the Natural History Museum of Los Angeles County. Hildreth Halliwell, September 21, 1971 interview recordings (with Al Turner and Bill Oster) in Valley Center, California; Tucson, Arizona: University of Arizona, 1971.

21. Lee A. Silva, *Wyatt Earp: A Biography of the Legend, Vol. I, The Cowtown Years*, 4-7.

22. Bailey and Chaput, *Cochise County Stalwarts*; Lynn R. Bailey, *Henry Clay Hooker and the Sierra Bonita Ranch* (Tucson, AZ: Westernlore Press, 1998). Forrestine Cooper Hooker, Edited by Don Taylor, *An Arizona Vendetta: The Truth About Wyatt Earp* (Tombstone, AZ: Old West Research and Publishing, 2011).

23. Josephine Earp was always referred to by close friends and family members as "Sadie." Hildreth Halliwell, September 21, 1971 interview recordings (with Al Turner and Bill Oster) in Valley Center, California; Tucson, Arizona: University of Arizona, 1971.

24. And quite possibly his greatest achievement, although it is somewhat difficult to top the historical significance of his amazing diaries; the George W. Parsons Collection at the Arizona Historical Society.

25. The George W. Parsons Collection at the Arizona Historical Society, consisting primarily of his diaries and correspondence, has as a focus greater Tombstone and Los Angeles, where for fifty years he was involved with many of the key personalities of those locations. Bailey and Chaput, *Cochise County Stalwarts*.

26. George W. Burton, *Men of Achievement in the Great Southwest* (Los Angeles: Los Angeles Times, 1904), 70–71. Obituary in Los Angeles Times, December 15, 1918.

BIBLIOGRAPHY

PRIMARY

Bisbee. Cochise County Recorder. Mine Files, Mines; Claims; Locations; Water Rights.

Los Angeles, Los Angeles Public Library. Sanborn Map Collection.

Los Angeles, Natural History Museum: Alcalde Papers (Spanish & Mexican administration); Incorporation Papers; Photographic/biographical files; William S. Hart Papers (Wyatt Earp correspondence).

Sacramento. California State Library. Registers of Voters (arranged by county).

San Marino, CA, Huntington Library. Stuart Lake Collection (a Wyatt Earp collection).

Tucson. Arizona Historical Society. Biographical/Photographic collections; George W. Parsons Collection.

Washington, D. C. National Archives, "Registers of Veterans at the National Home for Disabled Volunteer Soldiers, Pacific Branch in Sawtelle, California, 1888-1933." This contains a sheet for each individual with state of origin, military unit and years, admission and discharge from Home, burial location, and disposition of funds or personal property. The originals of these files are in the National Archives and Records Administration and are available at several online sites. They are easily accessible, without charge, through FamilySearch.com. More complete military and pension files are also in the National Archives, and portions of these files are also available online.

Washington, D. C. Library of Congress, Historical American Buildings Survey (HABS), containing files of the Pacific Branch, Soldiers' Home, Sawtelle.

OTHER INSTITUTIONS

Los Angeles County Library, Norwalk Branch

Santa Monica History Museum

Santa Monica Public Library

Sharlot Hall Museum Library & Archives

PRIVATE COLLECTIONS

Mary and David D. de Haas

Jim and Lynda Groom

Lee and Sue Silva Collection/Research Archives

Truman Rex Fisher Collection/Research Papers

Dr. Robert D. Pepper Research Archives

Karen Holliday Tanner and John Tanner Collection

Victor Clyde Forsythe Family Collection

John D. Gilchriese Collection

James Swinnerton Collection

GOVERNMENT DOCUMENTS

Annual Reports, War Department, for Pacific Branch, Soldiers' Home, various years.

California, Journal of the Assembly. Sacramento: Supt of State Printing, 1911

Federal Census of 1870, Deer Lodge County, Montana.

Message of the President of the United States. Senate, 31st Cong., 1st Sess., Rep. Com. No. 18, 1850

Official Boundaries of Congressional Districts. Los Angeles: Board of Supervisors, 1912.

Official Register of the United States.
    Washington, annual pub., lists of employees.

Penal Code of California. San Francisco, 1897.
    State law re distance, sale of liquor, Soldiers' Home.

Report of the Auditor of the City of Los Angeles. Los Angeles: City of Los Angeles, 1905.

Thirteenth Report of the State Mineralogist. Sacramento: Supt. of State Printing, 1896.

U. S. Congress. House. Disabled (or, Disabled Volunteer Soldiers). Various reports, 1895-1910.

U. S. War Department, Office of Inspector General, Knox Report, 57th Cong., 1st Sess, House Doc. 137 (1901).

U. S. War Department. Inspector General, or Inspection. Various reports, 1900-1914.

BOOKS

Ackerman, Rita K.W. *O.K. Corral Postscript: Death of Ike Clanton.* Honolulu, HI: Talei Publishers, 2006.

Ainsworth, Ed. Foreword by John Wayne, *The Cowboy in Art.* Cleveland, OH: The World Publishing Company, 1969.

———. *Painters of the Desert.* Palm Desert, CA: Desert Magazine, Inc., 1960.

Alexander, Bob. *John H. Behan: Sacrificed Sheriff.* Silver City, NM: High-Lonesome Books, 2002.

Bailey, Lynn R. *Henry Clay Hooker and the Sierra Bonita Ranch.* Tucson, AZ: Westernlore Press, 1998.

———, comp. and ed. *Tombstone from a Woman's Point of View: The Correspondence of Clara Spalding Brown July 7, 1880, to November 14, 1882.* Tucson, AZ: Westernlore Press, 1998.

———. *A Tale of the "Unkilled": The Life, Times, and Writings of Wells W. Spicer, The Man Who Defended John D. Lee, and Exonerated the Earps and Doc Holliday.* Tucson, AZ: Westernlore Press, 1999.

———. *The Valiants: The Tombstone Rangers and Apache War Frivolities.* Tucson, AZ: Westernlore Press, 1999.

———. *Tombstone, Arizona: "Too Tough to Die."* Tucson, AZ: Westernlore Press, 2010.

Bailey, Lynn R., and Don Chaput. *Cochise County Stalwarts,* 2 vols. Tucson, AZ: Westernlore Press, 2000.

Bicknell, Thomas C., and Chuck Parsons. Foreword by Robert K. DeArment. *Ben Thompson:Portrait of a Gunfighter.* Denton: University of North Texas Press, 2018.

Bell, Bob Boze. *The Illustrated Life and Times of Wyatt Earp.* Phoenix, AZ: Tri Star Boze Publications, 1993.

Boessenecker, John. *When Law Was in the Holster: The Frontier Life of Bob Paul.* Norman: University of Oklahoma Press, 2012.

Burdette, Robert J., ed. *American Biography and Genealogy: California Edition,* 2 vols. Chicago: Lewis Publishing Co., 1919.

Burton, George W. *Men of Achievement in the Great Southwest.* Los Angeles: Los Angeles Times, 1904.

Burns, Walter Noble. *Tombstone: An Iliad of the Southwest.* Garden City, NY: Double Day, Page & Company, 1927. Cochise County Deputy Sheriff Col. William Breckenridge's personal autographed copy from the collection of coauthor David D. de Haas.

Cataldo, Nicholas R. *The Earp Clan: The Southern California Years.* San Bernardino, CA: Back Roads Press, 2006.

Cataldo, Nick, and Fred Holladay. *The Earps of San Bernardino County.* San Bernardino, CA: City of San Bernardino Historical & Pioneer Society, 2001.

Chafin, Earl. *Wyatt Earp in Alaska: The Story of Wyatt and Josephine Earp from 1897 to 1901 in Rampart, St. Michael, and Nome, Alaska.* Riverside, CA: The Earl Chafin Press, 1999.

———. *Final Hours of Wyatt Earp: His Last Years, Funeral, Burial Place and Getting His Story Told.* Riverside, CA: Earl Chafin Press, 2001.

———, ed. *Sincerely Your Friend, Wyatt S. Earp: The Letters of Wyatt Earp.* Riverside, CA: The Earl Chafin Press, 2001.

Chaput, Donald. *The Earp Papers.* Encampment, WY: Affiliated Writers of America, 1994.

———. *Nellie Cashman and the North American Mining Frontier.* Tucson, AZ: Westernlore Press, 1995.

———. *Dr. Goodfellow: Physician to the Gunfighters.* Tucson, AZ: Westernlore Press, 1996.

———. *Virgil Earp: Western Peace Officer.* Norman, OK: University of Oklahoma Press, 1996.

———. *"Buckskin Frank" Leslie.* Tucson, AZ: Westernlore Press, 1999.

———. *Empire of Sand: The Ehrenberg-Quartzsite-Parker Triangle.* Santa Ana, CA: Graphic Publishers, 2015.

Clum, John P. Edited by Neil B. Carmony. *Apache Days and Tombstone Nights: John Clum's Autobiography.* Silver City, NM: High-Lonesome Books, 1997.

Clum, John P. Foreword and Annotations by John D. Gilchriese. *It All Happened in Tombstone.* Flagstaff, AZ: Northland Press, 1965

Cooper Hooker, Forrestine. Edited by Don Taylor. *An Arizona Vendetta: The Truth About Wyatt Earp.* Tombstone, AZ: Old West Research and Publishing, 2011.

DeArment, Robert K. *Bat Masterson: The Man and the Legend.* Norman: University of Oklahoma Press, 1979.

———. *Knights of the Green Cloth: The Saga of the Frontier Gamblers.* Norman: University of Oklahoma Press, 1982.

———. *Broadway Bat: Gunfighter in Gotham: The New York City Years of Bat Masterson.* Honolulu, HI: Talei Publishers, 2005.

DeMattos, Jack. *The Earp Decision.* College Station, TX: Creative Publishing Company, 1989.

DeMattos, Jack, and Chuck Parsons. Foreword by John Boessenecker. *They Called Him Buckskin Frank: The Life and Times of Nashville Franklyn Leslie.* Denton: University of North Texas Press, 2018.

———. Foreword by Rick Miller. *The Notorious Luke Short: Sporting Man of the Wild West.* Denton: University of North Texas Press, 2015.

Devere, Jr., Burton. *Bonanzas to Borrascas: The Mines of Tombstone, Arizona.* Tombstone, AZ: Rose Tree Museum, 2010.

Dodge, Fred. Edited by Carolyn Lake. *Undercover for Wells Fargo: The Unvarnished Recollections of Fred Dodge.* Boston, MA: Houghton Mifflin Company, 1969.

Dolph, Jerry, and Arthur Randall. *Wyatt Earp and Coeur d'Alene Gold: Stampede to Idaho Territory*. Post Falls, ID: Eagle City Publications, 1999.

Dworkin, Mark J. *American Mythmaker: Walter Noble Burns and the Legends of Billy the Kid, Wyatt Earp, and Joaquin Murrieta*. Norman: University of Oklahoma Press, 2015.

Earp-Edwards, Adelia. *Wild West Remembrances (1861–1941)*. Riverside, CA: Earl Chaffin Press, 1998.

Earp, Josephine S. Edited by Earl Chafin. *Wyatt's Woman: She Married Wyatt Earp: The Life and Times of Josephine Sarah Marcus*. 1938. Repr., Riverside, CA: The Earl Chafin Press, 1998.

Earp, Wyatt S. Collected and Introduction by Glenn G. Boyer. *Wyatt Earp: A Peace Officer of Tombstone*. Sierra Vista, AZ: Yoma V. Bissette, October 26, 1981. Personal copy of author Al Turner.

Earp, Wyatt. Edited by John Richard Stephens. *Wyatt Earp Speaks: My Side of the O.K. Corral Shootout, Plus Interviews with Doc Holliday*. Cambria Pines by the Sea, CA: Fern Canyon Press, 1998.

Erwin, Richard E. *The Truth About Wyatt Earp*. Carpinteria, CA: The O.K. Press, 1992.

Fattig, Timothy W. *Wyatt Earp: The Biography*. Honolulu, HI: Talei Publishers, 2002.

Fischer, Ron W. Preface Jane Candia Coleman, Introduction Ben T. Traywick, Foreword Glenn G. Boyer. *Nellie Cashman: Frontier Angel*. Honolulu, HI: Talei Publishers Inc., 2000.

———. *The Last Great Frontier Marshall: A Biography of William "Bill" Tilghman*. Tombstone, AZ: Ron W. Fischer Enterprises, 2001.

Fisher, Truman Rex, ed. *Correspondence Between Wyatt S. Earp and William S. Hart et al., from 1920 to 1929*. Newhall, CA: William S. Hart Museum, October 1984. With photos of Earp's L.A. residences.

Flood, Jr., John Henry. Edited by Don Taylor. *Wyatt Earp*. Tombstone, AZ: Old West Research & Publishing, 2011.

Flood Jr., John Henry. Edited by Earl Chafin. *Biography of Wyatt Earp: Gunfighter of the Old West (1926)*. Riverside, CA: Self-published, 1988.

Forrest, Earle R. *Arizona's Dark and Bloody Ground*. Caldwell, ID: Caxton Printers, 1936.

Gatto, Steve. *John Ringo: The Reputation of a Deadly Gunman*. Tucson, AZ: San Simon Publishing Company, 1995.

———. *Wyatt Earp: A Biography of a Western Lawman*. Tucson, AZ: San Simon Publishing Company, 1997.

———. *The Real Wyatt Earp: A Documentary Biography*. Silver City, NM: High Lonesome Books, 2000.

———. *Johnny Ringo*. Lansing, MI: Protar House, 2002.

———. *Curly Bill: Tombstone's Most Famous Outlaw*. Lansing, MI: Protar House, 2003.

Gilchriese, John D. *The Odyssey of Virgil Earp*. Tucson, AZ, 1968. Gilchriese's personal copy of the original manuscript (edited version subsequently published in *The Tombstone Epitaph*, National Edition, Fall 1968) in collection of coauthor David D. de Haas.

Grace, Fran. *Carrie A. Nation: Retelling the Life*. Bloomington: Indiana University Press, 2001.

Grey, Zane. *To the Last Man*. New York: Harper & Brothers, 1921.

Hand, George. Edited and Introduction by Neil Carmony. *Whiskey, Six-guns and Red-light Ladies: George Hand's Saloon Diary, Tucson, 1875–1878*. Silver City, NM: High-Lonesome Books, 1994.

Hattich, William. Foreword by John D. Gilchriese. *Tombstone: In History, Romance and Wealth*. Oklahoma: University of Oklahoma Press, 1981. Reprint, Originally published Tombstone, Arizona: *Tombstone Daily Prospector*, April 1903.

Hickey, Michael M. *The Street Fight Trilogy: Street Fight in Tombstone Near the O.K. Corral; Los Dos Pistoleros Earp, The Two Earp Pistoleers; The Cowboy Conspiracy to Convict The Earps;* Honolulu, HI: Talei Publishers, 1992, 1993, 1994.

———. *The Death of Warren Baxter Earp: A Closer Look*. Honolulu, HI: Talei Publishers, 2000.

History of Arizona Territory. San Francisco, California: Wallace W. Elliott & Co., 1884.

Hooker, Forrestine Cooper. *An Arizona Vendetta: The Truth About Wyatt Earp— and Some Others*. Los Angeles, CA: The Munk Library of Arizona Southwest Museum, ca. 1919. See also retyped copy Neil B. Carmony, 2000.

Hornung, Chuck. *Wyatt Earp's Cow-boy Campaign*. Jefferson, NC: McFarland & Co., 2016.

Ingersoll, Luther A. *Santa Monica Bay Cities*. Los Angeles: L. A. Ingersoll, 1908

James, George Wharton. *Tourist's Guide-Book to South California*. Los Angeles: B. R. Baumgardt, 1894.

John's Western Gallery and William B. Shillingberg. *Wyatt Earp, Tombstone and the West (Parts I, II, and III)*. John D. Gilchriese Collection Auction Catalogues. San Francisco, CA: John's Western Gallery, 2004/2005.

Kintop, Jeffrey, and Guy L. Rocha. *The Earps' Last Frontier: Wyatt and Virgil Earp in the Nevada Mining Camps, 1902-1905*. Reno, NV: Great Basin Press, 1989.

Kirschner, Ann. *Lady at the O.K. Corral: The True Story of Josephine Marcus Earp*. New York: Harper Collins Publishers, 2013.

Lake, Stuart N. *Wyatt Earp: Frontier Marshal*. Cambridge, MA: Houghton Mifflin Company, 1931. Tombstone Mayor John P. Clums's personal copy in collection ofDavid D. de Haas.

Ledoux, Gary. *Tombstone: A Chronicle in Perspective*. Victoria, BC: Trafford Publishing, 2002.

———. *Nantan: The Life and Times of John P. Clum (Volumes 1 and 2)*. Victoria, BC: Trafford Publishing, 2007/2008.

Los Angeles City Directories. Los Angeles: various publishers, 1890-1910.

Lubet, Steven. *Murder in Tombstone: The Forgotten Trial of Wyatt Earp.* New Haven, CT: Yale University Press, 2004.

Main, John E. *The Booze Route.* Los Angeles: Commercial Printing House, 1907.

Marks, Paula Mitchell. *And Die in the West: The Story of the O.K. Corral Gunfight.* New York: William Morrow and Company, 1989.

Men of Achievement, The Greater Southwest. Los Angeles: Los Angeles Times, 1904.

Newmans, Directory of Los Angeles. Los Angeles: T. Newman, 1903.

Memorial Addresses on the Life and Character of George Hearst. Washington. GPO, 1894.

Moak, Sim. *The Last of the Mill Creeks and Early Life in Northern California.* Chico, CA: np, 1923.

O'Neal, Bill. *Encyclopedia of Western Gunfighters.* Norman: University of Oklahoma Press, 1979.

Parsons, George W. Edited, Annotated, and with Introduction and Index by Lynn R. Bailey. *A Tenderfoot in Tombstone: The Private Journal of George Whitwell Parsons: The Turbulent Years, 1880–82.* Tucson, AZ: Westernlore Press, 1996.

Parsons, George W. Transcribed, Edited, Annotated, Indexed, and with Foreword by Lynn R. Bailey *The Devil Has Foreclosed: The Private Journal of George Whitwell Parsons, Volume II,: The Concluding Years, 1882–87,* Tucson, AZ: Westernlore Press, 1997.

Palenske, Garner A. *Wyatt Earp in San Diego: Life After Tombstone.* Santa Ana, CA:- Graphic Publishers, 2011.

Phelps, Alonzo. *Contemporary Biography of Representative Californians.* San Francisco: A. L. Bancroft & Co., 1881.

Press Reference Library: Notables of the West. Los Angeles: Los Angeles Examiner, 1913.

Reidhead, S.J. *Travesty: The Story of Frank Waters and The Earp Brothers of Tombstone.* Roswell, NM: Jinglebob Press, 2005.

Resident and Business Directory of Santa Monica, Ocean Park, Venice, Sawtelle, and Palms, California. Santa Monica: Santa Monica Bay Directory Co., 1908.

Roberts, Gary. *Doc Holliday: The Life and Legend.* Hoboken, NJ: John Wiley and Sons, Inc., 2013.

———, Roy Young, and Casey Tefertiller. *A Wyatt Earp Anthology: Long May His Story Be Told.* Denton: University of North Texas Press, 2019.

Robinson, W. W. *Santa Monica: A Calendar of Events in the Making of a City.* Los Angeles: Title Insurance and Trust Co., 1966.

Rodman, Willoughby. *History of the Bench and Bar of Southern California.* Los Angeles, California: Wm. J. Porter, 1909.

Ross, Thom. Foreword by Paul Andrew Hutton. *Gunfight at the O.K. Corral: In Words and Pictures.* Golden, CO: Fulcrum Publishing, 2001.

Santa Monica and Ocean Park Directory. Santa Monica: n.p., 1905.

Schultz, Henry. *Sawtelle, California: Its Excellent Business Advantages.* Sawtelle: L. D. Loomis & S. Cole, c. 1906.

Sherins, Robert S., MD. *Wadsworth Veterans Hospital. Sawtelle Veterans Soldiers' Home.* Los Angeles: UCLA School of Medicine, 2012.

Shillingberg, William B. *Tombstone, A. T.: A History of Early Mining, Milling, and Mayhem.* Spokane, WA: The Arthur H. Clark Company, 1999.

———. *Dodge City: The Early Years, 1872-1886.* Norman, OK: The Arthur H. Clark Company, 2009.

Silva, Lee A. *Wyatt Earp: A Biography of the Legend. Vol. I, The Cowtown Years.* Santa Ana, CA: Graphic Publishers, 2002.

———. *Wyatt Earp: A Biography of the Legend. Vol. II, Tombstone Before the Earps.* Santa Ana, CA: Graphic Publishers, 2010.

Taft, Fred H. *An Empire Builder of the Middle West* (biography of Stephen H. Taft). Los Angeles: Parker, Stone & Baird Co., 1929.

Tanner, Karen Holliday. *Doc Holliday: A Family Portrait.* Norman: University of Oklahoma Press, 1998.

The Sunset Club of Los Angeles. Los Angeles, California: Geo. Rice & Sons, 1916.

Tefertiller, Casey. *Wyatt Earp: The Life and Legend.* New York: John Wiley & Sons, 1997.

Traywick, Ben T. *Historical Documents and Photographs of Tombstone.* 1971. rev. ed., Tombstone, AZ: Red Marie's Bookstore, 1994.

———. *John Henry (The "Doc" Holliday Story).* Tombstone, AZ: Red Marie's Bookstore, 1996.

———. *The Clantons of Tombstone.* Tombstone, AZ: Red Marie's Bookstore, 1996.

———. *Wyatt Earp's Thirteen Dead Men,* Tombstone, AZ: Red Marie's Books, 1998.

———. *Wyatt Earp: Angel of Death.* Honolulu, HI: Talei Publishers, 2007.

———. *Tombstone's "Buckskin Frank": Nashville Franklyn Leslie.* Tombstone, AZ: Red Marie's Books, 2013.

Trimble, Marshall. *Wild West: Heroes and Rogues (Volume 1; Wyatt Earp: Showdown in Tombstone).* Phoenix, AZ: Golden West Publishers, 2008.

Turner, Alfred, ed. *The Earps Talk.* College Station, TX: The Early West/The Creative Publishing Company, 1980.

———. *The O.K. Corral Inquest.* College Station, TX: The Early West/The Creative Publishing Company, 1981.

Warren, Charles Sumner. *History of the Santa Monica Bay Region.* Santa Monica: A. H. Cawston, 1934.

Waters, Frank, *The Earp Brothers of Tombstone: The Story of Mrs. Virgil Earp,* New York: Clarkson N. Potter, Inc., 1960.

Young, Roy B. *Cochise County Cowboy War: "A Cast of Characters."* Apache, OK: Young & Sons Enterprises, 1999.

———. *Pete Spence: "Audacious Artist in Crime."* Apache, OK: Young & Sons Enterprises, 2000.

———. *James Cooksey Earp: Out of the Shadows.* Apache, OK: Young & Sons Enterprises, 2006.

———. *Robert Havlin Paul: Frontier Lawman, The Arizona Years.* Apache, OK: Young & Son Enterprises, 2009.

———. Foreword by Gary L. Roberts and Robert E. Palmquist. *Judge William H. Stilwell: Bench and Bar in Arizona Territory.* Apache, OK: Young & Sons Enterprises, 2011.

———, Gary L. Roberts and Casey Tefertiller, eds., *A Wyatt Earp Anthology: Long May His Story Be Told.* Denton: University of North Texas Press, 2019.

ARTICLES

"At the Bar of the Senate" (Soldiers' Home), *West Coast Magazine,* February 1911, 403–420.

Bell, Bob Boze. "Wyatt Earp in Hollywood." *True West Magazine,* October 2015.

Chaput, Don. "The Earp Brothers' Body Count." *NOLA Quarterly,* April–May 2000, 33–39.

de Haas MD, David D. "Clyde Forsythe Painted California Deserts; and One Little Vacant Lot in Tombstone." *Wild West Magazine,* October 2013, 1, 2, 22-23. Full/Extended online version: https://www.historynet.com/victor-clyde-forsythe-and-the-gunfightatcorral-a-new-perspective.htm

———. "Revisiting the 'O.K. Corral Fire Aftermath Photo'." *Wild West Magazine,* April 2016, 11. Extended online version: https://www.historynet.com/revisitingthe-ok-corral-fire-aftermath-photo.htm

———. "My Best Friend Lee." *Wild West History Association Journal,* October 2014, 8–19.

———. "Collectors Roundup." Tempe, Arizona. *Wild West History Association Journal,* February 2012, 49–52.

———. Letter to the Editor. Follow up to "Collectors Roundup." *Wild West History Association Journal,* August 2012, 3–4.

———. Letter to the Editor. Albert B. Fall and his Teapot Dome Scandal. *Wild West History Association Journal,* February 2012, 4–5.

"Dr. H. E. Hasse." *Southern California Practitioner* 20 (1905): 486.

Dunn, Hal V. "Virgil Earp and the Mystery of his Sawtelle Token." *Token and Medal Society Journal* 37 (Oct, 1997): 160-68.

Dyke, Scott, and Bob Palmquist. "Adelia Earp's Dubious Memoir." *Wild West Magazine,* October 2016.

Fisher, Truman Rex. "Wyatt Earp's Multitudinous Tombstones." *True West Magazine,* April 1997, 26 – 29.

Gilchriese, John D. "Wyatt Earp's Personal Diagrams of Prominent Historical Events." Mclean, VA: United States Marshals Foundation, Inc., 1989.

"Goldfield, The New Eldorado," *Putnam's Monthly,* March 1907, 658–72.

Greene, Jeffrey, MD, PhD, "Amnesia, Adverse Events, and the Angel of History," *Annals of Internal Medicine* 171, no. 6 (Philadelphia, PA: American College of Physicians) (September 17, 2019): 434 – 435. Hutton, Paul Andrew. "Showdown at the Hollywood Corral. Wyatt Earp and the Movies." *Montana: The Magazine of Western History,* Summer 1995.

Lee, Jane Matson, Mark Dworkin, and H.F. Sills. "Mystery Man of the O.K. Corral Shootout." *WOLA Journal,* Spring 2004.

Palmquist, Bob. "Justice in Tombstone." *Wild West Magazine,* October 2015.

Peterson, Roger S. "Wyatt Earp: Man Versus Myth." Harrisburg, Pennsylvania, *American History Magazine,* August 1994, pp. 54 – 61.

Roberts, Gary L. "Allie's Story: Mrs. Virgil Earp and the 'Tombstone Travesty.'" *WOLA Journal,* Fall 1999.

———. "'Suppose ... Suppose...': Wyatt Earp, Frontier Violence, Myth and History." Epilogue in *A Wyatt Earp Anthology: Long May His Story Be Told.* Denton: University of North Texas Press, 2019.

"Sawtelle—The Home Mecca." *The West Coast Magazine,* February 1909, p. 706.

"Sawtelle—Then and Now." *The West Coast Magazine,* December 1908, 544–546.

Silva, Lee A. "The Mysterious Morgan Earp." *Wild West Magazine,* October 2010, 28–35. Full original article manuscript and research material (and Wild West History Association "Outstanding Article on Western History" 2011 award plaque) in the collection of co-author David D. de Haas.

———. "In a Brother's Shadow." *Wild West Magazine,* December 2009, 26–33.

———. "Did Tom McLaury Have a Gun?" *Wild West Magazine,* October 2006, 34–41.

Silva, Susan L., and Lee A. Silva. "The Killing of Dora Hand." *Wild West Magazine.* December 2009, 40–47. Wild West History Association (WWHA) 2010 "Outstanding Article on Western History" award plaque in the collection of co-author David D. de Haas.

Taft, S. H. "Sawtelle, The Pioneer Awakener." *West Coast Magazine.* January 1909, 626.

"The First Through Train." *The Carson Daily Appeal.* Carson City, Nevada, May 13, 1869.

"Temperance Movement." *Southern California Practitioner* 23 (1908): 256.

"United States Soldiers' Home at Santa Monica." *Overland Monthly,* September 1888, 225–42.

Wilkinson, Cheryl Lynn. "The Soldiers' City: Sawtelle, California, 1897-1922." *Southern California Quarterly* 95 (Summer, 2013): 188-224.

NEWSPAPERS

Abilene Weekly Reflector (Kansas)

Anaconda Standard (Montana)

Arizona Republican (Phoenix)

Bakersfield Mountain Echo

Bisbee Daily Review

Butte Miner (Montana)

Carson Daily Appeal

Chicago Tribune

Coconino Sun (Flagstaff)

Copper Era (Clifton, AZ)

Daily Arizona Silver Belt (Globe)

Evening News (San Jose)

Grand Forks Herald (North Dakota)

Honolulu Republican (Hawaii)

La Cronica (Los Angeles)

Leavenworth Times (Kansas)

Los Angeles Evening Express

Los Angeles Herald

Los Angeles Times

Morning Press (Santa Barbara)

National Tribune (Washington, D. C.)

New North-West (Deer Lodge, Montana)

New York Age

New York Herald

New York Times

New York Tribune

Oakland Tribune

Oregonian (Portland)

Oshkosh Northwestern (Wisc.)

Oxnard Courier (CA)

Railroad & Street Railway Journal

Reno Evening Gazette

Sacramento Union

Salt Lake Herald Republican

San Bernardino Sun

San Francisco Call

San Francisco Chronicle

San Francisco Examiner

San Jose Mercury News

Santa Monica Outlook
Sawtelle Sentinel
Spokesman Review (Spokane, Washington)
Sterling Kansas Bulletin
Tombstone Epitaph
Tombstone Prospector
Vestkusten (San Francisco, Swedish)
Veteran-Enterprise (Sawtelle)
Weekly Arizona Journal-Miner (Prescott)
Weekly Gazette-Times (Corvallis)
Williams News (Arizona)

OTHER

Giela, Vick Cecile. "Sawtelle Renewed." M.A. Thesis, UCLA, Urban Planning, 1970.

In re Estate of Doolittle, 153 Cal. 29 (1908 pension case, Soldiers' Home).

Halliwell, Hildreth, September 21, 1971, Interview with Al Turner, recordings in her home in Valley Center, California; Tucson, Arizona: University of Arizona, 1971; copy in collection of David D. de Haas, MD.

Nevada Historical Society Quarterly 20 (Winter, 1977), Notes & Documents.

Newspapers.com

Rousseau, Sarah Jane, Rousseau diary, 1864.

Santa Monica: A Protected Harbor (pamphlet). Santa Monica: Press of the Outlook, 1894.

"Texas Jack" [James Wright]. "Texas, by God" and the Twin Territories. (New Mexico & Arizona). Internet Wild West discussion board.

"Wild West Collectors" Facebook page. de Haas, David D. and Mary D., Moderators.

Wilkinson, Cheryl Lynn. "The Veterans in Our Midst: Disabled Union Veterans in West Los Angeles, 1888–1914." M. A. Thesis, California State University, Northridge, 2013.

INDEX

Akin, Henry, Santa Monica liquor dealer, 40, 46

Albee, Charles, fight at Soldiers' Home, 57

Alcohol, a Santa Monica problem, 7, 23, 25-29; at Sawtelle, 20, 52-58, 66; legislation, 22, 27, 41, 60-68, 102-05, 112-17, 119-21, 143; and Home suicides, 49; incidents detailed, 40, 46; in nation's Soldiers' Homes, 43; Los Angeles situation, 87-92; see also Blind pig; Legislation

Alexandria Hotel, Los Angeles, Wyatt Earp bunco case, 93-94, 179

Allgren, Gus, opium smuggler, 125

Anderson, Thomas J., Home veteran, judge, 152

Annexation, incorporation, Sawtelle issues, 41, 63, 118-19, 143

Anti-Saloon League, 88, 120, 200 fn. 9; see also Alcohol; Prohibition; Taft

Arcadia Hotel, Santa Monica, 41, 131-34

Arrests, crimes, 27-29, 40, 43, 46, 52, 54, 57-58, 60, 62-64, 66, 87, 90, 99, 102-04, 112-17, 122- 25; see also Alcohol; Blind pig

Auble, Walter, Los Angeles Police Chief, 90

Aubright, Strickland, veteran, physician, 152

Bagg, S. C., Tombstone and Santa Monica, 132-33

Bailey, Edwin, veteran, 152

Bailey, Enos, veteran, Home undertaker, marries, 47, 152

Baker, Robert S., illus., 9; Santa Monica founder, 7, 9, 11, 13-17, 127, 129, 135, 195 fn. 15

Baldwin, Elias J. (Lucky), gambler, Wyatt Earp associate, 178; 211 fn 8

Ballona, 9, 11; gold mining, 128

Balloon Route, railroad map, 16; 41, 43, 44, 49, 68

Bandini, Arturo, Pasadena, 135

Bandini de Baker, Arcadia, Southern California entrepreneur, 11-13, 17, 127, 129, 132, 134-35

Barrett, Andrew W., Soldiers' Home manager, 19

Barrett Villa, lots sold, 22; name for Sawtelle, 19

Beach Boys, 182

Behan, John, mentioned, 75

Bell, Lewis Cass, veteran, marries, 47

Bennett, William True, veteran, photographer, 155

Benson, AZ, Santa Monica tourism, 134

Beverly Hills, formerly Morocco Junction, 41, 44, 49, preface

Beyer, John, veteran, suicide, 49

Bilicke, Albert C., and Earp family connections, 71-7, 177, 179, 186

Bilicke, Carl Gustave, and Earp family, 73, 178-79

Bilicke family, hotels, AZ, CA, Earp connections, 178-79

Billings, Mary, marries a veteran, 49

229